Black Hawk's War, 1832

Black Hawk's War, 1832
The Campaign against the Sauk & Fox Indians

Autobiography of Ma-Ka-Tai-Me-She-Kia-Kiak,
or Black Hawk
dictated by Himself

Wakefield's History of the Black Hawk War
Frank Everett Stevens

Black Hawk's War, 1832
The Campaign against the Sauk & Fox Indians
Autobiography of Ma-Ka-Tai-Me-She-Kia-Kiak, or Black Hawk
dictated by Himself
Wakefield's History of the Black Hawk War
by Frank Everett Stevens

FIRST EDITION

First published under the titles
T*Autobiography of Ma-Ka-Tai-Me-She-Kia-Kiak, or Black Hawk*
Wakefield's History of the Black Hawk War

Leonaur is an imprint of Oakpast Ltd
Copyright in this form © 2018 Oakpast Ltd

ISBN: 978-1-78282-750-4 (hardcover)
ISBN: 978-1-78282-751-1 (softcover)

http://www.leonaur.com

Publisher's Notes
The views expressed in this book are not necessarily those of the publisher.

Contents

Autobiography of Ma-Ka-Tai-Me-She-Kia-Kiak, or Black Hawk   11

Wakefield's History of the Black Hawk War   163

Autobiography of Ma-Ka-Tai-Me-She-Kia-Kiak, or Black Hawk

Contents

Original Dedication	13
Advertisement	15
Autobiography of Black Hawk	17
Starts for a New Home	102
The Black Hawk War	115
The Black Hawk War Continued	120
Kilbourn's Narrative	125
Appendix	149

As a Token of High Regard,
I Dedicate This Volume
to My Friend,
Hon. Bailey Davenport,
of Rock Island, Ill.

Indian Agency,
Rock Island, October 16, 1833.

I do hereby certify, that Makataimeshekiakiak, or Black Hawk, did call upon me, on his return to his people in August last, and expressed a great desire to have a history of his life written and published, in order (as he said) "that the people of the United States, (among whom he had been travelling, and by whom he had been treated with great respect, friendship and hospitality,) might know the *causes* that had impelled him to acts as he had done, and the *principles* by which he was governed."

In accordance with his request, I acted as interpreter; and was particularly cautious to understand distinctly the narrative of Black Hawk throughout—and have examined the work carefully since its completion, and have no hesitation in pronouncing it strictly correct, in all its particulars.

Given under my hand, at the Sac and Fox agency, the day and date above written.

Antoine Le Clair,
U.S. Interpreter for the Sacs and Foxes.

Original Dedication

Ne-Ka-Na-Wen.
Ma-Ne-So-No Oke-Maut Wap-Pi Mak-Quai.
Wa-Ta-Sai We-Yeu,
Ai nan-ni ta co-si-ya-quai, na-katch ai she-ke she-he-nack, hai-me-ka- ti ya-quai ke-she-he-nack, ken-e-chawe-he-ke kai-pec-kien a-cob, ai- we-ne-she we-he-yen; ne-wai-ta-sa-mak ke-kosh-pe kai-a-poi qui-wat. No-ta-wach-pai pai-ke se-na-mon nan-ni-yoo, ai-ke-kai na-o-pen. Ni-me- to sai-ne-ni-wen, ne-ta-to-ta ken ai mo-he-man ta-ta-que, ne-me-to- sai-ne-ne-wen.
Nin-a-kai-ka poi-pon-ni chi-cha-yen, kai-ka-ya ha-ma-we pa-she-to-he- yen. Kai-na-ya kai-nen-ne-naip, he-nok ki-nok ke-cha-kai-ya pai-no- yen ne-ket-te-sim-mak o-ke-te-wak ke-o-che, me-ka ti-ya-quois na-kach mai-quoi, a-que-qui pa-che-qui ke-kan-ni ta-men-nin. Ke-to-ta we-yen, a-que-ka-ni-co-te she-tai-hai-hai yen, nen, chai-cha-me-co kai-ke-me- se ai we-ke ken-na-ta-mo-wat ken-ne-wa-ha-o ma-quo-qua-yeai-quoi. Ken-wen-na ak-che-man wen-ni-ta-hai ke-men-ne to-ta-we-yeu, ke-kog-hai ke-ta-shi ke-kai na-we-yen, he-na-cha wai-che-we to-mo-nan, ai pe-che- qua-chi mo-pen ma-me-co, ma-che-we-ta na-mo-nan, ne-ya-we-nan qui-a- ha-wa pe-ta-kek, a que-year tak-pa-she-qui a-to-ta-mo-wat, chi-ye-tuk he-ne cha-wai-chi he-ni-nan ke-o-chi-ta mow-ta-swee-pai che-qua-que.
He-ni-cha-hai poi-kai-nen na-no-so-si-yen, ai o-sa-ke-we-yen, ke-pe-me-kai-mi-kat hai-nen hac-yai, na-na-co-si-peu, nen-a-kai-ne co-ten ne-co-ten ne-ka chi-a-quoi ne-me-cok me-to-sai ne-ne wak-kai ne-we- yen-nen, kai-shai ma-ni-to-ke ka-to-me-nak ke-wa-sai he-co-wai mi-a-me ka-chi pai-ko-tai-hear-pe kai-cee wa-wa-kia he-pe ha-pe-nach-he-cha, na-na-ke-na-way ni-taain ai we-pa-he-wea to-to-na ca, ke-to-ta-we- yeak, he-nok, mia-ni ai she-ke-ta ma-ke-si-yen, nen-a-kai na-co-ten ne-ka-he-nen e-ta-quois, wa toi-na-ka che-ma-ke-keu

na-ta-che tai-hai- ken ai mo-co-man ye-we-yeu ke-to-towe. E-nok ma-ni-hai she-ka-ta-ma ka-si-yen, wen-e-cha-hai nai-ne-mak, mai-ko-ten ke ka-cha ma-men-na- tuk we-yowe, keu-ke-nok ai she-me ma-na-ni ta-men-ke-yowe.

Ma-Ka-Tai-Me-She-Kia-Kiak
Ma-taus-we Ki-sis, 1833.

Dedication (translation)

To Brigadier General H. Atkinson:

Sir—The changes of fortune and vicissitudes of war made you my conqueror. When my last resources were exhausted, my warriors worn down with long and toilsome marches, we yielded, and I became your prisoner.

The story of my life is told in the following pages: it is intimately connected, and in some measure, identified, with a part of the history of your own: I have, therefore, dedicated it to you. The changes of many summers have brought old age upon me, and I can not expect to survive many moons. Before I set out on my journey to the land of my fathers, I have determined to give my motives and reasons for my former hostilities to the whites, and to vindicate my character from misrepresentation. The kindness I received from you whilst a prisoner of war assures me that you will vouch for the facts contained in my narrative, so far as they came under your observation.

I am now an obscure member of a nation that formerly honored and respected my opinions. The pathway to glory is rough, and many gloomy hours obscure it. May the Great Spirit shed light on yours, and that you may never experience the humility that the power of the American government has reduced me to, is the wish of him, who, in his native forests, was once as proud and bold as yourself.

Black Hawk.
10th Moon, 1833.

Advertisement

It is presumed that no apology will be required for presenting to the public the life of a hero who has lately taken such high rank among the distinguished individuals of America. In the following pages he will be seen in the character of a warrior, a patriot and a State prisoner; in every situation he is still the chief of his band, asserting their rights with dignity, firmness and courage. Several accounts of the late war having been published, in which he thinks justice is not done to himself or nation, he determined to make known to the world the injuries his people have received from the whites, the causes which brought on the war on the part of his nation, and a general history of it throughout the campaign. In his opinion this is the only method now left him to rescue his little band, the remnant of those who fought bravely with him, from the effects of the statements that have already gone forth.

The facts which he states, respecting the Treaty of 1804, in virtue of the provisions of which the government claimed the country in dispute and enforced its arguments with the sword, are worthy of attention. It purported to cede to the United States all of the country, including the village and cornfields of Black Hawk and his band, on the east side of the Mississippi. Four individuals of the tribe, who were on a visit to St. Louis to obtain the liberation of on of their people from prison, were prevailed upon, says Black Hawk, to make this important treaty, without the knowledge or authority of the tribes, or nation.

In treating with the Indians for their country, it has always been customary to assemble the whole nation; because, as has been truly suggested by the Secretary of War, the nature of the authority of the chiefs of the tribe is such, that it is not often that they dare make a treaty of much consequence, and we might add, never, when involving so much magnitude as the one under consideration, without the presence of their young men. A rule so reasonable and just ought never to be violated, and the Indians might well question the right of the government to dispossess them, when such violation was made the basis of its right.

The editor has written this work according to the dictation of Black Hawk, through the United States interpreter, at the Sac and Fox Agency of Rock Island. He does not, therefore, consider himself responsible for any of the facts, or views, contained in it, and leaves the old chief and his story with the public, whilst he neither asks, nor expects, any fame for his services as an amanuensis.

The (original) Editor.

Autobiography of Black Hawk

I was born at the Sac village, on Rock River, in the year 1767, and am now in my 67th year. My great grandfather, Nanamakee, or Thunder, according to the tradition given me by my father, Pyesa, was born in the vicinity of Montreal, Canada, where the Great Spirit first placed the Sac nation, and inspired him with a belief that, at the end of four years he should see a *white man*, who would be to him a father. Consequently he blacked his face, and eat but once a day, just as the sun was going down, for three years, and continued dreaming, throughout all this time whenever he slept. When the Great Spirit again appeared to him, and told him that, at the end of one year more, he should meet his father, and directed him to start seven days before its expiration, and take with him his two brothers, Namah, or Sturgeon, and Paukahummawa, or Sunfish, and travel in a direction to the left of sun-rising. After pursuing this course for five days, he sent out his two brothers to listen if they could hear a noise, and if so, to fasten some grass to the end of a pole, erect it, pointing in the direction of the sound, and then return to him.

Early next morning they returned, and reported that they had heard sounds which appeared near at hand, and that they had fulfilled his order. They all then started for the place where the pole had been erected; when, on reaching it, Nanamakee left his party and went alone to the place from whence the sounds proceeded, and found, that the white man had arrived and pitched his tent. When he came in sight, his father came out to meet him. He took him by the hand and welcomed him into his tent.

He told him that he was the son of the King of France; that he had been dreaming for four years; that the Great Spirit had directed him to come here, where he should meet a nation of people who had never yet seen a white man; that they should be his children and he should be their father; that he had communicated these things to the King, his father, who laughed at him and called him Mashena, but he insisted on coming here to meet his children where the Great Spirit had directed him. The king had told him that he would find neither land nor people; that this was an uninhabited region of lakes and mountains, but, finding that he would have no peace without it, he fitted out a *napequa*, manned it, and gave him charge of it, when he immediately loaded it, set sail and had now landed on the very day that the Great Spirit had told him in his dreams he should meet his children. He had now met the man who should, in future, have charge of all the nation.

He then presented him with a medal which he hung round his neck. Nanamakee informed him of his dreaming, and told him that his two brothers remained a little way behind. His father gave him a shirt, a blanket and a handkerchief besides a variety of other presents, and told him to go and bring his brethren. Having laid aside his buffalo robe and dressed himself in his new dress, he started to meet his brothers. When they met he explained to them his meeting with the white man and exhibited to their view the presents that he had made him. He then took off his medal and placed it on his elder brother Namah, and requested them both to go with him to his father.

They proceeded thither, were where ushered into the tent, and after some brief ceremony his father opened a chest and took presents therefrom for the newcomers. He discovered that Nanamakee had given his medal to his elder brother Namah. He told him that he had done wrong; that he should wear that medal himself, as he had others for his brothers. That which he had given him was typical of the rank he should hold in the nation; that his brothers could only rank as *civil chiefs*, and that their duties should consist of taking care of the village and attending to its civil concerns, whilst his rank, from his superior knowledge, placed him over all. If the nation should get into any difficulty with another, then his *puccohawama*, or sovereign decree, must be obeyed. If he declared war he must lead them on to battle; that the Great Spirit had made him a great and brave general, and had sent him here to give him that medal and make presents to him for his people.

His father remained four days, during which time he gave him guns, powder and lead, spears and lances, and taught him their use, so that in war he might be able to chastise his enemies, and in peace they could kill buffalo, deer and other game necessary for the comforts and luxuries of life. He then presented the others with various kinds of cooking utensils and taught them their uses. After having given them large quantities of goods as presents, and everything necessary for their comfort, he set sail for France, promising to meet them again, at the same place, after the 12th moon.

The three newly made chiefs returned to their village and explained to Mukataquet, their father, who was the principal chief of the nation, what had been said and done.

The old chief had some dogs killed and made a feast preparatory to resigning his scepter, to which all the nation were invited. Great anxiety prevailed among them to know what the three brothers had seen and heard. When the old chief arose and related to them the sayings and doings of his three sons, and concluded by saying that the Great Spirit had directed that these, his three sons, should take the rank and power that had once been his, and that he yielded these honors and duties willingly to them, because it was the wish of the Great Spirit, and he could never consent to make him angry.

He now presented the great medicine bag to Nanamakee, and told him that he "cheerfully resigned it to him, it is the soul of our nation, it has never yet been disgraced and I will expect you to keep it unsullied."

Some dissensions arose among them, in consequence of so much power being given to Nanamakee, he being so young a man. To quiet them, Nanamakee, during a violent thunder storm, told them that he had caused it, and that it was an exemplification of the name the Great Spirit had given him. During the storm the lightning struck, and set fire to a tree near by, a sight they had never witnessed before. He went to it and brought away some of its burning branches, made a fire in the lodge and seated his brothers around it opposite to one another, while he stood up and addressed his people as follows:

> I am yet young, but the Great Spirit has called me to the rank I hold among you. I have never sought to be more than my birth entitled me to. I have not been ambitious, nor was it ever my wish while my father was yet among the living to take his place, nor have I now usurped his powers. The Great Spirit caused me to dream for four years. He told me where to go and meet the white man who would be a kind father to us all. I obeyed. I went, and have seen and know our new father.
>
> You have all heard what was said and done. The Great Spirit directed him to come and meet me, and it is his order that places me at the head of my nation, the place which my father

has willingly resigned.

You have all witnessed the power that has been given me by the Great Spirit, in making that fire, and all that I now ask is that these, my two chiefs, may never let it go out. That they may preserve peace among you and administer to the wants of the needy. And should an enemy invade our country, I will then, and not until then, assume command, and go forth with my band of brave warriors and endeavour to chastise them.

At the conclusion of this speech every voice cried out for Nanamakee. All were satisfied when they found that the Great Spirit had done what they had suspected was the work of Nanamakee, he being a very shrewd young man.

The next spring according to promise their French father returned, with his *napequa* richly laden with goods, which were distributed among them. He continued for a long time to keep up a regular trade with them, they giving him in exchange for his goods furs and peltries.

After a long time the British overpowered the French, the two nations being at war, and drove them away from Quebec, taking possession of it themselves. The different tribes of Indians around our nation, envying our people, united their forces against them and by their combined strength succeeded in driving them to Montreal, and from thence to Mackinac. Here our people first met our British father, who furnished them with goods. Their enemies still wantonly pursued them and drove them to different places along the lake. At last they made a village near Green Bay, on what is now called Sac River, having derived its name from this circumstance. Here they held a council with the Foxes, and a national treaty of friendship and alliance was agreed upon. The Foxes abandoned their village and joined the Sacs.

This arrangement, being mutually obligatory upon both parties, as neither were sufficiently strong to meet their enemies with any hope of success, they soon became as one band or nation of people. They were driven, however, by the combined forces of their enemies to the Wisconsin. They remained here for some time, until a party of their young men, who descended Rock River to its mouth, had returned and made a favourable report of the country. They all descended Rock River, drove the Kaskaskias from the country and commenced the erection of their village, determined never to leave it.

At this village I was born, being a lineal descendant of the first chief, Nanamakee, or Thunder. Few, if any events of note transpired within my recollection until about my fifteenth year. I was not allowed to paint or wear feathers, but distinguished myself at an early age by wounding an enemy; consequently I was placed in the ranks of the braves.

Soon after this a leading chief of the Muscow nation came to our village for recruits to go to war against the Osages, our common enemy.

I volunteered my services to go, as my father had joined him, and was proud to have an opportunity to prove to him that I was not an unworthy son, and that I had courage and bravery. It was not long before we met the enemy and a battle immediately ensued. Standing by my father's side, I saw him kill his antagonist and tear the scalp from off his head. Fired with valor and ambition, I rushed furiously upon another and smote him to the earth with my tomahawk. I then ran my lance through his body, took off his scalp and returned in triumph to my father. He said nothing but looked well pleased. This was the first man I killed. The enemy's loss in this engagement having been very great, they immediately retreated, which put an end to the war for the time being. Our party then returned to the village and danced over the scalps we had taken. This was the first time I was permitted to join in a scalp dance.

After a few moons had passed, being acquired considerable reputation as a brave, I led a party of seven and attacked one hundred Osages! I killed one man and left him for my comrades to scalp while I was taking observations of the strength and preparations of the enemy. Finding that they were equally well armed with ourselves, I ordered a retreat and came off without the loss of a man. This excursion gained for me great applause, and enabled me, before a great while, to raise a party of one hundred and eighty to march against the Osages. We left our village in high spirits and marched over a rugged country, until we reached the land of the Osages, on the borders of the Missouri.

We followed their trail until we arrived at the village, which we approached with exceeding caution, thinking that they were all here, but found, to our sorrow, that they had deserted it. The party became dissatisfied in consequence of this disappointment, and all, with the exception of five noble braves, dispensed and went home. I then placed myself at the head of this brave little band, and thanked the Great Spirit that so *many* had remained. We took to the trail of our enemies, with a full determination never to return without some trophy of victory. We followed cautiously on for several days, killed one man and a boy, and returned home with their scalps.

In consequence of this mutiny in camp, I was not again able to raise a sufficient force to go against the Osages until about my nineteenth year. During this interim they committed many outrages on our nation; hence I succeeded in recruiting two hundred efficient warriors, and early one morning took up the line of march. In a few days we were in the enemy's country, and we had not gone far before we met a force equal to our own with which to contend. A general battle immediately commenced, although my warriors were considerably fatigued by forced marches. Each party fought desperately. The enemy seemed unwilling to yield the ground and we were determined to conquer or die.

A great number of Osages were killed and many wounded before they commenced a retreat. A band of warriors more brave, skilful and efficient than mine could not be found. In this engagement I killed five men and one squaw, and had the good fortune to take the scalps of all I struck with one exception—that of the squaw, who was accidentally killed. The enemy's loss in this engagement was about one hundred braves. Ours nineteen. We then returned to our village well pleased with our success, and danced over the scalps which we had taken.

The Osages, in consequence of their great loss in this battle, became satisfied to remain on their own lands. This stopped for a while their depredations on our nation. Our attention was now directed towards an ancient enemy who had decoyed and murdered some of our helpless women and children. I started with my father, who took command of a small party, and proceeded against the enemy to chastise them for the wrongs they had heaped upon us. We met near the Merimac and an action ensued; the Cherokees having a great advantage in point of numbers. Early in this engagement my father was wounded in the thigh, but succeeded in killing his enemy before he fell. Seeing that he had fallen, I assumed command, and fought desperately until the enemy commenced retreating before the well directed blows of our braves. I returned to my father to administer to his necessities, but nothing could be done for him. The medicine man said the wound was mortal, from which he soon after died. In this battle I killed three men and wounded several. The enemy's loss was twenty-eight and ours seven.

I now fell heir to the great medicine bag of my forefathers, which had belonged to my father. I took it, buried our dead, and returned with my party, sad and sorrowful, to our village, in consequence of the loss of my father.

Owing to this misfortune I blacked my face, fasted and prayed to the Great Spirit for five years, during which time I remained in a civil capacity, hunting and fishing.

The Osages having again commenced aggressions on our people, and the Great Spirit having taken pity on me, I took a small party and went against them. I could only find six of them, and their forces being so weak, I thought it would be cowardly to kill them, but took them prisoners and carried them to our Spanish father at St. Louis, gave them up to him and then returned to our village.

Determined on the final and complete extermination of the dastardly Osages, in punishment for the injuries our people had received from them, I commenced recruiting a strong force, immediately on my return, and stated in the third moon, with five hundred Sacs and Foxes, and one hundred Iowas, and marched against the enemy. We continued our march for many days before we came upon their trail, which was discovered late in the day. We encamped for the night, made an early start next morning, and before sundown we fell upon forty lodges, killed all the inhabitants except two squaws, whom I took as prisoners. Doing this engagement I killed seven men and two boys with my own hands. In this battle many of the bravest warriors among the Osages were killed, which caused those who yet remained of their nation to keep within the boundaries of their own land and cease their aggressions upon our hunting grounds.

The loss of my father, by the Cherokees, made me anxious to avenge his death by the utter annihilation, if possible, of the last remnant of their tribe. I accordingly commenced collecting another party to go against them. Having succeeded in this, I started with my braves and went into their country, but I found only five of their people, whom I took prisoners. I afterwards released four of them, the other, a young squaw, we brought home. Great as was my hatred of these people, I could not kill so small a party.

About the close of the ninth moon, I led a large party against the Chippewas, Kaskaskias and Osages. This was the commencement of a long and arduous campaign, which terminated in my thirty-fifth year, after having had seven regular engagements and numerous small skirmishes. During this campaign several hundred of the enemy were slain. I killed thirteen of their bravest warriors with my own hands.

Our enemies having now been driven from our hunting grounds, with so great a loss as they sustained, we returned in peace to our village. After the seasons of mourning and burying our dead braves and of feasting and dancing had passed, we commenced preparations for our winter's hunt. When all was ready we started on the chase and returned richly laden with the fruits of the hunter's toil.

We usually paid a visit to St. Louis every summer, but in consequence of the long protracted war in which we had been engaged, I had not been there for some years.

Our difficulties all having been settled, I concluded to take a small party and go down to see our Spanish father during the summer. We went, and on our arrival put up our lodges where the market house now stands. After painting and dressing we called to see our Spanish father and were kindly received. He gave us a great variety of presents and an abundance of provisions. We danced through the town as usual, and the inhabitants all seemed well pleased. They seemed to us like brothers, and always gave us good advice. On my next and last visit to our Spanish father, I discovered on landing, that all was not right. Every countenance seemed sad and gloomy. I inquired the cause and was informed that the Americans were coming to take possession of the town and country, and that we were to lose our Spanish father. This news made me and my band exceedingly sad, because we had always heard bad accounts of the Americans from the Indians who had lived near them. We were very sorry to lose our Spanish father, who had always treated us with great friendship.

A few days afterwards the Americans arrived. I, in company with my band, went to take leave for the last time of our father. The Americans came to see him also. Seeing their approach, we passed out at one door as they came in at another. We immediately embarked in our canoes for our village on Rock River, not liking the change any more than our friends at St. Louis appeared to.

On arriving at our village we gave out the news that a strange people had taken possession of St. Louis and that we should never see our generous Spanish father again. This information cast a deep gloom over our people.

Sometime afterwards a boat came up the river with a young American chief, at that time Lieutenant, and afterwards General Pike, and a small party of soldiers aboard. The boat at length arrived at Rock River and the young chief came on shore with his interpreter. He made us a speech and gave us some presents, in return for which we gave him meat and such other provisions as we could spare.

We were well pleased with the speech of the young chief. He gave us good advice and said our American father would treat us well. He presented us an American flag which we hoisted. He then requested us to lower the *British colours*, which were waving in the air, and to give him our British medals, promising to send others on his return to St: Louis. This we declined to do as we wished to have two fathers.

When the young chief started we sent runners to the village of the Foxes, some miles distant, to direct them to treat him well as he passed, which they did. He went to the head of the Mississippi and then returned to St. Louis. We did not see any Americans again for some time, being supplied with goods by British traders.

We were fortunate in not giving up our medals, for we learned afterwards, from our traders, that the chiefs high up the Mississippi, who gave theirs, never received any in exchange for them. But the fault was not with the young American chief. He was a good man, a great brave, and I have since learned, died in his country's service.

Some moons after this young chief had descended the Mississippi, one of our people killed an American, was taken prisoner and was confined in the prison at St. Louis for the offence. We held a council at our village to see what could be done for him, and determined that Quashquame, Pashepaho, Ouchequaka and Hashequarhiqua should go down to St. Louis, see our American father and do all they could to have our friend released by paying for the person killed, thus covering the blood and satisfying the relations of the murdered man. This being the only means with us for saving a person who had killed another, and we then thought it was the same way with the whites.

The party started with the good wishes of the whole nation, who had high hopes that the emissaries would accomplish the object of their mission. The relations of the prisoner blacked their faces and fasted, hoping the Great Spirit would take pity on them and return husband and father to his sorrowing wife and weeping children.

Quashquame and party remained a long time absent. They at length returned and encamped near the village, a short distance below it, and did not come up that day, nor did any one approach their camp. They appeared to be dressed in fine coats and had medals. From these circumstances we were in hopes that they had brought good news. Early the next morning the Council Lodge was crowded, Quashquame and party came up and gave us the following account of their mission:

On our arrival at St. Louis we met our American father and explained to him our business, urging the release of our friend. The American chief told us he wanted land. We agreed to give him some on the west side of the Mississippi, likewise more on the Illinois side opposite Jeffreon. When the business was all arranged we expected to have our friend released to come home with us. About the time we were ready to start our brother was let out of the prison. He started and ran a short distance when he was *shot dead!*

This was all they could remember of what had been said and done. It subsequently appeared that they had been drunk the greater part of the time while at St. Louis.

This was all myself and nation knew of the treaty of 1804. It has since been explained to me. I found by that treaty, that all of the country east of the Mississippi, and south of Jeffreon was ceded to the United States for one thousand dollars a year. I will leave it to the people of the United States to say whether our nation was properly represented in this treaty? Or whether we received a fair compensation for the extent of country ceded by these four individuals?

I could say much more respecting this treaty, but I will not at this time. It has been the origin of all our serious difficulties with the whites.

Sometime after this treaty was made, a war chief with a party of soldiers came up in keel boats, encamped a short distance above the head of the Des Moines rapids, and commenced cutting timber and building houses. The news of their arrival was soon carried to all our villages, to confer upon which many councils were held. We could not understand the intention, or comprehend the reason why the Americans wanted to build homes at that place. We were told that they were a party of soldiers, who had brought great guns with them, and looked like a war party of whites.

A number of people immediately went down to see what was going on, myself among them. On our arrival we found that they were building a fort. The soldiers were busily engaged in cutting timber, and I observed that they took their arms with them when they went to the woods. The whole party acted as they would do in an enemy's country. The chiefs held a council with the officers, or headmen of the party, which I did not attend, but understood from them that the war chief had said that they were building homes for a trader who was coming there to live, and would sell us goods very cheap, and that the soldiers were to remain to keep him company. We were pleased at this information ad hoped that it was all true, but we were not so credulous as to believe that all these buildings were intended merely for the accommodation of a trader. Being distrustful of their intentions, we were anxious for them to leave off building and go back down the river.

By this time a considerable number of Indians had arrived to see what was doing. I discovered that the whites were alarmed. Some of our young men watched a party of soldiers, who went out to work, carrying their arms, which were laid aside before they commenced. Having stolen quietly to the spot they seized the guns and gave a wild yell! The party threw down their axes and ran for their arms, but found them gone, and themselves surrounded. Our young men laughed at them and returned their weapons.

When this party came to the fort they reported what had been done, and the war chief made a serious affair of it. He called our chiefs to council inside his fort. This created considerable excitement in our camp, everyone wanting to know what was going to be done. The picketing which had been put up, being low, every Indian crowded around the fort, got upon blocks of wood and old barrels that they might see what was going on inside. Some were armed with guns and others with bows and arrows. We used this precaution, seeing that the soldiers had their guns loaded and having seen them load their big guns in the morning.

A party of our braves commenced dancing and proceeded up to the gate with the intention of, going in, but were stopped. The council immediately broke up, the soldiers with their guns in hands rushed out from the rooms where they had been concealed. The cannon were hauled to the gateway, and a soldier came running with fire in his hand, ready to apply the match. Our braves gave way and retired to the camp. There was no preconcerted plan to attack the whites at that time, but I am of the opinion now that had our braves got into the fort all of the whites would have been killed, as were the British soldiers at Mackinac many years before.

We broke up our camp and returned to Rock River. A short time afterward the party at the fort received reinforcements, among whom we observed some of our old friends from St. Louis.

Soon after our return from Fort Madison runners came to our village from the Shawnee Prophet. Others were despatched by him to the village of the Winnebagoes, with invitations for us to meet him on the Wabash. Accordingly a party went from each village.

All of our party returned, among whom came a prophet, who

explained to us the bad treatment the different nations of Indians had received from the Americans, by giving them a few presents and taking their land from them.

I remember well his saying: "If you do not join your friends on the Wabash, the Americans will take this very village from you!" I little thought then that his words would come true, supposing that he used these arguments merely to encourage us to join him, which we concluded not to do. He then returned to the Wabash, where a party of Winnebagoes had preceded him, and preparations were making for war. A battle soon ensued in which several Winnebagoes were killed. As soon as their nation heard of this battle, and that some of their people had been killed, they sent several war parties in different directions. One to the mining county, one to Prairie du Chien, and another to Fort Madison. The latter returned by our village and exhibited several scalps which they had taken. Their success induced several parties to go against the fort.

Myself and several of my band joined the last party, and were determined to take the fort. We arrived in the vicinity during the night. The spies that we had sent out several days before to watch the movements of those at the garrison, and ascertain their numbers, came to us and gave the following information: "A keel arrived from below this evening with seventeen men. There are about fifty men in the fort and they march out every morning to exercise." It was immediately determined that we should conceal ourselves in a position as near as practicable to where the soldiers should come out, and when the signal was given each one was to fire on them and rush into the fort. With my knife I dug a hole in the ground deep enough that by placing a few weeds around it, succeeded in concealing myself. I was so near the fort that I could hear the sentinels walking on their beats. By daybreak I had finished my work and was anxiously awaiting the rising of the sun. The morning drum beat.

I examined the priming of my gun, and eagerly watched for the gate to open. It did open, but instead of the troops, a young man came out alone and the gate closed after him. He passed so close to me that I could have killed him with my knife, but I let him pass unharmed. He kept the path toward the river, and had he gone one step from it, he must have come upon us and would have been killed. He returned immediately and entered the gate. I would now have rushed for the gate and entered it with him, but I feared that our party was not prepared to follow me.

The gate opened again when four men emerged and went down to the river for wood. While they were gone another man came out, walked toward the river, was fired on and killed by a Winnebago. The others started and ran rapidly towards the fort, but two of them were shot down dead. We then took shelter under the river's bank out of reach of the firing from the fort.

The firing now commenced from both parties and was kept up without cessation all day. I advised our party to set fire to the fort, and commenced preparing arrows for that purpose. At night we made the attempt, and succeeded in firing the buildings several times, but without effect, as the fire was always instantly extinguished.

The next day I took my rifle and shot in two the cord by which they hoisted their flag, and prevented them from raising it again. We continued firing until our ammunition was expended. Finding that we could not take the fort, we returned home, having one Winnebago killed and one wounded during the siege.

I have since learned that the trader who lived in the fort, wounded the Winnebago while he was scalping the first man that was killed. The Winnebago recovered, and is now living, and is very friendly disposed towards the trader, believing him to be a great brave.

Soon after our return home, news reached us that a war was going to take place between the British and the Americans.

Runners continued to arrive from different tribes, all confirming the reports of the expected war. The British agent, Colonel Dixon, was holding talks with, and making presents to the different tribes. I had not made up my mind whether to join the British or remain neutral. I had not discovered yet one good trait in the character of the Americans who had come to the country. They made fair promises but never fulfilled them, while the British made but few, and we could always rely implicitly on their word.

One of our people having killed a Frenchman at Prairie du Chien, the British took him prisoner and said they would shoot him next day. His family were encamped a short distance below the mouth of the Wisconsin. He begged for permission to go and see them that night, as he was to die the next day. They permitted him to go after he had promised them to return by sunrise the next morning.

He visited his family, which consisted of his wife and six children. I can not describe their meeting and parting so as to be understood by the whites, as it appears that their feelings are acted upon by certain rules laid down by their preachers, while ours are governed by the monitor within us. He bade his loved ones the last sad farewell and hurried across the prairie to the fort and arrived in time. The soldiers were ready and immediately marched out and shot him down. I visited the stricken family, and by hunting and fishing provided for them until they reached their relations.

Why did the Great Spirit ever send the whites to this island to drive us from our homes and introduce among us poisonous liquors, disease and death? They should have remained in the land the Great Spirit allotted them. But I will proceed with my story. My memory, however, is not very good since my late visit to the white people. I have still a buzzing noise in my ear from the noise and bustle incident to travel. I may give some parts of my story out of place, but will make my best endeavours to be correct.

Several of our chiefs were called upon to go to Washington to see our Great Father. They started and during their absence I went to Peoria, on the Illinois River, to see an old friend and get his advice. He was a man who always told us the truth, and knew everything that was going on. When I arrived at Peoria he had gone to Chicago, and was not at home. I visited the Pottawattomie villages and then returned to Rock River. Soon after which our friends returned from their visit to the Great Father and reported what had been said and done. Their Great Father told them that in the event of a war taking place with England, not to interfere on either side, but remain neutral. He did not want our help, but wished us to hunt and supply our families, and remain in peace. He said that British traders would not be allowed to come on the Mississippi to furnish us with goods, but that we would be well supplied by an American trader.

Our chiefs then told him that the British traders always gave us credit in the fall for guns, powder and goods, to enable us to hunt and clothe our families. He replied that the trader at Fort Madison would have plenty of goods, and if we should go there in the autumn of the year, he would supply us on credit, as the British traders had done. The party gave a good account of what they had seen and the kind treatment they had received. This information pleased us all very much. We all agreed to follow our Great Father's advice and not interfere in the war. Our women were much pleased at the good news. Everything went on cheerfully in our village. We resumed our pastimes of playing ball, horse-racing and dancing, which had been laid aside when this great war was first talked about. We had fine crops of corn which were now ripe, and our women were busily engaged in gathering it and making caches to contain it.

In a short time we were ready to start to Fort Madison to get our supply of goods, that we might proceed to our hunting grounds. We passed merrily down the river, all in high spirits. I had determined to spend the winter at my old favourite hunting ground on Skunk River. I left part of my corn and mats at its mouth to take up as we returned and many others did the same.

The next morning we arrived at the fort and made our encampment. Myself and principal men paid a visit to the war chief at the fort. He received us kindly and gave us some tobacco, pipes and provisions.

The trader came in and we all shook hands with him, for on him all our dependence was placed, to enable us to hunt and thereby support our families. We waited a long time, expecting the trader would tell us that he had orders from our Great Father to supply us with goods, but he said nothing on the subject. I got up and told him in a short speech what we had come for, and hoped he had plenty of goods to supply us. I told him that he should be well paid in the spring, and concluded by informing him that we had decided to follow our Great Father's advice and not go to war.

He said that he was happy to hear that we had concluded to remain in peace. That he had a large quantity of goods, and that if we had made a good hunt we should be well supplied, but he remarked that he had received no instructions to furnish us anything on credit, nor could he give us any without receiving the pay for them on the spot!

We informed him what our Great Father had told our chiefs at Washington, and contended that he could supply us if he would, believing that our Great Father always spoke the truth. The war chief said the trader could not furnish us on credit, and that he had received no instructions from our Great Father at Washington. We left the fort dissatisfied and went to camp. What was now to be done we knew not. We questioned the party that brought us the news from our Great Father, that we could get credit for our winter supplies at this place. They still told the same story and insisted on its truth. Few of us slept that night. All was gloom and discontent.

In the morning a canoe was seen descending the river, bearing an express, who brought intelligence that La Gutrie, a British trader, had landed at Rock Island with two boat loads of goods. He requested us to come up immediately as he had good news for us, and a variety of presents. The express presented us with tobacco, pipes and *wampum*.

The news ran through our camp like fire through dry grass on the prairie. Our lodges were soon taken down and we all started for Rock Island. Here ended all hopes of our remaining at peace, having been forced into war by being deceived.

Our party were not long in getting to Rock Island. When we came in sight and saw tents pitched, we yelled, fired our guns and beat our drums. Guns were immediately fired at the island, returning our salute, and a British flag hoisted. We loaded, were cordially received by La Gutrie, and then smoked the pipe with him. After which he made a speech to us, saying that he had been sent by Colonel Dixon. He gave us a number of handsome presents, among them a large silk flag and a keg of rum. He then told us to retire, take some refreshments and rest ourselves, as he would have more to say to us next day.

We accordingly retired to our lodges, which in the meantime had been put up, and spent the night. The next morning we called upon him and told him we wanted his two boat loads of goods to divide among our people, for which he should be well paid in the spring in furs and peltries. He consented for us to take them and do as we pleased with them. While our people were dividing the goods, he took me aside and informed me that Colonel Dixon was at Green Bay with twelve boats loaded with goods, guns and ammunition. He wished to raise a party immediately and go to him. He said our friend, the trader at Peoria, was collecting the Pottawattomies and would be there before us. I communicated this information to my braves, and a party of two hundred warriors were soon collected and ready to depart. I paid a visit to the lodge of an old friend, who had been the comrade of my youth, and had been in many war parties with me, but was now crippled and no longer able to travel.

He had a son that I had adopted as my own, and who had hunted with me the two winters preceding. I wished my old friend to let him go with me. He objected, saying he could not get his support if he did attend me, and that I, who had always provided for him since his misfortune, would be gone, therefore he could not spare him as he had no other dependence. I offered to leave my son in his stead but he refused to give his consent. He said that he did not like the war, as he had been down the river and had been well treated by the Americans and could not fight against them. He had promised to winter near a white settler above Salt river, and must take his son with him. We parted and I soon concluded my arrangements and started with my party for Green Bay. On our arrival there we found a large encampment; were well received by Colonel Dixon and the war chiefs who were with him. He gave us plenty of provisions, tobacco and pipes, saying that he would hold a council with us the next day. In the encampment I found a great number of Kickapoos, Ottawas and Winnebagoes. I visited all their camps and found them in high spirits. They had all received new guns, ammunition and a variety of clothing.

In the evening a messenger came to visit Colonel Dixon. I went to his tent, in which them were two other war chiefs and an interpreter. He received me with a hearty shake of the hand; presented me to the other chiefs, who treated me cordially, expressing themselves as being much. Pleased to meet me. After I was seated Colonel Dixon said:

> General Black Hawk, I sent for you to explain to you what we are going to do and give you the reasons for our coming here. Our friend, La Gutrie, informs us in the letter you brought from him, of what has lately taken place. You will now have to hold us fast by the hand. Your English Father has found out that the Americans want to take your country from you and has sent me and my braves to drive them back to their own country. He has, likewise, sent a large quantity of arms and ammunition, and we want all your warriors to join us.

He then placed a medal around my neck and gave me a paper, which I lost in the late war, and a silk flag, saying: "You are to command all the braves that will leave here the day after tomorrow, to join our braves at Detroit."

I told him I was very much disappointed, as I wanted to descend the Mississippi and make war upon the settlements. He said he had been ordered to lay in waste the country around St. Louis. But having been a trader on the Mississippi for many years himself, and always having been treated kindly by the people there, he could not send brave men to murder helpless women and innocent children. There were no soldiers there for us to fight, and where he was going to send us there were a great many of them. If we defeated them the Mississippi country should be ours. I was much pleased with this speech, as it was spoken by a brave.

I inquired about my old friend, the trader at Peoria, and observed, "that I had expected that he would have been here before me." He shook his head and said, "I have sent express after express for him, and have offered him great sums of money to come and bring the Pottawatomies and Kickapoos with him." He refused, saying, "Your British father has not enough money to induce me to join you. I have now laid a trap for him. I have sent Gomo and a party of Indians to take him prisoner and bring him here alive. I expect him in a few days."

The next day arms and ammunition, knives, tomahawks and clothing were given to my band. We had a great feast in the evening, and the morning following I started with about five hundred braves to join the British Army. We passed Chicago and observed that the fort had been evacuated by the Americans, and their soldiers had gone to Fort Wayne. They were attacked a short distance from the fort and defeated. They had a considerable quantity of powder in the fort at Chicago, which they had promised to the Indians, but the night before they marched away they destroyed it by throwing it into a well. If they had fulfilled their word to the Indians, they doubtless would have gone to Fort Wayne without molestation. On our arrival, I found that the Indians had several prisoners, and I advised them to treat them well. We continued our march, joining the British below Detroit, soon after which we had a battle. The Americans fought well, and drove us back with considerable loss. I was greatly surprised at this, as I had been told that the Americans would not fight.

Our next movement was against a fortified place. I was stationed with my braves to prevent any person going to, or coming from the fort. I found two men taking care of cattle and took them prisoners. I would not kill them, but delivered them to the British war chief. Soon after, several boats came down the river fail of American soldiers. They landed on the opposite side, took the British batteries, and pursued the soldiers that had left them. They went too far without knowing the strength of the British and were defeated. I hurried across the river, anxious for an opportunity to show the courage of my braves, but before we reached the scene of battle all was over.

The British had taken many prisoners and the Indians were killing them. I immediately put a stop to it, as I never thought it brave, but base and cowardly to kill in unarmed and helpless foe. We remained here for some time. I can not detail what took place, as I was stationed with my braves in the woods. It appeared, however, that the British could not take this fort, for we marched to another, some distance off. When we approached it, I found a small stockade, and concluded that there were not many men in it. The British war chief sent a flag of truce. Colonel Dixon carried it, but soon returned, reporting that the young war chief in command would not give up the fort without fighting. Colonel Dixon came to me and said, "you will see tomorrow, how easily we will take that fort." I was of the same opinion, but when the morning came I was disappointed. The British advanced and commenced the attack, fighting like true braves, but were defeated by the braves in the fort, and a great number of our men were killed.

The British Army was making preparations to retreat. I was now tired of being with them, our success being bad, and having got no plunder. I determined on leaving them and returning to Rock River, to see what had become of my wife and children, as I had not heard from them since I left home. That night I took about twenty of my braves, and left the British camp for home. On our journey we met no one until we came to the Illinois River. Here we found two lodges of Pottawattomies. They received us in a very friendly manner, and gave us something to eat. I inquired about their friends who were with the British. They said there had been some fighting on the Illinois river, and that my friend, the Peoria trader, had been taken prisoner. "By Gomo and his party?" I immediately inquired.

They replied, "no, but by the Americans, who came up with boats. They took him and the French settlers prisoners, and they burned the village of Peoria." They could give us no information regarding our friends on Rock River. In three days more we were in the vicinity of our village, and were soon after surprised to find that a party of Americans had followed us from the British camp. One of them, more daring than his comrades, had made his way through the thicket on foot, and was just in the act of shooting me when I discovered him. I then ordered him to surrender, marched him into camp, and turned him over to a number of our young men with this injunction: "Treat him as a brother, as I have concluded to adopt him in our tribe."

A little while before this occurrence I had directed my party to proceed to the village, as I had discovered a smoke ascending from a hollow in the bluff, and wished to go alone to the place from whence the smoke proceeded, to see who was there. I approached the spot, and when I came in view of the fire, I saw an old man sitting in sorrow beneath a mat which he had stretched over him. At any other time I would have turned away without disturbing him, knowing that he came here to be alone, to humble himself before the Great Spirit, that he might take pity on him. I approached and seated myself beside him. He gave one look at me and then fixed his eyes on the ground.

It was my old friend. I anxiously inquired for his son, my adopted child, and what had befallen our people. My old comrade seemed scarcely alive. He must have fasted a long time. I lighted my pipe and put it into his mouth. He eagerly drew a few puffs, cast up his eyes which met mine, and recognised me. His eyes were glassy and he would again have fallen into forgetfulness, had I not given him some water, which revived him. I again inquired, "what has befallen our people, and what has become of our son?"

In a feeble voice he said:

> Soon after your departure to join the British, I descended the river with a small party, to winter at the place I told you the white man had asked me to come to. When we arrived I found that a fort had been built, and the white family that had invited me to come and hunt near them had removed to it. I then paid a visit to the fort to tell the white people that my little band were friendly, and that we wished to hunt in the vicinity of the fort. The war chief who commanded there, told me that we might hunt on the Illinois side of the Mississippi, and no person would trouble us. That the horsemen only ranged on the Missouri side, and he had directed them not to cross the river. I was pleased with this assurance of safety, and immediately crossed over and made my winter's camp.
>
> Game was plenty. We lived happy, and often talked of you. My boy regretted your absence and the hardships you would have to undergo. We had been here about two moons, when my boy went out as usual to hunt. Night came on and he did not return. I was alarmed for his safety and passed a sleepless night. In the morning my old woman went to the other lodges and gave the alarm and all turned out to hunt for the missing one. There being snow upon the ground they soon came upon his track, and after pursuing it for some distance, found he was on the trail of a deer, which led toward the river. They soon came to the place where he had stood and fired, and near by, hanging on the branch of a tree, found the deer, which he had killed and skinned.
>
> But here were also found the tracks of white men. They had taken my boy prisoner. Their tracks led across the river and then down towards the fort. My friends followed on the trail, and soon found my boy lying dead. He had been most cruelly murdered. His face was shot to pieces, his body stabbed in several places and his head scalped. His arms were pinioned behind him.

The old man paused for some time, and then told me that his wife had died on their way up the Mississippi. I took the hand of my old friend in mine and pledged myself to avenge the death of his son. It was now dark, and a terrible storm was raging. The rain was descending in heavy torrents, the thunder was rolling in the heavens, and the lightning flashed athwart the sky. I had taken my blanket off and wrapped it around the feeble old man. When the storm abated I kindled a fire and took hold of my old friend to remove him nearer to it. He was dead! I remained with him during the night. Some of my party came early in the morning to look for me, and assisted me in burying him on the peak of the bluff. I then returned to the village with my friends. I visited the grave of my old friend as I ascended Rock River the last time.

On my arrival at the village I was met by the chiefs and braves and conducted to the lodge which was prepared for me. After eating, I gave a fall account of all that I had seen and done. I explained to my people the manner in which the British and Americans fought. Instead of stealing upon each other and taking every advantage to kill the enemy and save their own people as we do, which, with us is considered good policy in a war chief, they march out in open daylight and fight regardless of the number of warriors they may lose. After the battle is over they retire to feast and drink wine as if nothing had happened. After which they make a statement in writing of what they have done, each party claiming the victory, and neither giving an account of half the number that have been killed on their own side They all fought like braves, but would not do to lead a party with us. Our maxim is: "*Kill the enemy and save our own men.*" Those chiefs will do to paddle a canoe but not to steer it. The Americans shot better than the British, but their soldiers were not so well clothed, nor so well provided for.

The village chief informed me that after I started with my braves and the parties who followed, the nation was reduced to a small party of fighting men; that they would have been unable to defend themselves if the Americans had attacked them. That all the children and old men and women belonging to the warriors who had joined the British were left with them to provide for. A council had been called which agreed that Quashquame, the Lance, and other chiefs, with the old men, women and children, and such others as chose to accompany them, should descend the Mississippi to St. Louis, and place themselves under the American chief stationed there. They accordingly went down to St. Louis, were received as the friendly band of our nation, were sent up the Missouri and provided for, while their friends were assisting the British!

Keokuk was then introduced to me as the war chief of the braves then in the village. I inquired how he had become chief? They said that a large armed force was seen by their spies going toward Peoria. Fears were entertained that they would come up and attack the village and a council had been called to decide as to the best course to be adopted, which concluded upon leaving the village and going to the west side of the Mississippi to get out of the way. Keokuk, during the sitting of the council, had been standing at the door of the lodge, not being allowed to enter, as he had never killed an enemy, where he remained until old Wacome came out. He then told him that he heard what they had decided upon, and was anxious to be permitted to speak before the council adjourned.

Wacome returned and asked leave for Keokuk to come in and make a speech. His request was granted. Keokuk entered and addressed the chiefs. He said:

> I have heard with sorrow that you have determined to leave our village and cross the Mississippi, merely because you have been told that the Americans were coming in this direction. Would you leave our village, desert our homes and fly before an enemy approaches? Would you leave all, even the graves of our fathers, to the mercy of an enemy without trying to defend them? Give me charge of your warriors and I'll defend the village while you sleep in safety.

The council consented that Keokuk should be war chief. He marshalled his braves, sent out his spies and advanced with a party himself on the trail leading to Peoria. They returned without seeing an enemy. The Americans did not come by our village. All were satisfied with the appointment of Keokuk. He used every precaution that our people should not be surprised. This is the manner in which and the cause of his receiving the appointment.

I was satisfied, and then started to visit my wife and children. I found them well, and my boys were growing finely. It is not customary for us to say much about our women, as they generally perform their part cheerfully and never interfere with business belonging to the men. This is the only wife I ever had or ever will have. She is a good woman, and teaches my boys to be brave. Here I would have rested myself and enjoyed the comforts of my lodge, but I could not. I had promised to avenge the death of my adopted son.

I immediately collected a party of thirty braves, and explained to them the object of my making this war party, it being to avenge the death of my adopted son, who had been cruelly and wantonly murdered by the whites. I explained to them the pledge I had made to his father, and told them that they were the last words that he had heard spoken. All were willing to go with me to fulfil my word. We started in canoes, and descended the Mississippi, until we arrived near the place where Fort Madison had stood. It had been abandoned and burned by the whites, and nothing remained but the chimneys. We were pleased to see that the white people had retired from the country. We proceeded down the river again. I landed with one brave near Cape Gray, the remainder of the party went to the mouth of the Quiver. I hurried across to the tail that led from the mouth of the Quiver to a fort, and soon after heard firing at the mouth of the creek.

Myself and brave concealed ourselves on the side of the road. We had not remained here long before two men, riding one horse, came at full speed from the direction of the sound of the firing. When they came sufficiently near we fired; the horse jumped and both men fell. We rushed toward them and one rose and ran. I followed him and was gaining on him, when he ran over a pile of rails that had lately been made, seized a stick and struck at me. I now had an opportunity to see his face, and I knew him. He had been at Qaashquame's village to teach his people how to plough. We looked upon him as a good man. I did not wish to kill him, and pursued him no further. I returned and met my brave. He said he had killed the other man and had his scalp in his hand. We had not proceeded far before we met the man supposed to be killed, coming up the road, staggering like a drunken man, and covered all over with blood.

This was the most terrible sight I had ever seen. I told my comrade to kill him to put him out of his misery. I could not look at him. I passed on and heard a rustling in the bushes. I distinctly saw two little boys concealing themselves in the undergrowth, thought of my own children, and passed on without noticing them. My comrade here joined me, and in a little while we met the other detachment of our party. I told them that we would be pursued, and directed them to follow me. We crossed the creek and formed ourselves in the timber. We had not been here long, when a party of mounted men rushed at full speed upon us. I took deliberate aim and shot the leader of the party.

He fell lifeless from his horse. All my people fired, but without effect. The enemy rushed upon us without giving us time to reload. They surrounded us and forced us into a deep sink-hole, at the bottom of which there were some bushes.

We loaded our gun and awaited the approach of the enemy. They rushed to the edge of the hole, fired on us and killed one of our men. We instantly returned their fire, killing one of their party. We reloaded and commenced digging holes in the side of the bank to protect ourselves, while a party watched the enemy, expecting their whole force would be upon us immediately. Some of my warriors commenced singing their death songs. I heard the whites talking, and called to them to come out and fight. I did not like my situation and wished the matter settled. I soon heard chopping and knocking. I could not imagine what they were doing.

Soon after they ran up a battery on wheels and fired without hurting any of us. I called to them again, and told them if they were brave men to come out and fight us. They gave up the siege and returned to their fort about dusk. There were eighteen in this trap with me. We came out unharmed, with the exception of the brave who was killed by the enemy's first fire, after we were entrapped. We found one white man dead at the edge of the sink-hole, whom they did not remove for fear of our fire, and scalped him, placing our dead brave upon him, thinking we could not leave him in a better situation than on the prostrate form of a fallen foe.

We had now effected our purpose and concluded to go back by land, thinking it unsafe to use our canoes. I found my wife and children, and the greater part of our people, at the mouth of the Iowa river. I now determined to remain with my family and hunt for them, and to humble myself before the Great Spirit, returning thanks to him for preserving me through the war. I made my hunting camp on English river, which is a branch of the Iowa. During the winter a party of Pottawattomies came from the Illinois to pay me a visit, among them was Washeown, an old man who had formerly lived in our village. He informed as that in the fall the Americans had built a fort at Peoria and had prevented them from going down the Sangamon to hunt. He said they were very much distressed.

Gomo had returned from the British Army, and brought news of their defeat near Malden. He told us that he went to the American chief with a flag, gave up fighting, and told him he desired to make peace for his nation. The American chief gave him a paper to the war chief at Peoria, and I visited that fort with Gomo. It was then agreed that there should be no more hostilities between the Americans and the Pottawattomies. Two of the white chiefs, with eight Pottawattomie braves, and five others, Americans, had gone down to St. Louis to have the treaty of peace confirmed. This, said Washeown, is good news; for we can now go to our hunting grounds, and, for my part, I never had anything to do with this war. The Americans never killed any of our people before the war, nor interfered with our hunting grounds, and I resolved to do nothing against them. I made no reply to these remarks as the speaker was old and talked like a child.

We gave the Pottawattomies a great feast. I presented Washeown with a good horse. My braves gave one to each of his party, and, at parting, said they wished us to make peace, which we did not promise, but told them that we would not send out war parties against the settlements.

A short time after the Pottawattomies had gone, a party of thirty braves belonging to our nation, from the peace camp on the Missouri, paid us a visit. They exhibited five scalps which they had taken on the Missouri, and wished us to join in a dance over them, which we willingly did. They related the manner in which they had taken these scalps. Myself and braves showed them the two we had taken near the Quiver, and told them the cause that induced us to go out with the war party, as well as the manner in which we took these scalps, and the difficulty we had in obtaining them.

They recounted to us all that had taken place, the number that had been slain by the peace party, as they were called and recognized to be, which far surpassed what our warriors, who had joined the British, had done. This party came for the purpose of joining the British, but I advised them to return to the peace party, and told them the news which the Pottawattomies had brought. They returned to the Missouri, accompanied by some of my braves whose families were there.

After "sugar-making" was over in the spring, I visited the Fox village at the lead mines. They had nothing to do with the war, and consequently were not in mourning. I remained there some days, spending my time very pleasantly with them in dancing and feasting. I then paid a visit to the Pottawattomie village on the Illinois River, and learned that Sanatuwa and Tatapuckey had been to St. Louis. Gomo told me that "peace had been made between his people and the Americans, and that seven of his band remained with the war chief to make the peace stronger." He then told me: "Washeown is dead! He had gone to the fort to carry some wild fowl to exchange for tobacco, pipes and other articles. He had secured some tobacco and a little flour, and left the fort before sunset, but had not proceeded far when he was *shot dead* by a white war chief, who had concealed himself near the path for that purpose. He then dragged him to the lake and threw him in, where I afterwards found him. I have since given two homes and a rifle to his relatives, not to break the peace, to which they have agreed."

I remained for some time at the village of Gomo, and went with him to the fort to pay a visit to the war chief. I spoke the Pottawattomie tongue well, and was taken for one of their people by him. He treated us friendly, and said he was very much displeased about the murder of Washeown. He promised us he would find out and punish the person who killed him. He made some inquiries about the Sacs, which I answered. On my return to Rock River, I was informed that a party of soldiers had gone up the Mississippi to build a fort at Prairie du Chien. They stopped near our village, appearing very friendly, and were treated kindly by our people.

We commenced repairing our lodges, putting our village in order, and clearing our cornfields. We divided the fields belonging to the party on the Missouri among those who wanted them, on condition that they should be relinquished to their owners on their return from the peace establishment. We were again happy in our village. Our women went cheerfully to work and all moved on harmoniously.

Some time afterward, five or six boats arrived loaded with soldiers on their way to Prairie du Chien to reinforce the garrison at that place. They appeared friendly and were well received, and we held a council with the war chief. We had no intention of hurting him or any of his party, for we could easily have defeated them. They remained with us all day and gave our people plenty of whisky. Doing the night a party arrived, by way of Rock River, who brought us six kegs of powder. They told us that the British had gone to Prairie du Chien and taken the fort. They wished us to again join them in the war, which we agreed to do. I collected my warriors and determined to pursue the boats, which had sailed with a fair wind. If we had known the day before, we could easily have taken them all, as the war chief used no precaution to prevent it.

I started immediately with my party, by land, in pursuit, thinking that some of their boats might get aground, or that the Great Spirit would put them in our power, if he wished them taken and their people killed. About half way up the rapids I had a full view of the boats all sailing with a strong wind. I discovered that one boat was badly managed, and was suffered to be drawn ashore by the wind. They landed by running hard aground and lowered their sail. The others passed on. This boat the Great Spirit gave to us.

All that could, hurried aboard, but they were unable to push off, being fast aground. We advanced to the river's bank undercover, and commenced firing on the boat. I encouraged my braves to continue firing. Several guns were fired from the boat, but without effect. I prepared my bow and arrows to throw fire to the sail, which was lying on the boat. After two or three attempts, I succeeded in setting it on fire. The boat was soon in flames. About this time, one of the boats that had passed returned, dropped anchor and swung in close to one which was on fire, taking off all the people except those who were killed or badly wounded. We could distinctly see them passing from one boat to the other, and fired on them with good effect. We wounded the war chief in this way.

Another boat now came down, dropped her anchor, which did not take hold, and drifted ashore. The other boat cut her cable and drifted down the river, leaving their comrades without attempting to assist them. We then commenced an attack upon this boat, firing several rounds, which was not returned. We thought they were afraid or only had a few aboard. I therefore ordered a rush toward the boat, but when we got near enough they fired, killing two of our braves— these being all we lost in the engagement. Some of their men jumped out and shoved the boat off, and thus got away without losing a man. I had a good opinion of this war chief, as he managed so much better than the others. It would give me pleasure to shake him by the hand.

We now put out the fire on the captured boat to save the cargo, when a skiff was seen coming down the river. Some of our people cried out, "Here comes an express from Prairie du Chien." We hoisted the British flag, but they would not land. They turned their little boat around, and rowed up the river. We directed a few shots at them, but they were so far off that we could not hurt them. I found several barrels of whisky on the captured boat, knocked in the heads and emptied the bad medicine into the river. I next found a box full of small bottles and packages, which appeared to be bad medicine also, such as the medicine men kill the white people with when they are sick. This I threw into the river.

Continuing my search for plunder, I found several guns, some large barrels filled with clothing, and a number of cloth lodges, all of which

I distributed among my warriors. We now disposed of the dead, and returned to the Fox village opposite the lower end of Rock Island, where we put up our new lodges, and hoisted the British flag. A great many of our braves were dressed in the uniform clothing which we had taken from the Americans, which gave our encampment the appearance of a regular camp of soldiers. We placed out sentinels and commenced dancing over the scalps we had taken. Soon after several boats passed down, among them a very large one carrying big guns. Our young men followed them some distance, but could do them no damage more than scare them. We were now certain that the fort at Prairie du Chien had been taken, as this large boat went up with the first party who built the fort.

In the course of the day some of the British came down in a small boat. They had followed the large one, thinking it would get fast in the rapids, in which case they were sure of taking her. They had summoned her on her way down to surrender, but she refused to do so, and now, that she had passed the rapids in safety, all hope of taking her had vanished. The British landed a big gun and gave us three soldiers to manage it. They complimented us for our bravery in taking the boat, and told us what they had done at Prairie do Chien. They gave us, a keg of rum, and joined with us in our dancing and feasting. We gave them some things which we had taken from the boat, particularly books and papers. They started the next morning, promising to return in a few days with a large body of soldiers.

We went to work under the direction of the men left with us, and dug up the ground in two places to put the big gun in, that the men might remain in with it and be safe. We then sent spies down the river to reconnoitre, who sent word by a runner that several boats were coming up filled with men. I marshalled my forces and was soon ready for their arrival. I resolved to fight, as we had not yet had a fair fight with the Americans during the war. The boats arrived in the evening, stopping at a small willow island, nearly opposite to us. During the night we removed our big gun further down, and at daylight next morning commenced firing. We were pleased to see that almost every shot took effect. The British being good gunners, rarely missed. They pushed off as quickly as possible, although I had expected they would land and give us battle.

I was fully prepared to meet them but was sadly disappointed by the boats all sailing down the river. A party of braves followed to watch where they landed, but they did not stop until they got below the Des Moines rapids, where they came ashore and commenced building a fort. I did not want a fort in our country, as we wished to go down to the Two River country in the fall and hunt, it being our choice hunting ground, and we concluded that if this fort was built, it would prevent us from going there. We arrived in the vicinity in the evening, and encamped on a high bluff for the night. We made no fire, for fear of being observed, and our young men kept watch by turns while others slept.

I was very tired, and was soon asleep. The Great Spirit, during my slumber, told me to go down the bluff to a creek, that I would there find a hollow tree cut down, and by looking in at the top of it, I would see a large snake with head erect—to observe the direction he was looking, and I would see the enemy close by and unarmed. In the morning I communicated to my braves what the Great Spirit had said to me, took one of them and went down a ravine that led to the creek. I soon came in sight of the place where they were building the fort, which was on a hill at the opposite side of the creek. I saw a great many men. We crawled cautiously on our hands and knees until we got to the bottom land, then through the grass and weeds until we reached the bank of the creek. Here I found a tree that had been cut down; I looked in at the top of it and saw a large snake, with his head raised, looking across the creek.

I raised myself cautiously, and discovered nearly opposite to me, two war chiefs walking arm in arm, without guns. They turned and walked back toward the place where the men were working at the fort. In a little while they returned, walking directly towards the spot where we lay concealed, but did not come so near as before. If they had they would have been killed, for each of us had a good rifle. We crossed the creek and crawled to a cluster of bushes. I again raised myself a little to see if they were coming; but they went into the fort, and by this they saved their lives.

We recrossed the creek and I returned alone, going up the same ravine I came down. My brave went down the creek, and I, on raising the brow of a hill to the left of the one we came down, could plainly see the men at work. I saw a sentinel walking in the bottom near the mouth of the creek. I watched him attentively, to see if he perceived my companion, who had gone toward him. The sentinel stopped for some time and looked toward where my brave was concealed. He walked first one way and then the other.

I observed my brave creeping towards him, at last he lay still for a while, not even moving the grass, and as the sentinel turned to walk away, my brave fired and he fell. I looked towards the fort, and saw the whites were in great confusion, running wildly in every direction, some down the steep bank toward a boat. My comrade joined me, we returned to the rest of the party and all hurried back to Rock River, where we arrived in safety at our village. I hung up my medicine bag, put away my rifle and spear, feeling as if I should want them no more, as I had no desire to raise other war parties against the whites unless they gave me provocation. Nothing happened worthy of note until spring, except that the fort below the rapids had been abandoned and burned by the Americans.

Soon after I returned from my wintering ground we received information that peace had been made between the British and Americans, and that we were required to make peace also, and were invited to go down to Portage des Sioux, for that purpose. Some advised that we should go down, others that we should not. Nomite, our principal civil chief, said he would go, as soon as the Foxes came down from the mines.

They came and we all started from Rock River, but we had not gone far before our chief was taken sick and we stopped with him at the village on Henderson River. The Foxes went on and we were to follow as soon as our chief got better, but he rapidly became worse and soon died. His brother now became the principal chief. He refused to go down, saying, that if he started, he would be taken sick and die as his brother had done. This seemed to be reasonable, so we concluded that none of us would go at this time. The Foxes returned. They said, "we have smoked the pipe of peace with our enemies, and expect that the Americans will send a war party against you if you do not go down." This I did not believe, as the Americans had always lost by their armies that were sent against us. La Gutrie and other British traders arrived at our village in the fall. La Gutrie told us that we must go down and make peace, as this was the wish of our English father. He said he wished us to go down to the Two River country to winter, where game was plenty, as there had been no hunting there for several years.

Having heard the principal war chief had come up with a number of troops, and commenced the erection of a fort near the Rapids des Moines, we consented to go down with the traders to visit the American chief, and tell him the reason why we had not been down sooner. When we arrived at the head of the rapids, the traders left their goods, and all of their boats with one exception, in which they accompanied us to see the Americans. We visited the war chief on board his boat, telling him what we had to say, and explaining why we had not been down sooner. He appeared angry and talked to La Gutrie for some time. I inquired of him what the war chief said. He told me that he was threatening to hang him up to the yard arm of his boat. "But" said he, "I am not afraid of what he says. He dare not put his threats into execution. I have done no more than I had a right to do as a British subject."

I then addressed the chief, asking permission for ourselves and some Menomonees, to go down to the Two River country for the purpose of hunting. He said we might go down but must return before the ice came, as he did not intend that we should winter below the fort. "But," he inquired, "what do you want the Menomonee to go with you for?"

I did not know at first what reply to make, but told him that they had a great many pretty squaws with them, and we wished them to go with us on that account. He consented. We all went down the river and remained all winter, as we had no intention of returning before spring when we asked leave to go. We made a good hunt. Having loaded our trader's boats with furs and peltries, they started to Mackinac, and we returned to our village.

There is one circumstance that I did not relate at the proper place. It has no reference to myself or people, but to my friend Gomo, the Pottawattomie chief. He came to Rock River to pay me a visit, and during his stay he related to me the following story:

> The war chief at Peoria is a very good man. He always speaks the truth and treats our people well. He sent for me one day, told me he was nearly out of provisions, and wished me to send my young men hunting to supply his fort. I promised to do so, immediately returned to my camp and told my young men the wishes and wants of the war chief. They readily agreed to go and hurt for our friend and returned with plenty of deer. They carried them to the fort, laid them down at the gate and returned to our camp. A few days afterward I went again to the fort to see if they wanted any more meat. The chief gave me powder and lead and said he wanted, me to send my hunters out again. When I returned to camp, I told my young men that the chief wanted more meat.

Matatah, one of my principal braves, said he would take a party and go across the Illinois, about one day's travel, where game was plenty, and make a good hunt for our friend the war chief. He took eight hunters with him, and his wife and several other squaws went with them. They had travelled about half the day in the prairie when they discovered a party of white men coming towards them with a drove of cattle. Our hunters apprehended no danger or they would have kept out of the way of the whites, who had not yet perceived them. Matatah changed his course, as he wished to meet and speak to the whites. As soon as the whites saw our party, some of them put off at full speed, and came up to our hunters. Matatah gave up his gun to them, and endeavoured to explain to them that he was friendly and was hunting for the war chief.

They were not satisfied with this but fired at and wounded him. He got into the branches of a tree that had blown down, to keep the horses from running over him. He was again fired on several times and badly wounded. He, finding that he would be murdered, and, mortally wounded already, sprang at the man nearest him, seized his gun and shot him from his horse. He then fell, covered with blood from his wounds, and immediately expired. The other hunters being in the rear of Matatah attempted to escape, after seeing their leader so basely murdered by the whites. They were pursued and nearly all of the party killed. My youngest brother brought me the news in the night, he having been with the party and was slightly wounded. He said the whites had abandoned their cattle and gone back towards the settlement. The rest of the night we spent in mourning for our friends.

At daylight I blacked my face and started for the fort to see the chief. I met him at the gate and told him what had happened. His countenance changed and I could see sorrow depicted in it for the death of my people. He tried to persuade me that I was mistaken, as he could not believe that the whites would act so cruelly. But when I convinced him, he said to me, 'those cowards who murdered your people shall be punished.' I told him that my people would have revenge, that they would not trouble any of his people at the fort, as we did not blame him or any of his soldiers, but that a party of my braves would go towards the Wabash to avenge the death of their friends and relations. The next day I took a party of hunters, killed several deer, and left them at the fort gate as I passed.

Here Gomo ended his story. I could relate many similar ones that have come within my own knowledge and observation, but I dislike to look back and bring on sorrow afresh. I will resume my narrative.

The great chief at St. Louis having sent word for us to come down and confirm the treaty, we did not hesitate, but started immediately that we might smoke the peace pipe with him. On our arrival we met the great chiefs in council. They explained to us the words of our Great Father at Washington, accusing us of heinous crimes and many misdemeanours, particularly in not coming down when first invited. We knew very well that our Great Father had deceived us and thereby forced us to join the British, and could not believe that he had put this speech into the mouths of those chiefs to deliver to us. I was not a civil chief and consequently made no reply, but our civil chiefs told the commissioner that, "What you say is a lie. Our Great Father sent us no such speech, he knew that the situation in which we had been placed was caused by him."

The white chiefs appeared very angry at this reply and said, "We will break off the treaty and make war against you, as you have grossly insulted us."

Our chiefs had no intention of insulting them and told them so, saying, "we merely wish to explain that you have told us a lie, without any desire to make you angry, in the same manner that you whites do when you do not believe what is told you." The council then proceeded and the pipe of peace was smoked.

Here for the first time, I touched the goose quill to the treaty not knowing, however, that, by the act I consented to give away my village. Had that been explained to me I should have opposed it and never would have signed their treaty, as my recent conduct will clearly prove.

What do we know of the manners, the laws, and the customs of the white people? They might buy our bodies for dissection, and we would touch the goose quill to confirm it and not know what we were doing. This was the case with me and my people in touching the goose quill for the first time.

We can only judge of what is proper and right by our standard of what is right and wrong, which differs widely from the whites, if I have been correctly informed. The whites may do wrong all their lives, and then if they are sorry for it when about to die, all is well, but with us it is different. We must continue to do good throughout our lives. If we have corn and meat, and know of a family that have none, we divide with them. If we have more blankets than we absolutely need, and others have not enough, we must give to those who are in want. But I will presently explain our customs and the manner in which we live.

We were treated friendly by the whites and started on our return to our village on Rock River. When we arrived we found that the troops had come to build a fort on Rock Island. This, in our opinion, was a contradiction to what we had done—"to prepare for war in time of peace." We did not object, however, to their building their fort on the island, but were very sorry, as this was the best one on the Mississippi, and had long been the resort of our young people during the summer. It was our garden, like the white people have near their big villages, which supplied us with strawberries, blackberries, gooseberries, plums, apples and nuts of different kinds. Being situated at the foot of the rapids its waters supplied us with the finest fish.

In my early life I spent many happy days on this island. A good spirit had charge of it, which lived in a cave in the rocks immediately under the place where the fort now stands. This guardian spirit has often been seen by our people. It was white, with large wings like a swan's, but ten times larger. We were particular not to make much noise in that part of the island which it inhabited, for fear of disturbing it. But the noise at the fort has since driven it away, and no doubt a bad spirit has taken its place.

Our village was situated on the north side of Rock River, at the foot of the rapids, on the point of land between Rock River and the Mississippi.

In front a prairie extended to the Mississippi, and in the rear a continued bluff gently ascended from the prairie.

Black Hawk's Tower

On its highest peak our watch tower was situated, from which we had a fine view for many miles up and down Rock River, and in every direction. On the side of this bluff we had our cornfields, extending about two miles up parallel with the larger river, where they adjoined those of the Foxes, whose village was on the same stream, opposite the lower end of Rock Island, and three miles distant from ours. We had eight hundred acres in cultivation including what we had on the islands in Rock River. The land around our village which remained unbroken, was covered with blue-grass which furnished excellent pasture for our horses. Several fine springs poured out of the bluff near by, from which we were well supplied with good water.

The rapids of Rock River furnished us with an abundance of excellent fish, and the land being very fertile, never failed to produce good crops of corn, beans, pumpkins and squashes. We always had plenty; our children never cried from hunger, neither were our people in want. Here our village had stood for more than a hundred years, during all of which time we were the undisputed possessors of the Mississippi Valley, from the Wisconsin to the Portage des Sioux, near the mouth of the Missouri, being about seven hundred miles in length.

At this time we had very little intercourse with the whites except those who were traders. Our village was healthy, and there was no place in the country possessing such advantages, nor hunting grounds better than those we had in possession. If a prophet had come to our village in those days and told us that the things were to take place which have since come to pass, none of our people would have believed him. What! to be driven from our village, and our hunting grounds, and not even to be permitted to visit the graves of our forefathers and relatives and our friends?

This hardship is not known to the whites. With us it is a custom to visit the graves of our friends and keep them in repair for many years. The mother will go alone to weep over the grave of her child. The brave, with pleasure, visits the grave of his father, after he has been successful in war, and repaints the post that marks where he lies. There is no place like that where the bones of our forefathers lie to go to when in grief. Here prostrate by the tombs of our fathers will the Great Spirit take pity on us.

But how different is our situation now from what it was in those happy days. Then were we as happy as the buffalo on the plains, but now, we are as miserable as the hungry wolf on the prairie. But I am digressing from my story. Bitter reflections crowd upon my mind and must find utterance.

When we returned to our village in the spring, from our wintering grounds, we would finish bartering with our traders, who always followed us to our village. We purposely kept some of our fine furs for this trade, and, as there was great opposition among them, who should get these furs, we always got our goods cheap. After this trade was met, the traders would give us a few kegs of rum, which were generally promised in the fall, to encourage us to make a good hunt and not go to war. They would then start with their furs and peltries, for their homes, and our old men would take a frolic. At this time our young men never drank. When this was ended, the next thing to be done was to bury our dead; such as had died during the year. This is a great medicine feast.

The relations of those who have died, give all the goods they have purchased, as presents to their friends, thereby reducing themselves to poverty, to show the Great Spirit that they are humble, so that he will take pity on them. We would next open the caches, take out the corn and other provisions which had been put up in the fall. We would then commence repairing our lodges. As soon as this was accomplished, we repair the fences around our cornfields and clean them off ready for planting. This work was done by the women. The men during this time are feasting on dried venison, bear's meat, wild fowl and corn prepared in different ways, while recounting to one another what took place during the winter.

Our women plant the corn, and as soon as they are done we make a feast, at which we dance the crane dance in which they join us, dressed in their most gaudy attire, and decorated with feathers. At this feast the young men select the women they wish to have for wives. He then informs his mother, who calls on the mother of the girl, when the necessary arrangements are made and the time appointed for him to come. He goes to the lodge when all are asleep, or pretend to be, and with his flint and steel strikes a light and soon finds where his intended sleeps. He then awakens her, holds the light close to his face that she may know him, after which he places the light close to her. If she blows it out the ceremony is ended and he appears in the lodge next morning as one of the family. If she does not blow out the light, but leaves it burning he retires from the lodge.

The next day he places himself in full view of it and plays his flute. The young women go out one by one to see who he is playing for. The tune changes to let them know he is not playing for them. When his intended makes her appearance at the door, he continues his courting tune until she returns to the lodge. He then quits playing and makes another trial at night which mostly turns out favourable. During the first year they ascertain whether they can agree with each other and be happy, if not they separate and each looks for another companion. If we were to live together and disagree, we would be as foolish as the whites. No indiscretion can banish a woman from her parental lodge; no difference how many children she may bring home she is always welcome—the kettle is over the fire to feed them.

The crane dance often lasts two or three days. When this is over, we feast again and have our national dance. The large square in the village is swept and prepared for the purpose. The chiefs and old warriors take seats on mats, which have been spread on the upper end of the square, next come the drummers and singers, the braves and women form the sides, leaving a large space in the middle. The drums beat and the singing commences. A warrior enters the square keeping time with the music. He shows the manner he started on a war party, how he approached the enemy, he strikes and shows how he killed him. All join in the applause, and he then leaves the square and another takes his place. Such of our young men have not been out in war parties and killed an enemy stand back ashamed, not being allowed to enter the square. I remember that I was ashamed to look where our young men stood, before I could take my stand in the ring as a warrior.

What pleasure it is to an old warrior, to see his son come forward and relate his exploits. It makes him feel young, induces him to enter the square and "fight his battles o'er again."

This national dance makes our warriors. When I was travelling last summer on a steamboat on the river, going from New York to Albany, I was shown the place where the Americans dance the war-dance, (West Point), where the old warriors recount to their young men what they have done to stimulate them to go and do likewise. This surprised me, as I did not think the whites understood our way of making braves.

When our national dance is over, our cornfields hoed, every weed dug up and our corn about knee high, all our young men start in a direction toward sundown, to hunt deer and buffalo and to kill Sioux if any are found on our hunting grounds. A part of our old men and women go to the lead mines to make lead, and the remainder of our people start to fish and get meat stuff. Everyone leaves the village and remains away about forty days. They then return, the hunting party bringing in dried buffalo and deer meat, and sometimes Sioux scalps, when they are found trespassing on our hunting grounds. At other times they are met by a party of Sioux too strong for them and are driven in. If the Sioux have killed the Sacs last, they expect to be retaliated upon and will fly before them, and so with us. Each party knows that the other has a right to retaliate, which induces those who have killed last to give way before their enemy, as neither wishes to strike, except to avenge the death of relatives.

All our wars are instigated by the relations of those killed, or by aggressions on our hunting grounds. The party from the lead mines brings lead, and the others dried fish, and mats for our lodges. Presents are now made by each party, the first giving to the others dried buffalo and deer, and they in return presenting them lead, dried fish and mats. This is a happy season of the year, having plenty of provisions, such as beans, squashes and other produce; with our dried meat and fish, we continue to make feasts and visit each other until our corn is ripe. Some lodge in the village a feast daily to the Great Spirit. I cannot explain this so that the white people will understand me, as we have no regular standard among us.

Everyone makes his feast as he thinks best, to please the Great Spirit, who has the care of all beings created. Others believe in two Spirits, one good and one bad, and make feasts for the Bad Spirit, to keep him quiet. They think that if they can make peace with him, the Good Spirit will not hurt them. For my part I am of the opinion, that so far as we have reason, we have a right to use it in determining what is right or wrong, and we should always pursue that path which we believe to be right, believing that "whatsoever is, is right." If the Great and Good Spirit wished us to believe and do as the whites, he could easily change our opinions, so that we could see, and think, and act as they do. We are nothing compared to his power, and we feel and know it. We have men among us, like the whites, who pretend to know the right path, but will not consent to show it without pay. I have no faith in their paths, but believe that every man must make his own path.

When our corn is getting ripe, our young people watch with anxiety for the signal to pull roasting ears, as none dare touch them until the proper time. When the corn is fit for use another great ceremony takes place, with feasting and returning thanks to the Great Spirit for giving us corn.

I will has relate the manner in which corn first came. According to tradition handed down to our people, a beautiful woman was seen to descend from the clouds, and alight upon the earth, by two of our ancestors who had killed a deer, and were sitting by a fire roasting a part of it to eat. They were astonished at seeing her, and concluded that she was hungry and had smelt the meat. They immediately went to her, taking with them a piece of the roasted venison. They presented it to her, she ate it, telling them to return to the spot where she was sitting at the end of one year, and they would find a reward for their kindness and generosity. She then ascended to the clouds and disappeared.

The men returned to their village, and explained to the tribe what they had seen, done and heard, but were laughed at by their people. When the period had arrived for them to visit this consecrated ground, where they were to find a reward for their attention to the beautiful woman of the clouds, they went with a large party, and found where her right hand had rested on the ground corn growing, where the left hand had rested beans, and immediately where she had been seated, tobacco.

The two first have ever since been cultivated by our people as our principal provisions, and the last is used for smoking. The white people have since found out the latter, and seem to it relish it as much as we do, as they use it in different ways: Smoking, snuffing and chewing.

We thank the Great Spirit for all the good he has conferred upon us. For myself, I never take a drink of water from a spring without being mindful of his goodness.

We next have our great ball play, from three to five hundred on a side play this game. We play for guns, lead, homes and blankets, or any other kind of property we may have. The successful party takes the stakes, and all return to our lodges with peace and friendship. We next commence horse racing, and continue on, sport and feasting until the corn is secured. We then prepare to leave our village for our hunting grounds.

The traders arrive and give us credit for guns, flints, powder, shot and lead, and such articles as we want to clothe our, families with and enable us to hunt. We first, however, hold a council with them, to ascertain the price they will give for our skins, and then they will charge us for the goods. We inform them where we intend hunting, and tell them where to build their houses. At this place we deposit a part of our corn, and leave our old people. The traders have always been kind to them and relieved them when in want, and consequently were always much respected by our people, and never since we were it nation, has one of them been killed by our people.

We then disperse in small parties to make our hunt, and as soon as it is over, we return to our trader's establishment, with our skins, and remain feasting, playing cards and at other pastimes until the close of the winter. Our young men then start on the beaver hunt, others to hunt raccoons and muskrats; the remainder of our people go to the sugar camps to make sugar. All leave our encampment and appoint a place to meet on the Mississippi, so that we may return together to our village in the spring. We always spend our time pleasantly at the sugar camp. It being the season for wild fowl, we lived well and always had plenty, when the hunters came in that we might make a feast for them. After this is over we return to our village, accompanied sometimes by our traders. In this way the time rolled round happily. But these are times that were.

While on the subject of our manners and customs, it might be well to relate an instance that occurred near our village just five years before we left it for the last time.

In 1827, a young Sioux Indian got lost on the prairie, in a snow storm, and found his way into a camp of the Sacs. According to Indian customs, although he was an enemy, he was safe while accepting their hospitality. He remained there for some time on account of the severity of the storm. Becoming well acquainted he fell in love with the daughter of the Sac at whose village he had been entertained, and before leaving for his own country, promised to come to the Sac village for her at a certain time during the approaching summer. In July he made his way to the Rock River village, secreting himself in the woods until he met the object of his love, who came out to the field with her mother to assist her in hoeing corn.

Late in the afternoon her mother left her and went to the village. No sooner had she got out of hearing, than he gave a loud whistle which assured the maiden that he had returned. She continued hoeing leisurely to the end of the row, when her lover came to meet her, and she promised to come to him as soon as she could go to the lodge and get her blanket, and together they would flee to his country. But unfortunately for the lovers the girl's two brothers had seen the meeting, and after procuring their guns started in pursuit of them. A heavy thunderstorm was coming on at the time. The lovers hastened to, and took shelter under a cliff of rocks, at Black Hawk's watchtower. Soon after a loud peal of thunder was heard, the cliff of rocks was shattered in a thousand pieces, and the lovers buried beneath, while in full view of her pursuing brothers. This, their unexpected tomb, still remains undisturbed.

This tower to which my name had been applied, was a favourite resort and was frequently visited by me alone, when I could sit and smoke my pipe, and look with wonder and pleasure, at the grand scenes that were presented by the sun's rays, even across the mighty water. On one occasion a Frenchman, who had been making his home in our village, brought his violin with him to the tower, to play and dance for the amusement of a number of our people, who had assembled there, and while dancing with his back to the cliff accidentally fell over it and was killed by the fall. The Indians say that always at the same time of the year, soft strains of the violin can be heard near that spot.

On returning in the spring from our hunting grounds, I had the pleasure of meeting our old friend, the trader of Peoria, at Rock Island. He came up in a boat from St. Louis, not as a trader, but as our agent. We were well pleased to see him. He told us that he narrowly escaped falling into the hands of Dixon. He remained with us a short time, gave us good advice, and then returned to St. Louis.

The Sioux having committed depredations on our people, we sent out war parties that summer, who succeeded in killing fourteen.

I paid several visits to Fort Armstrong, at Rock Island, during the summer, and was always well received by the gentlemanly officers stationed there, who were distinguished for their bravery, and they never trampled upon an enemy's rights. Colonel George Davenport resided near the garrison, and being in connection with the American Fur Company, furnished us the greater portion of our goods. We were not as happy then, in our village, as formerly. Our people got more liquor from the small traders than customary. I used all my influence to prevent drunkenness, but without effect. As the settlements progressed towards us, we became worse off and more unhappy.

Many of our people, instead of going to the old hunting grounds, when game was plenty, would go near the settlements to hunt, and, instead of saving their skins, to pay the trader for goods furnished them in the fall, would sell them to the settlement for whisky, and return in the spring with their families almost naked, and without the means of getting anything for them.

About this time my eldest son was taken sick and died. He had always been a dutiful child and had just grown to manhood. Soon after, my youngest daughter, an interesting and affectionate child, died also. This was a hard stroke, because I loved my children. In my distress I left the noise of the village and built my lodge on a mound in the cornfield, and enclosed it with a fence, around which I planted corn and beans. Here I was with my family alone. I gave everything I had away, and reduced myself to poverty. The only covering I retained was a piece of buffalo robe. I blacked my face and resolved on fasting for twenty-four moons, for the loss of my two children—drinking only of water during the day, and eating sparingly of boiled corn at sunset. I fulfilled my promise, hoping that the Great Spirit would take pity on me.

My nation had now some difficulty with the Iowas. Our young men had repeatedly killed some of them, and the breaches had always been made up by giving presents to the relations of those killed. But the last council we had with them, we promised that in case any more of their people were killed ours, instead of presents, we would give up the person or persons, who had done the injury. We made this determination known to our people, but notwithstanding this, one of our young men killed an Iowa the following winter.

A party of our people were about starting for the Iowa village to give the young man up, and I agreed to accompany them. When we were ready to start, I called at the lodge for the young man to go with us. He was sick, but willing to go, but his brother, however, prevented him and insisted on going to die in his place, as he was unable to travel. We started, and on the seventh day arrived in sight of the Iowa village, and within a short distance of it we halted ad dismounted. We all bid farewell to our young brave, who entered the village singing his death song, and sat down on the square in the middle of the village. One of the Iowa chiefs came out to us. We told him that we had fulfilled our promise, that we had brought the brother of the young man who had killed one of his people—that he had volunteered to come in his place, in consequence of his brother being unable to travel from sickness.

We had no further conversation but mounted our horses and rode off. As we started I cast my eye toward the village, and observed the Iowas coming out of their lodges with spears and war clubs. We took the backward trail and travelled until dark—then encamped and made a fire. We had not been there long before we heard the sound of horses coming toward us. We seized our arms, but instead of an enemy it was our young brave with two horses. He told me that after we had left him, they menaced him with death for some time—then gave him something to eat—smoked the pipe with him and made him a present of the two horses and some goods, and started him after us. When we arrived at our village our people were much pleased, and for their noble and generous conduct on this occasion, not one of the Iowa people has been killed since by our nation.

That fall I visited Malden with several of my band, and was well treated by the agent of our British Father, who gave us a variety of presents. He also gave me a medal, and told me there never would be war between England and America again; but for my fidelity to the British, during the war that had terminated some time before, requested me to come with my band and get presents every year, as Colonel Dixon had promised me.

I returned and hunted that winter on the Two Rivers. The whites were now settling the country fast. I was out one day hunting in a bottom, and met three white men. They accused me of killing their hogs. I denied it, but they would not listen to me. One of them took my gun out of my hand and fired it off—then took out the flint, gave it back to me and commenced beating me with sticks, ordering me at the same time to be off. I was so much bruised that I could not sleep for several nights.

Some time after this occurrence, one of my camp cut a bee tree and carried the honey to his lodge. A party of white men soon followed him, and told him the bee tree was theirs, and that he had no right to cut it. He pointed to the honey and told them to take it. They were not satisfied with this, but took all the packs of skins that he had collected during the winter, to pay his trader and clothe his family with in the spring, and carried them off.

How could we like a people who treated us so unjustly? We determined to break up our camp for fear they would do worse, and when we joined our people in the spring a great many of them complained of similar treatment.

This summer our agent came to live at Rock Island. He treated us well and gave us good advice. I visited him and the trader very often during the summer, and for the first time heard talk of our having to leave our village. The trader, Colonel George Davenport, who spoke our language, explained to me the terms of the treaty that had been made, and said we would be obliged to leave the Illinois side of the Mississippi, and advised us to select a good place for our village and remove to it in the spring. He pointed out the difficulties we would have to encounter if we remained at our village on Rock River. He had great influence with the principal Fox chief, his adopted brother, Keokuk. He persuaded him to leave his village, go to the west side of the Mississippi and build another, which he did the spring following.

Nothing was talked of but leaving our village. Keokuk had been persuaded to consent to go, and was using all his influence, backed by the war chief at Fort Armstrong and our agent and trader at Rock Island, to induce others to go with him. He sent the crier through our village, to inform our people that it was the wish of our Great Father that we should remove to the west side of the Mississippi, and recommended the Iowa River as a good place for the new village. He wished his party to make such arrangements, before they started on their winter's hunt, an to preclude the necessity of their returning to the village in the spring.

The party opposed to removing called on me for my opinion. I gave it freely, and after questioning Quashquame about the sale of our lands, he assured me that he "never had consented to the sale of our village." I now promised this party to be the leader, and raised the standard of opposition to Keokuk, with a full determination not to leave our village. I had an interview with Keokuk, to see if this difficulty could not be settled with our Great Father, and told him to propose to give any other land that our Great Father might choose, even our lead mines, to be peaceably permitted to keep the small point of land on which our village was situated. I was of the opinion that the white people had plenty of land and would never take our village from us. Keokuk promised to make an exchange if possible, and applied to our agent, and the great chief at St. Louis, who had charge of all the agents, for permission to go to Washington for that purpose.

This satisfied us for a time. We started to our hunting grounds with good hopes that something would be done for us. Doing the winter I received information that three families of whites had come to our village and destroyed some of our lodges, were making fences and dividing our cornfields for their own use. They were quarrelling among themselves about their lines of division. I started immediately for Rock River, a distance of ten days' travel, and on my arrival found the report true. I went to my lodge and saw a family occupying it. I wished to talk to them but they could not understand me.

I then went to Rock Island; the agent being absent, I told the interpreter what I wanted to say to these people, *viz*:

> Not to settle on our lands, nor trouble our fences, that there was plenty of land in the country for them to settle upon, and that they must leave our village, as we were coming back to it in the spring.

The interpreter wrote me a paper, I went back to the village and showed it to the intruders, but could not understand their reply. I presumed, however, that they would remove as I expected them to. I returned to Rock Island, passed the night there and had a long conversation with the trader. He advised me to give up and make my village with Keokuk on the Iowa River. I told him that I would not. The next morning I crossed the Mississippi on very bad ice, but the

Great Spirit had made it strong, that I might pass over safe. I travelled three days farther to see the Winnebago sub-agent and converse with him about our difficulties. He gave no better news than the trader had done. I then started by way of Rock River, to see the Prophet, believing that he as a man of great knowledge. When we met, I explained to him everything as it was. He at once agreed that I was right, and advised me never to give up our village, for the whites to plough up the bones of our people. He said, that if we remained at our village, the whites would not trouble us, and advised me to get Keokuk, and the party that consented to go with him to the Iowa in the spring, to return and remain at our village.

I returned to my hunting ground, after an absence of one moon, and related what I had done. In a short time we came up to our village, and found that the whites had not left it, but that others had come, and that the greater part of our cornfields had been enclosed. When we landed the whites appeared displeased because we came back. We repaired the lodges that had been left standing and built others. Keokuk came to the village, but his object was to persuade others to follow him to the Iowa. He had accomplished nothing towards making arrangements for us to remain, or to exchange other lands for our village. There was no more friendship existing between us. I looked upon him as a coward and no brave, to abandon his village to be occupied by strangers. What right had these people to our village, and our fields, which the Great Spirit had given us to live upon?

My reason teaches me that land cannot be sold. The Great Spirit gave it to his children to live upon and cultivate as far as necessary for their subsistence, and so long as they occupy and cultivate it they have the right to the soil, but if they voluntarily leave it, then any other people have a right to settle on it. Nothing can be sold but such things as can be carried away.

In consequence of the improvements of the intruders on our fields, we found considerable difficulty to get ground to plant a little corn. Some of the whites permitted us to plant small patches in the fields they had fenced, keeping all the best ground for themselves. Our women had great difficulty in climbing their fences, being unaccustomed to the kind, and were ill treated if they left a rail down.

One of my old friends thought he was safe. His cornfield was on a small island in Rock River. He planted his corn, it came up well, but the white man saw it; he wanted it, and took his teams over, ploughed up the crop and replanted it for himself. The old man shed tears, not for himself but on account of the distress his family would be in if they raised no corn. The white people brought whisky to our village, made our people drink, and cheated them out of their homes, guns and traps. This fraudulent system was carried to such an extent that I apprehended serious difficulties might occur, unless a stop was put to it. Consequently I visited all the whites and begged them not to sell my people whisky. One of them continued the practice openly; I took a party of my young men, went to his house, took out his barrel, broke in the head and poured out the whisky. I did this for fear some of the whites might get killed by my people when they were drunk.

Our people were treated very badly by the whites on many occasions. At one time a white man beat one of our women cruelly, for pulling a few suckers of corn out of his field to suck when she was hungry. At another time one of our young men was beat with clubs by two white men, for opening a fence which crossed our road to take his horse through. His shoulder blade was broken and his body badly bruised, from the effects of which be soon after died.

Bad and cruel as our people were treated by the whites, not one of them was hurt or molested by our band. I hope this will prove that we are a peaceable people—having permitted ten men to take possession of our cornfields, prevent us from planting corn, burn our lodges, ill-treat our women, and beat to death our men without offering resistance to their barbarous cruelties. This is a lesson worthy for the white man to learn: to use forbearance when injured.

We acquainted our agent daily with our situation, and through him the great chief at St. Louis, and hoped that something would be done for us. The whites were complaining at the same time that we were intruding upon their rights. They made it appear that they were the injured party, and we the intruders. They called loudly to the great war chief to protect their property.

How smooth must be the language of the whites, when they can make right look like wrong, and wrong like right.

During this summer I happened at Rock Island, when a great chief arrived, whom I had known as the great chief of Illinois, (Governor Cole) in company with another chief who I have been told is a great writer (judge James Hall.) I called upon them and begged to explain the grievances to them, under which my people and I were labouring, hoping that they could do something for us. The great chief however, did not seem disposed to council with, me. He said he was no longer the chief of Illinois; that his children had selected another father in his stead, and that he now only ranked as they did. I was surprised at this talk, as I had always heard that he was a good brave and great chief. But the white people appear to never be satisfied. When they get a good father, they hold councils at the suggestion of some bad, ambitious man, who wants the place himself, and conclude among themselves that this man, a, some other equally ambitious, would make a better father than they have, and nine times out of ten they don't get as good a one again.

I insisted on explaining to these chiefs the true situation of my people. They gave their assent. I rose and made a speech, in which I explained to them the treaty made by Quashquame, and three of our braves, according to the manner the trader and others had explained it to me. I then told them that Quashquame and his party positively denied having ever sold my village, and that as I had never known them to lie, I was determined to keep it in possession.

I told them that the white people had already entered our village, burned our lodges, destroyed our fences, ploughed up our corn and beat our people. They had brought whisky into our country, made our people drunk, and taken from them their homes, guns and traps, and that I had borne all this injury, without suffering any of my braves to raise a hand against the whites.

My object in holding this council was to get the opinion of these two chiefs as to the best course for me to pursue. I had appealed in vain, time after time to our agent, who regularly represented our situation to the chief at St. Louis, whose duty it was to call upon the Great Father to have justice done to us, but instead of this we are told that the white people wanted our county and we must leave it for them!

I did not think it possible that our Great Father wished us to leave our village where we had lived so long, and where the bones of so many of our people had been laid. The great chief said that as he no longer had any authority he could do nothing for us, and felt sorry that it was not in his power to aid us, nor did he know how to advise us. Neither of them could do anything for us, but both evidently were very sorry. It would give me great pleasure at all times to take these two chiefs by the hand.

That fall I paid a visit to the agent before we started to our hunting grounds, to hear if he had any good news for me. He had news. He said that the land on which our village now stood was ordered to be sold to individuals, and that when sold our right to remain by treaty would be at an end, and that if we returned next spring we would be forced to remove.

We learned during the winter, that part of the land where our village stood had been sold to individuals, and that the trader at Rock Island, Colonel Davenport, had bought the greater part that had been sold. The reason was now plain to me why he urged us to remove. His object, we thought, was to get our lands. We held several councils that winter to determine what we should do. We resolved in one of them, to return to our village as usual in the spring. We concluded that if we were removed by force, that the trader, agent and others must be the cause, and that if they were found guilty of having driven us from our village they should be killed. The trader stood foremost on this list. He had purchased the land on which my lodge stood, and that of our graveyard also. We therefore proposed to kill him and the agent, the interpreter, the great chief at St. Louis, the war chiefs at Forts Armstrong, Rock Island and Keokuk, these being the principal persons to blame for endeavouring to remove us.

Our women received bad accounts from the women who had been raising corn at the new village, of the difficulty of breaking the new prairie with hoes, and the small quantity of corn raised. We were nearly in the same condition with regard to the latter, it being the first time I ever knew our people to be in want of provisions.

I prevailed upon some of Keokuk's band to return this spring to the Rock River village, but Keokuk himself would not come. I hoped that he would get permission to go to Washington to settle our affairs with our Great Father. I visited the agent at Rock Island. He was displeased because we had returned to our village, and told me that we must remove to the west of the Mississippi. I told him plainly that we would not. I visited the interpreter at his house, who advised me to do as the agent had directed me. I then went to see the trader and upbraided him for buying our lands. He said that if he had not purchased them some person else would, and that if our Great Father would make an exchange with us, he would willingly give up the land he had purchased to the government. This I thought was fair, and began to think that he had not acted so badly as I had suspected. We again repaired our lodges and built others, as most of our village had been burnt and destroyed. Our women selected small patches to plant corn, where the whites had not taken them in their fences, and worked hard to raise something for our children to subsist upon.

I was told that according to the treaty, we had no right to remain on the lands sold, and that the government would force us to leave them. There was but a small portion however that had been sold, the balance remaining in the hands of the government. We claimed the right, if we had no other, to "live and hunt upon it as long as it remained the property of the government," by a stipulation in the treaty that required us to evacuate it after it had been sold. This was the land that we wished to inhabit and thought we had a right to occupy.

I heard that there was a great chief on the Wabash, and sent a party to get his advice. They informed him that we had not sold our village. He assured them then, that if we had not sold the land on which our village stood, our Great Father would not take it from us.

I started early to Malden to see the chief of my British Father, and told him my story. He gave the same reply that the chief on the Wabash had given, and in justice to him I must say he never gave me any bad advice, but advised me to apply to our American Father, who, he said, would do us justice. I next called on the great chief at Detroit and made the same statement to him that I had made to the chief of our British Father. He gave me the same reply. He said if we had not sold our lands, and would remain peaceably on them, that we would not be disturbed. This assured me that I was right, and determined me to hold out as I had promised my people. I returned from Malden late in the fall. My people were gone to their hunting ground, whither I followed.

Here I learned that they had been badly treated all summer by the whites, and that a treaty had been held at Prairie du Chien. Keokuk and some of our people attended it, and found that our Great Father had exchanged a small strip of the land that had been ceded by Quashquame and his party, with the Pottowattomies for a portion of their land near Chicago. That the object of this treaty was to get it back again, and that the United States had agreed to give them sixteen thousand dollars a year, forever for this small strip of land, it being less than a twentieth part of that taken from our nation for one thousand dollars a year.

This bears evidence of something I cannot explain. This land they say belonged to the United States. What reason then, could have induced them to exchange it with the Pottowattomies if it was so valuable? Why not keep it? Or if they found they had made a bad bargain with the Pottowattomies, why not take back their land at a fair proportion of what they gave our nation for it! If this small portion of the land that they took from us for one thousand dollars a year, be worth sixteen thousand dollars a year forever to the Pottowattomies, then the whole tract of country taken from us ought to be worth, to our nation, twenty times as much a this small fraction.

Here I was again puzzled to find out how the white people reasoned, and began to doubt whether they had any standard of right and wrong.

Communication was kept up between myself and the Prophet. Runners were sent to the Arkansas, Red river and Texas, not on the subject of our lands, but on a secret mission, which I am not at present permitted to explain.

It was related to me that the chiefs and head men of the Foxes had been invited to Prairie du Chien, to hold a council for the purpose of settling the difficulties existing between them and the Sioux.

The chiefs and head men, amounting to nine, started for the place designated, taking with them one woman, and were met by the Menonomees and Sioux, near the Wisconsin and killed, all except one man. Having understood that the whole matter was published shortly after it occurred, and is known to the white people, I will say no more about it.

I would here remark, that our pastimes and sports had been laid aside for two years. We were a divided people, forming two parties. Keokuk being at the head of one, willing to barter our rights merely for the good opinion of the whites, and cowardly enough to desert our village to them. I was at the head of the other division, and was determined to hold on to my village, although I had been ordered to leave it. But, I considered, as myself and band had no agency in selling our county, and that, as provision had been made in the treaty, for us all to remain on it as long as it belonged to the United States, that we could not be forced away. I refused therefore to quit my village. It was here that I was born, and here lie the bones of many friends and relations. For this spot I felt a sacred reverence, and never could consent to leave it without being forced therefrom.

When I called to mind the scenes of my youth and those of later days, when I reflected that the theatre on which these were acted, had been so long the home of my fathers, who now slept on the hills around it, I could not bring my mind to consent to leave this country to the whites for any earthly consideration.

The winter passed off in gloom. We made a bad hunt for want of guns, traps and other necessaries which the whites had taken from our people for whisky. The prospect before me was a bad one. I fasted and called upon the Great Spirit to direct my steps to the right path. I was in great sorrow because all the whites with whom I was acquainted and had been on terms of intimacy, advised me contrary to my wishes, that I began to doubt whether I had a friend among them.

Keokuk, who has a smooth tongue, and is a great speaker, was busy in persuading my band that I was wrong, and thereby making many of them dissatisfied with me. I had one consolation, for all the women were on my side on account of their cornfields.

On my arrival again at my village, with my band increased, I found it worse than before. I visited Rock Island and the agent again ordered me to quit my village. He said that if we did not, troops would be sent to drive us off. He reasoned with me and told me it would be better for us to be with the rest of our people, so that we might avoid difficulty and live in peace. The interpreter joined him and gave me so many good reasons that I almost wished I had not undertaken the difficult task I had pledged myself to my brave band to perform. In this mood I called upon the trader, who is fond of talking, and had long been my friend, but now amongst those who advised me to give up my village.

He received me very friendly and went on to defend Keokuk in what he had done, endeavouring to show me that I was bringing distress on our women and children. He inquired if some terms could not be made that would be honourable to me and satisfactory to my braves, for us to remove to the west side of the Mississippi. I replied that if our Great Father could do us justice and make the proposition, I could then give up honourably. He asked me "if the great chief at St. Louis would give us six thousand dollars to purchase provisions and other articles, if I would give up peaceably and remove to the west side of the Mississippi?"

After thinking some time I agreed that I could honourably give up, being paid for it, according to our customs, but told him that I could not make the proposal myself, even if I wished, because it would be dishonourable in me to do so. He said that he would do it by sending word to the great chief at St. Louis that he could remove us peaceably for the amount stated, to the west side of the Mississippi. A steamboat arrived at the island during my stay. After its departure the trader told me that he had requested a war chief, who was stationed at Galena, and was on board the steamboat, to make the offer to the great chief at St. Louis, and that he would soon be back and bring his answer. I did not let my people know what had taken place for fear they would be displeased. I did not much like what had been done myself, and tried to banish it from my mind.

After a few days had passed the war chief returned and brought an answer that "the great chief at St. Louis would give us nothing, and that if we did not remove immediately we would be driven off."

I was not much displeased with the answer they brought me, because I would rather have laid my bones with those of my forefathers than remove for any consideration. Yet if a friendly offer had been made as I expected, I would, for the sake of our women and children have removed peaceably.

I now resolved to remain in my village, and make no resistance if the military came, but submit to my fate. I impressed the importance of this course on all my band, and directed them in case the military came not to raise an arm against them.

About this time our agent was put out of office, for what reason I could never ascertain. I then thought it was for wanting to make us leave our village and if so it was right, because I was tired of hearing him talk about it. The interpreter, who had been equally as bad in trying to persuade us to leave our village was retained in office, and the young man who took the place of our agent, told the same old story over about removing us. I was then satisfied that this could not have been the cause.

Our women had planted a few patches of corn which was growing finely, and promised a subsistence for our children, but the white people again commenced ploughing it up. I now determined to put a stop to it by clearing our county of the intruders. I went to their principal men and told them that they should and must leave our country, giving them until the middle of the next day to remove. The worst left within the time appointed, but the one who remained, represented that his family, which was large, would be in a starving condition, if he went and left his crop. He promised to behave well, if I would consent to let him remain until fall, in order to secure his crop. He spoke reasonably and I consented.

We now resumed some of our games and pastimes, having been assured by the prophet that we would not be removed. But in a little while it was ascertained that a great war chief, General Gaines, was on his way to Rock River with a great number of soldiers. I again called upon the prophet, who requested a little time to see into the matter. Early next morning he came to me and said he had been dreaming; that he saw nothing bad in this great war chief, General Gaines, who was now near Rock River. That his object was merely to frighten us from our village, that the white people might get our land for nothing. He assured us that this great war chief dare not, and would not, hurt any of us. That the Americans were at peace with the British, and when they made peace, the British required, and the Americans agreed to it, that they should never interrupt any nation of Indians that was at peace, and that all we had to do to retain our village was to refuse any and every offer that might be made by this war chief.

The war chief arrived and convened a council at the agency. Keokuk and Wapello were sent for, and with a number of their band were present.

The council house was opened and all were admitted, and myself and band were sent for to attend. When we arrived at the door singing a war song, and armed with lances, spears, war clubs, bows and arrows, as if going to battle, I halted and refused to enter, as I could see no necessity or propriety in having the room crowded with those who were already there. If the council was convened for us, why then have others in our room. The war chief having sent all out except Keokuk, Wapello and a few of their chiefs and braves, we entered the council in this warlike appearance, being desirous of showing the war chief that we were not afraid. He then rose and made a speech. He said:

> The president is very sorry to be put to the trouble and expense of sending so large a body of soldiers here to remove you from the lands you have long since ceded to the United States. Your Great Father has already warned you repeatedly, through your agent, to leave the country, and he is very sorry to find that you have disobeyed his orders. Your Great Father wishes you well, and asks nothing from you but what is reasonable and right. I hope you will consult your own interests, and leave the country you are occupying, and go to the other side of the Mississippi.

I replied:

> We have never sold our country. We never received any annuities from our American father, and we are determined to hold on to our village.

The war chief, apparently angry, rose and said
"Who is *Black Hawk? Who is Black Hawk?*"
I replied:
"I am a *Sac!* My forefather was a *Sac!* I and all the nations call me a *Sac!!*"

The war chief said:

"I came here neither to beg nor hire you to leave your village. My business is to remove you, peaceably if I can, forcibly if I must! I will now give you two days in which to remove, and if you do not cross the Mississippi by that time, I will adopt measures to force you away."

I told him that I never would consent to leave my village and was determined not to leave it.

The council broke up and the war chief retired to his fort. I consulted the prophet again. He said he had been dreaming, and that the Great Spirit had directed that a woman, the daughter of Mattatas, the old chief of the village, should take a stick in her hand and go before the war chief, and tell him that she is the daughter of Mattatas, and that he had always been the white man's friend. That he had fought their battles, been wounded in their service and had always spoken well of them, and she had never heard him say that he had sold their village. The whites are numerous, and can take it from us if they choose, but she hoped they would not be so unfriendly. If they were, he had one favour to ask; she wished her people to be allowed to remain long enough to gather their provisions now growing in their fields; that she was a woman and had worked hard to raise something to support her children. And now, if we are driven from our village without being allowed to save our corn, many of our little children must perish with hunger.

Accordingly Mattatas' daughter was sent to the fort, accompanied by several of our young men and was admitted. She went before the war chief and told the story of the prophet. The war chief said that the president did not send him here to make treaties with the women, nor to hold council with them. That our young men most leave the fort, but she might remain if she wished.

All our plans were defeated. We must cross the river, or return to our village and await the coming of the war chief with his soldiers. We determined on the latter, but finding that our agent, interpreter, trader and Keokuk, were determined on breaking my ranks, and had induced several of my warriors to cross the Mississippi, I sent a deputation to the agent, at the request of my band, pledging myself to leave the county in the fall, provided permission was given us to remain, and secure our crop of corn then growing, as we would be in a starving situation if we were driven off without the means of subsistence.

The deputation returned with an answer from the war chief, "That no further time would be given than that specified, and if we were not then gone he would remove us."

I directed my village crier to proclaim that my orders were, in the event of the war chief coming to our village to remove us, that not a gun should be fired or any resistance offered. That if he determined to fight, for them to remain quietly in their lodges, and let him kill them if he chose.

I felt conscious that this great war chief would not hurt our people, and my object was not war. Had it been, we would have attacked and killed the war chief and his braves, when in council with us, as they were then completely in our power. But his manly conduct and soldierly deportment, his mild yet energetic manner, which proved his bravery, forbade it.

Some of our young men who had been out as spies came in and reported that they had discovered a large body of mounted men coming toward our village, who looked like a war party. They arrived and took a position below Rock River, for their place of encampment. The great war chief, General Gaines, entered Rock River in a steamboat, with his soldiers and one big gun. They passed and returned close by our village, but excited no alarm among my braves. No attention was paid to the boat; even our little children who were playing on the bank of the river, as usual, continued their amusement. The water being shallow, the boat got aground, which gave the whites some trouble. If they had asked for assistance, there was not a brave in my band who would not willingly have aided them. Their people were permitted to pass and repass through our village, and were treated with friendship by our people.

The war chief appointed the next day to remove us. I would have remained and been taken prisoner by the regulars, but was afraid of the multitude of pale faced militia, who were on horse back, as they were under no restraint of their chiefs.

We crossed the river during the night, and encamped some distance below Rock Island. The great war chief convened another council, for the purpose of making a treaty with us. In this treaty he agreed to give us corn in place of that we had left growing in our fields. I touched the goose quill to this treaty, and was determined to live in peace.

The corn that had been given us was soon found to be inadequate to our wants, when loud lamentations were heard in the camp by the women and children, for their roasting ears, beans and squashes. To satisfy them, a small party of braves went over in the night to take corn from their own fields. They were discovered by the whites and fired upon. Complaints were again made of the depredations committed by some of my people, on their own cornfields.

I understood from our agent, that there had been a provision made in one of our treaties for assistance in agriculture, and that we could have our fields ploughed if we required it. I therefore called upon him, and requested him to have a small log home built for me, and a field ploughed that fall, as I wished to live retired. He promised to have it done. I then went to the trader, Colonel Davenport, and asked for permission to be buried in the graveyard at our village, among my old friends and warriors, which he gave cheerfully. I then returned to my people satisfied.

A short time after this, a party of Foxes went up to Prairie du Chien to avenge the murder of their chiefs and relations, which had been committed the summer previous, by the Menomonees and Sioux. When they arrived in the vicinity of the encampment of the Menomonees, they met with a Winnebago, and inquired for the Menomonee camp. They requested him to go on before them and see if there were any Winnebagoes in it, and if so, to tell them that they had better return to their own camp. He went and gave the information, not only to the Winnebagoes, but to the Menomonees, that they might be prepared. The party soon followed, killed twenty-eight Menomonees, and made their escape.

This retaliation which with us is considered lawful and right, created considerable excitement among the whites. A demand was made for the Foxes to be surrendered to, and tried by, the white people. The principal men came to me during the fall and asked my advice. I conceived that they had done right, and that our Great Father acted very unjustly in demanding them, when he had suffered all their chiefs to be decoyed away, and murdered by the Menomonees, without ever having made a similar demand of them. If he had no right in the first instance he had none now, and for my part, I conceived the right very questionable, if not an act of usurpation in any case, where a difference exists between two nations, for him to interfere. The Foxes joined my band with the intention to go out with them on the fall hunt.

About this time, Neapope, who started to Malden when it was ascertained that the great war chief, General Gaines, was coming to remove us, returned. He said he had seen the chief of our British Father, and asked him if the Americans could force us to leave our village. He said:

If you had not sold your land the Americans could not take your village from you. That the right being vested in you only, could be transferred by the voice and will of the whole nation, and that as you have never given your consent to the sale of your country, it yet remains your exclusive property, from which the American government never could force you away, and that in the event of war, you should have nothing to fear, as we would stand by and assist you.

He said that he had called at the prophet's lodge on his way down, and there had learned for the first time, that we had left our village. He informed me privately, that the prophet was anxious to see me, as he had much good news to tell me, and that I would hear good news in the spring from our British father.

The prophet requested me to give you all the particulars, but I would much rather you would see him yourself and learn all from him. But I will tell you that he has received expresses from our British father, who says that he is going to send us guns, ammunition, provisions and clothing early in the spring. The vessels that bring them will come by way of Milwaukee. The prophet has likewise received *wampum* and tobacco from the different nations on the lakes, Ottawas, Chippewas, and Pottowattomies, and as to the Winnebagoes he has them all at his command. We are going to be happy once more.

I told him I was pleased that our British Father intended to see us righted. That we had been driven from our lands without receiving anything for them, and I now began to hope from his talk, that my people would once more be happy. If I could accomplish this I would be satisfied. I am now growing old and could spend the remnant of my time anywhere. But I wish first to see my people happy. I can then leave them cheerfully. This has always been my constant aim, and I now begin to hope that our sky will soon be clear.

Neapope said:

The prophet told me that all the tribes mentioned would fight for us if necessary, and the British father will support us. If we should be whipped, which is hardly possible, we will still be safe, the prophet having received a friendly talk from the chief of Wassicummico, at Selkirk's settlement, telling him, that if we were not happy in our own country, to let him know and he would make us happy. He had received information from our British father that we had been badly treated by the Americans. We must go and see the prophet. I will go first; you had better remain and get as many of your people to join you as you can. You know everything that we have done. We leave the matter with you to arrange among your people as you please. I will return to the prophet's village tomorrow. You can in the meantime make up your mind an to the course you will take and send word to the prophet by me, as he is anxious to assist us, and wishes to know whether you will join us, and assist to make your people happy.

During the night I thought over everything that Neapope had told me, and was pleased to think that by a little exertion on my part, I could accomplish the object of all my wishes. I determined to follow the advice of the prophet, and sent word by Neapope, that I would get all my braves together, explain everything that I had heard to them, and recruit as many as I could from the different villages.

Accordingly I sent word to Keokuk's band and the Fox tribe, explaining to them all the good news I had heard. They would not hear. Keokuk said that I had been imposed upon by liars, and had much better remain where I was and keep quiet. When he found that I was determined to make an attempt to recover my village, fearing that some difficulty would arise, he made application to the agent and great chief at St. Louis, asking permission for the chiefs of our nation to go to Washington to see our Great Father, that we might have our difficulties settled amicably. Keokuk also requested the trader, Colonel Davenport, who was going to Washington, to call on our Great Father and explain everything to him, and ask permission for us to come on and see him.

Having heard nothing favourable from the great chief at St. Louis, I concluded that I had better keep my band together, and recruit as many as possible, so that I would be prepared to make the attempt to rescue my village in the spring, provided our Great Father did not send word for us to go to Washington. The trader returned. He said he had called on our Great Father and made a full statement to him in relation to our difficulties, and had asked leave for us to go to Washington, but had received no answer.

I had determined to listen to the advice of my friends, and if permitted to go to see our Great Father, to abide by his counsel, whatever it might be. Every overture was made by Keokuk to prevent difficulty, and I anxiously hoped that something would be done for my people that it might be avoided. But there was bad management somewhere, or the difficulty that has taken place would have been avoided.

When it was ascertained that we would not be permitted to go to Washington, I resolved upon my course, and again tied to recruit some braves from Keookuk's band, to accompany me, but could not.

Conceiving that the peaceable disposition of Keokuk and his people had been in a great measure the cause of our having been driven from our village, I ascribed their present feelings to the same cause, and immediately went to work to recruit all my own band, and making preparations to ascend Rock River, I made my encampment on the Mississippi, where Fort Madison had stood. I requested my people to rendezvous at that place, sending out soldiers to bring in the warriors, and stationed my sentinels in a position to prevent any from moving off until all were ready.

My party having all come in and got ready, we commenced our march up the Mississippi; our women and children in canoes, carrying such provisions as we had, camp equipage, &c. My braves and warriors were on horseback, armed and equipped for defence. The prophet came down and joining us below Rock River, having called at Rock Island on his way down, to consult the war chief, agent and trader; who, he said, used many arguments to dissuade him from going with us, requesting him to come and meet us and turn us back. They told him also there was a war chief on his way to Rock Island with a large body of soldiers.

The prophet said he would not listen to this talk, because no war chief would dare molest us so long as we were at peace. That we had a right to go where we pleased peaceably, and advised me to say nothing to my braves and warriors until we encamped that night. We moved onward until we arrived at the place where General Gaines had made his encampment the year before, and encamped for the night. The prophet then addressed my braves and warriors. He told them to:

> Follow us and act like braves, and we have nothing to fear and much to gain. The American war chief may come, but will not, nor dare not interfere with us so long as we act peaceably. We are not yet ready to act otherwise. We must wait until we ascend Rock River and receive our reinforcements, and we will then be able to withstand any army.

That night the White Beaver, General Atkinson, with a party of soldiers passed up in a steamboat. Our party became alarmed, expecting to meet the soldiers at Rock River, to prevent us going up. On our arrival at its mouth, we discovered that the steamboat had passed on.

I was fearful that the war chief had stationed his men on some high bluff, or in some ravine, that we might be taken by surprise. Consequently, on entering Rock River we commenced beating our drums and singing, to show the Americans that we were not afraid.

Having met with no opposition, we moved up Rock River leisurely for some distance, when we were overtaken by an express from White Beaver, with an order for me to return with my band and recross the Mississippi again. I sent him word that I would not, not recognizing his right to make such a demand, as I was acting peaceably, and intended to go to the prophet's village at his request, to make corn.

The express returned. We moved on and encamped some distance below the prophet's village. Here another express came from the White Beaver, threatening to pursue us and drive us back, if we did not return peaceably. This message roused the spirit of my band, and all were determined to remain with me and contest the ground with the war chief, should he come and attempt to drive us. We therefore directed the express to say to the war chief "if he wished to fight us he might come on." We were determined never to be driven, and equally so, not to make the first attack, our object being to act only on the defensive. This we conceived to be our right.

Soon after the express returned, Mr. Gratiot, sub-agent for the Winnebagoes, came to our encampment. He had no interpreter, and was compelled to talk through his chiefs. They said the object of his mission was to persuade us to return. But they advised us to go on—assuring us that the further we went up Rock River the more friends we would meet, and our situation would be bettered. They were on our side and all of their people were our friends. We must not give up, but continue to ascend Rock River, on which, in a short time, we would receive reinforcements sufficiently strong to repulse any enemy. They said they would go down with their agent, to ascertain the strength of the enemy, and then return and give us the news. They had to use some stratagem to deceive their agent in order to help us.

During this council several of my braves hoisted the British flag, mounted their horses and surrounded the council lodge. I discovered that the agent was very much frightened. I told one of his chiefs to tell him that he need not be alarmed, and then went out and directed my braves to desist. Every warrior immediately dismounted and returned to his lodge. After the council adjourned I placed a sentinel at the agent's lodge to guard him, fearing that some of my warriors might again frighten him. I had always thought he was a good man and was determined that he should not be hurt. He started with his chiefs to Rock Island.

Having ascertained that White Beaver would not permit us to remain where we were, I began to consider what was best to be done, and concluded to keep on up the river, see the Pottowattomies and have a talk with them. Several Winnebago chiefs were present, whom I advised of my intentions, as they did not seem disposed to render us any assistance. I asked them if they had not sent us *wampum* during the winter, and requested us to come and join their people and enjoy all the rights and privileges of their country. They did not deny this; and said if the white people did not interfere, they had no objection to our making corn this year, with our friend the prophet, but did not wish us to go any further up.

The next day I started with my party to Kishwacokee. That night I encamped a short distance above the prophet's village. After all was quiet in our camp I sent for my chiefs, and told them that we had been deceived. That all the fair promises that had been held out to us through Neapope were false. But it would not do to let our party know it. We must keep it secret among ourselves, move on to Kishwacokee, as if all was right, and say something on the way to encourage our people. I will then call on the Pottowattomies, hear what they say, and see what they will do.

We started the next morning, after telling our people that news had just come from Milwaukee that a chief of our British Father would be there in a few days. Finding that all our plans were defeated, I told the prophet that he must go with me, and we would see what could be done with the Pottowattomies. On our arrival at Kishwacokee an express was sent to the Pottowattomie villages. The next day a deputation arrived. I inquired if they had corn in their villages. They said they had a very little and could not spare any. I asked them different questions and received very unsatisfactory answers.

This talk was in the presence of all my people. I afterwards spoke to them privately, and requested them to come to my lodge after my people had gone to sleep. They came and took seats. I asked them if they had received any news from the British on the lake. They said no. I inquired if they had heard that a chief of our British Father was coming to Milwaukee to bring us guns, ammunition, goods and provisions. They said no. I told them what news had been brought to me, and requested them to return to their village and tell the chiefs that I wished to see them and have a talk with them.

After this deputation started, I concluded to tell my people that if White Beaver came after us, we would go back, as it was useless to think of stopping or going on without more provisions and ammunition. I discovered that the Winnebagoes and Pottowattomies were not disposed to render us any assistance. The next day the Pottowattomie chiefs arrived in my camp. I had a dog killed, and made a feast. When it was ready, I spread my medicine bags, and the chiefs began to eat. When the ceremony was about ending, I received news that three or four hundred white men on horseback had been seen about eight miles off. I immediately started three young men with a white flag to meet them and conduct them to our camp, that we might hold a council with them and descend Rock River again.

I also directed them, in case the whites had encamped, to return, and I would go and see them. After this party had started I sent five young men to see what might take place. The first party went to the camp of the whites, and were taken prisoners. The last party had not proceeded far before they saw about twenty men coming toward them at full gallop. They stopped, and, finding that the whites were coming toward them in such a warlike attitude, they turned and retreated, but were pursued, and two of them overtaken and killed. The others then made their escape. When they came in with the news, I was preparing my flags to meet the war chief. The alarm was given. Nearly all my young men were absent ten miles away. I started with what I had left, about forty, and had proceeded but a short distance, before we saw a part of the army approaching. I raised a yell, saying to my braves, "Some of our people have been killed. Wantonly and cruelly murdered! We must avenge their death!"

In a little while we discovered the whole army coming towards us at a full gallop. We were now confident that our first party had been killed. I immediately placed my men behind a cluster of bushes, that we might have the first fire when they had approached close enough. They made a halt some distance from us. I gave another yell, and ordered my brave warriors to charge upon them, expecting that they would all be killed. They did charge. Every man rushed towards the enemy and fired, and they retreated in the utmost confusion and consternation before my little but brave band of warriors.

After following the enemy for some distance, I found it useless to pursue them further, as they rode so fast, and returned to the encampment with a few braves, as about twenty-five of them continued in pursuit of the flying enemy. I lighted my pipe and sat down to thank the Great Spirit for what he had done. I had not been meditating long, when two of the three young men I had sent with the flag to meet the American war chief, entered. My astonishment was not greater than my joy to see them living and well. I eagerly listened to their story, which was as follows:

> When we arrived near the encampment of the whites, a number of them rushed out to meet us, bringing their guns with them. They took us into their camp, where an American who spoke the Sac language a little told us that his chief wanted to know how we were, where we were going, where our camp was, and where was Black Hawk? We told him that we had come to see his chief, that our chief had directed us to conduct him to our camp, in case he had not encamped, and in that event to tell him that he, Black Hawk, would come to see him; he wished to hold a council with him, as he had given up all intention of going to war.

This man had once been a member of our tribe, having been adopted by me many years before and treated with the same kindness as was shown to our young men, but like the caged bird of the woods, he yearned for freedom, and after a few years residence with us an opportunity for escape came and he left us. On this occasion he would have respected our flag and carried back the message I had sent to his chief, had he not been taken prisoner, with a comrade, by some of my braves who did not recognize him, and brought him into camp. They were securely tied with cords to trees and left to meditate, but were occasionally buffeted by my young men when passing near them. When I passed by him there was a recognition on the part of us both, but on account of former friendship I concluded to let him go, and some little time before the sun went down I released him from his captivity by untying the cords that bound him and accompanied him outside of our lines so that he could escape safely. His companion had previously made a desperate effort to escape from his guards and was killed by them.

They continued their story:

> At the conclusion of this talk a party of white men came in

on horseback. We saw by their countenances that something had happened. A general tumult arose. They looked at us with indignation, talked among themselves for a moment, when several of them cocked their guns and fired at us in the crowd. Our companion fell dead. We rushed through the crowd and made our escape. We remained in ambush but a short time, before we heard yelling like Indians running an enemy. In a little while we saw some of the whites in full speed. One of them came near us. I threw my tomahawk and struck him on the head which brought him to the ground; I ran to him and with his own knife took off his scalp. I took his gun, mounted his horse, and brought my friend here behind me. We turned to follow our braves, who were chasing the enemy, and had not gone far before we overtook a white man, whose horse had mired in a swamp.

My friend alighted and tomahawked the man, who was apparently fast under his horse. He took his scalp, horse and gun. By this time our party was some distance ahead. We followed on and saw several white men lying dead on the way. After riding about six miles we met our party returning. We asked them how many of our men had been killed. . They said none after the Americans had retreated. We inquired how many whites had been killed. They replied that they did not know, but said we will soon ascertain, as we must scalp them as we go back. On our return we found ten men, besides the two we had killed before we joined our friends.

Seeing that they did not yet recognize us, it being dark, we again asked how many of our braves had been killed? They said five. We asked who they were? They replied that the first party of three who went out to meet the American war chief, had all been taken prisoners and killed in the encampment, and that out of a party of five, who followed to see the meeting of the first party with the whites, two had been killed. We were now certain that they did not recognise us, nor did we tell who we were until we arrived at our camp. The news of our death had reached it some time before, and all were surprised to see us again.

The next morning I told the crier of my village to give notice that we must go and bury our dead. In a little while all were ready. A small deputation was sent for our absent warriors, and the remainder started to bury the dead. We first disposed of them and then commenced an examination in the enemy's deserted encampment for plunder. We found arms and ammunition and provisions, all of which we were sadly in want of, particularly the latter, as we were entirely without. We found also a variety of saddle bags, which I distributed among my braves, a small quantity of whisky and some little barrels that had contained this bad medicine, but they were empty. I was surprised to find that the whites carried whisky with them, as I had understood that all the pale faces, when acting is soldiers in the field, were strictly temperate.

The enemy's encampment was in a skirt of woods near a run, about half a day's travel from Dixon's Ferry. We attacked them in the prairie, with a few bushes between us, about sundown, and I expected that my whole party would be killed. I never was so much surprised in all the fighting I have seen, knowing, too, that the Americans generally shoot well, as I was to see this army of several hundreds retreating, without showing fight, and passing immediately through their encampment, I did think they intended to halt there, as the situation would have forbidden attack by my party if their number had not exceeded half of mine, as we would have been compelled to take the open prairie whilst they could have picked trees to shield themselves from our fire.

I was never so much surprised in my life as I was in this attack. An army of three or four hundred men, after having learned that we were suing for peace, to attempt to kill the flag bearers that had gone unarmed to ask for a meeting of the war chiefs of the two contending parties to hold a council, that I might return to the west side of the Mississippi, to come forward with a full determination to demolish the few braves I had with me, to retreat when they had ten to one, was unaccountable to me. It proved a different spirit from any I had ever before seen among the pale faces. I expected to see them fight as the Americans did with the British during the last war, but they had no such braves among them.

At our feast with the Pottowattomies I was convinced that we had been imposed upon by those who had brought in reports of large re-enforcements to my band and resolved not to strike a blow; and in order to get permission from White Beaver to return and re-cross the Mississippi, I sent a flag of peace to the American war chief, who was reported to be close by with his army, expecting that he would convene a council and listen to what we had to say. But this chief, instead of pursuing that honourable and chivalric course, such as I have always practiced, shot down our flag-bearer and thus forced us into war with less than five hundred warriors to contend against three or four thousand soldiers.

The supplies that Neapope and the prophet told us about, and the reinforcements we were to have, were never more heard of, and it is but justice to our British Father to say were never promised, his chief being sent word in lieu of the lies that were brought to me, "for us to remain at peace as we could accomplish nothing but our own ruin by going to war."

What was now to be done? It was worse than folly to turn back and meet an enemy where the odds were so much against us and thereby sacrifice ourselves, our wives and children to the fury of an enemy who had murdered some of our brave and unarmed warriors when they were on a mission to sue for peace.

Having returned to our encampment, and found that all our young men had come in, I sent out spies to watch the movements of the army, and commenced moving up Kishwacokee with the balance of my people. I did not know where to go to find a place of safety for my women and children, but expected to find a good harbour about the head of Rock River. I concluded to go there, and thought my best route would be to go round the head of Kishwacokee, so that the Americans would have some difficulty if they attempted to follow us.

On arriving at the head of Kishwacokee, I was met by a party of Winnebagoes, who seemed to rejoice at our success. They said they had come to offer their services, and were anxious to join in. I asked them if they knew where there was a safe place for our women and children. They told us that they would send two old men with us to guide us to a good safe place.

I arranged war parties to send out in different directions, before I proceeded further. The Winnebagoes went alone. The war parties having all been fitted out and started, we commenced moving to the Four Lakes, the place where our guides were to conduct us. We had not gone far before six Winnebagoes came in with one scalp. They said they had killed a man at a grove, on the road from Dixon's to the lead mines. Four days after, the party of Winnebagoes who had gone out from the head of Kishwacokee, overtook us, and told me that they had killed four men and taken their scalps: and that one of them was Keokuk's father, (the agent). They proposed to have a dance over their scalps.

I told them that I could have no dancing in my camp, in consequence of my having lost three young braves; but they might dance in their own camp, which they did. Two days after, we arrived in safety at the place where the Winnebagoes had directed us. In a few days a great number of our warriors came in. I called them all around me, and addressed them. I told them: "Now is the time, if any of you wish to come into distinction, and be honoured with the medicine bag! Now is the time to show you, courage and bravery, and avenge the murder of our three braves !"

Several small parties went out, and returned again in a few days, with success—bringing in provisions for our people. In the mean time, some spies came in, and reported that the army had fallen back to Dixon's Ferry; and others brought news that the horsemen had broken up their camp, disbanded, and returned home.

Finding that all was safe, I made a dog feast, preparatory to leaving my camp with a large party, (as the enemy were stationed so far off). Before my braves commenced feasting, I took my medicine bags, and addressed them in the following language:

Braves and Warriors:
These are the medicine bags of our forefather, Mukataquet, who was the father of the Sac nation. They were handed down to the great war chief of our nation, Nanamakee, who has been at war with all the nations of the plains, and have never yet been disgraced! I expect you all to protect them!

After the ceremony was over and our feasting done I started, with about two hundred warriors following my great medicine bags. I directed my, course toward sunset and dreamed, the second night after we started, that there would be a great feast prepared for us after one day's travel. I told my warriors my dream in the morning and we started for Moscohocoynak, (Apple River). When we arrived in the vicinity of a fort the white people had built there we saw four men on horseback. One of my braves fired and wounded a man when the others set up a yell as if a large force were near and ready to come against us. We concealed ourselves and remained in this position for some time watching to see the enemy approach, but none came. The four men, in the meantime, ran to the fort and gave the alarm. We followed them and attacked their fort.

One of their braves, who seemed more valiant than the rest, raised his head above the picketing to fire at us when one of my braves, with a well-directed shot, put an end to his bravery. Finding that these people could not be killed without setting fire to their houses and fort I thought it more prudent to be content with what flour, provisions, cattle and horses we could find than to set fire to their buildings, as the light would be seen at a distance and the army might suppose we were in the neighbourhood and come upon us with a strong force. Accordingly we opened a house and filled our bags with flour and provisions, took several horses and drove off some of their cattle.

We started in a direction toward sunrise. After marching a considerable time I discovered some white men coming towards us. I told my braves that we would go into the woods and kill them when they approached. We concealed ourselves until they came near enough and then commenced yelling and firing and made a rush upon them. About this time their chief, with a party of men, rushed up to rescue the men we had fired upon. In a little while they commenced retreating and left their chief and a few braves who seemed willing and anxious to fight. They acted like men, but were forced to give way when I rushed upon them with my braves. In a short time the chief returned with a larger party. He seemed determined to fight, and anxious for a battle.

When he came near enough I raised the yell and firing commenced from both sides. The chief, who seemed to be a small man, addressed his warriors in a loud voice, but they soon retreated, leaving him and a few braves on the battlefield. A great number of my warriors pursued the retreating party and killed a number of their horses as they ran.

The chief and his few braves were unwilling to leave the field. I ordered my braves to rush upon them, and had the mortification of seeing two of my chiefs killed before the enemy retreated.

This young chief deserves great praise for his courage and bravery, but fortunately for us, his army was not all composed of such brave men.

During this attack we killed several men and about forty horses and lost two young chiefs and seven warriors. My braves were anxious to pursue them to the fort, attack and burn it, but I told them it was useless to waste our powder as there was no possible chance of success if we did attack them, and that as we had ran the bear into his hole we would there leave him and return to our camp.

On arriving at our encampment we found that several of our spies had returned, bringing intelligence that the army had commenced moving. Another party of five came in and said they had been pursued for several hours, and were attacked by twenty-five or thirty whites in the woods; that the whites rushed in upon them as they lay concealed and received their fire without seeing them. They immediately retreated whilst we reloaded. They entered the thicket again and as soon as they came near enough we fired. Again they retreated and again they rushed into the thicket and fired. We returned their fire and a skirmish ensued between two of their men and one of ours, who was killed by having his throat cut. This was the only man we lost, the enemy having had three killed; they again retreated.

Another party of three Sacs had come in and brought two young white squaws, whom they had given to the Winnebagoes to take to the whites. They said they had joined a party of Pottowattomies and went with them as a war party against the settlers of Illinois.

The leader of this party, a Pottowattomie, had been severely whipped by this settler, some time before, and was anxious to avenge the insult and injury. While the party was preparing to start, a young Pottowattomie went to the settler's house and told him to leave it, that a war party was coming to murder them. They started, but soon returned again, as it appeared that they were all there when the war party arrived. The Pottowattomies killed the whole family, except two young squaws, whom the Sacs took up on their horses and carried off, to save their lives. They were brought to our encampment, and a messenger sent to the Winnebagoes, as they were friendly on both sides, to come and get them, and carry them to the whites. If these young men, belonging to my band, had not gone with the Pottowattomies, the two young squaws would have shared the same fate as their friends.

During our encampment at the Four Lakes we were hard pressed to obtain enough to eat to support nature. Situated in a swampy, marshy country, (which had been selected in consequence of the great difficulty required to gain access thereto,) there was but little game of any sort to be found, and fish were equally scarce. The great distance to any settlement, and the impossibility of bringing supplies therefrom, if any could have been obtained, deterred our young men from making further attempts. We were forced to dig roots and bark trees, to obtain something to satisfy hunger and keep us alive. Several of our old people became so reduced, as to actually die with hunger! Learning that the army had commenced moving, and fearing that they might come upon and surround our encampment, I concluded to remove our women and children across the Mississippi, that they might return to the Sac nation again. Accordingly, on the next day we commenced moving, with five Winnebagoes acting as our guides, intending to descend the Wisconsin.

Neapope, with a party of twenty, remained in our rear, to watch for the enemy, whilst we were proceeding to the Wisconsin, with our women and children. We arrived, and had commenced crossing over to an island, when we discovered a large body of the enemy coming towards us. We were now compelled to fight, or sacrifice our wives and children to the fury of the whites. I met them with fifty warriors, (having left the balance to assist our women and children in crossing) about a mile from the river, When an attack immediately commenced, I was mounted on a fine horse, and was pleased to see my warriors so brave. I addressed them in a load voice, telling them to stand their ground and never yield it to the enemy. At this time I was on the rise of a hill, where I wished to form my warriors, that we might have some advantage over the whites.

But the enemy succeeded in gaining this point, which compelled us to fall into a deep ravine, from which we continued firing at them and they at us, until it began to grow dark. My horse having been wounded twice during this engagement, and fearing from his loss of blood that he would soon give out, and finding that the enemy would not come near enough to receive our fire, in the dusk of the evening, and knowing that our women and children had had sufficient time to reach the island in the Wisconsin, I ordered my warriors to return, by different routes, and meet me at the Wisconsin, and was astonished to find that the enemy were not disposed to pursue us.

In this skirmish with fifty braves, I defended and accomplished my passage over the Wisconsin, with a loss of only six men, though opposed by a host of mounted militia. I would not have fought there, but to gain time for our women and children to cross to an island. A warrior will duly appreciate the embarrassments I laboured under—and whatever may be the sentiments of the white people in relation to this battle, my nation, though fallen, will award to me the reputation of a great brave in conducting it.

The loss of the enemy could not be ascertained by our party; but I am of the opinion that it was much greater, in proportion, than mine. We returned to the Wisconsin and crossed over to our people.

Here some of my people left me, and descended the Wisconsin, hoping to escape to the west side of the Mississippi, that they might return home. I had no objection to their leaving me, as my people were all in a desperate condition, being worn out with travelling and starving with hunger. Our only hope to save ourselves was to get across the Mississippi. But few of this party escaped. Unfortunately for them, a party of soldiers from Prairie du Chien were stationed on the Wisconsin, a short distance from its mouth, who fired upon our distressed people. Some were killed, others drowned, several taken prisoners, and the balance escaped to the woods and perished with hunger. Among this party were a great many women and children.

I was astonished to find that Neapope and his party of spies had not yet come in, they having been left in my rear to bring the news, if the enemy were discovered. It appeared, however, that the whites had come in a different direction and intercepted our trail but a short distance from the place where we first saw them, leaving our spies considerably in the rear. Neapope and one other retired to the Winnebago village, and there remained during the war. The balance of his party, being brave men, and considering our interests as their own, returned, and joined our ranks.

Myself and band having no means to descend the Wisconsin, I started over a rugged country, to go to the Mississippi, intending to cross it and return to my nation. Many of our people were compelled to go on foot, for want of horses, which, in consequence of their having had nothing to eat for a long time, caused our march to be very slow. At length we arrived at the Mississippi, having lost some of our old men and little children, who perished on the way with hunger.

We had been here but a little while before we saw a steamboat (the *Warrior*,) coming. I told my braves not to shoot, as I intended going on board, so that we might save our women and children. I knew the captain (Throckmorton) and was determined to give myself up to him. I then sent for my white flag. While the messenger was gone, I took a small piece of white cotton and put it on a pole, and called to the captain of the boat, and told him to send his little canoe ashore and let me come aboard. The people on board asked whether we were Sacs or Winnebagoes. I told a Winnebago to tell them that we were Sacs, and wanted to give ourselves up! A Winnebago on the boat called out to us "to run and hide, that the whites were going to shoot!"

About this time one of my braves had jumped into the river, bearing a white flag to the boat, when another sprang in after him and brought him to the shore. The firing then commenced from the boat, which was returned by my braves and continued for some time. Very few of my people were hurt after the first fire, having succeeded in getting behind old logs and trees, which shielded them from the enemy's fire.

The Winnebago on the steamboat must either have misunderstood what was told, or did not tell it to the captain correctly; because I am confident he would not have allowed the soldiers to fire upon us if he had known my wishes. I have always considered him a good man, and too great a brave to fire upon an enemy when suing for quarters.

After the boat left us, I told my people to cross if they could, and wished; that I intended going into the Chippewa country. Some commenced crossing, and such as had determined to follow them, remained; only three lodges going with me. Next morning, at daybreak, a young man overtook me, and said that all my party had determined to cross the Mississippi—that a number had already got over safely and that he had heard the white army last night within a few miles of them. I now began to fear that the whites would come up with my people and kill them before they could get across. I had determined to go and join the Chippewas; but reflecting that by this I could only save myself, I concluded to return, and die with my people, if the Great Spirit would not give us another victory. During our stay in the thicket, a party of whites came close by us, but passed on without discovering us.

Early in the morning a party of whites being in advance of the army, came upon our people, who were attempting to cross the Mississippi. They tried to give themselves up; the whites paid no attention to their entreaties, but commenced slaughtering them. In a little while the whole army arrived. Our braves, but few in number, finding that the enemy paid no regard to age or sex, and seeing that they were murdering helpless women and little children, determined to fight until they were killed. As many women as could, commenced swimming the Mississippi, with their children on their backs. A number of them were drowned, and some shot before they could reach the opposite shore.

One of my braves, who gave me this information, piled up some saddles before him, (when the fight commenced), to shield himself from the enemy's fire, and killed three white men. But seeing that the whites were coming too close to him, he crawled to the bank of the without being perceived, and hid himself under the bank until the enemy retired. He then came to me and told me what had been done. After hearing this sorrowful news, I started with my little party to the Winnebago village at Prairie La Cross. On my arrival there I entered the lodge of one of the chiefs, and told him that I wished him to go with me to his father, that I intended giving myself up to the American war chief and die, if the Great Spirit saw proper. He said he would go with me.

I then took my medicine bag and addressed the chief. I told him that it was "the soul of the Sac nation—that it never had been dishonoured in any battle, take it, it is my life— dearer than life—and give it to the American chief!" He said he would keep it, and take care of it, and if I was suffered to live, he would send it to me.

During my stay at the village, the squaws made me a white dress of deer skin. I then started with several Winnebagoes, and went to their agent, at Prairie du Chien, and gave myself up.

On my arrival there, I found to my sorrow, that a large body of Sioux had pursued and killed a number of our women and children, who had got safely across the Mississippi. The whites ought not to have permitted such conduct, and none but cowards would ever have been guilty of such cruelty, a habit which had always been practiced on our nation by the Sioux.

The massacre, which terminated the war, lasted about two hours. Our loss in killed was about sixty, besides a number that was drowned. The loss of the enemy could not be ascertained by my braves, exactly; but they think that they killed about sixteen during the action.

I was now given up by the agent to the commanding officer at Fort Crawford, the White Beaver having gone down the river. We remained here a short time, and then started for Jefferson Barracks, in a steamboat, under the charge of a young war chief, (Lieutenant Jefferson Davis) who treated us all with much kindness. He is a good and brave young chief, with whose conduct I was much pleased. On our way down we called at Galena and remained a short time. The people crowded to the boat to see us: but the war chief would not permit them to enter the apartment where we were—knowing, from what his feelings would have been if he had been placed in a similar situation, that we did not wish to have a gaping crowd around us.

We passed Rock Island without stopping. The great war chief, General Scott, who was then at Fort Armstrong, came out in a small boat to see us, but the captain of the steamboat would not allow anybody from the fort to come on board his boat, in consequence of the cholera raging among the soldiers. I did think that the captain ought to have permitted the war chief to come on board to see me, because I could see no danger to be apprehended by it. The war chief looked well, and I have since heard was constantly among his soldiers, who were sick and dying, administering to their wants, and had not caught the disease from them and I thought it absurd to think that any of the people on the steamboat could be afraid of catching the disease from a well man. But these people are not brave like war chiefs, who never fear anything.

On our way down, I surveyed the country that had cost us so much trouble, anxiety and blood, and that now caused me to be a prisoner of war. I reflected upon the ingratitude of the whites when I saw their fine houses, rich harvests and everything desirable around them; and recollected that all this land had been ours, for which I and my people had never received a dollar, and that the whites were not satisfied until they took our village and our graveyards from us and removed us across the Mississippi.

On our arrival at Jefferson Barracks we met the great war chief, White Beaver, who had commanded the American army against my little band. I felt the humiliation of my situation; a little while before I had been leader of my braves, now I was a prisoner of war, but had surrendered myself. He received us kindly and treated us well.

We were now confined to the barracks and forced to wear the ball and chain. This was extremely mortifying and altogether useless. Was the White Beaver afraid I would break out of his barracks and run away? Or was he ordered to inflict this punishment upon me? If I had taken him prisoner on the field of battle I would not have wounded his feelings so much by such treatment, knowing that a brave war chief would prefer death to dishonour. But I do not blame the White Beaver for the course he pursued, as it is the custom among the white soldiers, and I suppose was a part of his duty.

The time dragged heavily and gloomily along throughout the winter, although the White Beaver did everything is his power to render us comfortable. Having been accustomed, throughout a long life, to roam the forests o'er, to go and come at liberty, confinement, and under such circumstances, could not be less than torture.

We passed away the time making pipes until spring, when we were visited by the agent, trader and interpreter, from Rock Island, Keokuk and several chiefs and braves of our nation, and my wife and daughter. I was rejoiced to see the two latter and spent my time very agreeably with them and my people as long as they remained.

The trader, Sagenash, (Colonel Davenport) presented me with some dried venison, which had been killed and cured by some of my friends. This was a valuable present, and although he had given me many before, none ever pleased me so much. This was the first meat I had eaten for a long time that reminded me of the former pleasures of my own *wigwam*, which had always been stored with plenty.

Keokuk and his chiefs, during their stay at the barracks, petitioned our Great Father, the president, to release us, and pledged themselves for our good conduct. I now began to hope I would soon be restored to liberty and the enjoyment of my family and friends, having heard that Keokuk stood high in the estimation of our Great Father, because he did not join me in the war, but I was soon disappointed in my hopes. An order came from our Great Father to the White Beaver to send us on to Washington.

In a little while all were ready and left Jefferson Barracks on board of a steamboat, under charge of a young war chief and one soldier, whom the White Beaver sent along as a guide to Washington. We were accompanied by Keokuk, wife and son, Appanooce, Wapello, Poweshiek, Pashippaho, Nashashuk, Saukee, Musquaukee, and our interpreter. Our principal traders, Colonel Geo. Davenport, of Rock Island, and S. S. Phelps and clerk, William Cousland, of the Yellow Banks, also accompanied us. On our way up the Ohio we passed several large villages, the names of which were explained to me. The first is called Louisville, and is a very petty village, situated on the bank of the Ohio River. The next is Cincinnati, which stands on the bank of the same river. This is a large and beautiful village and seemed to be in a thriving condition. The people gathered on the bank as we passed, in great crowds, apparently anxious to see us.

On our arrival at Wheeling the streets and river banks were crowded with people, who flocked from every direction to see us. While we remained here many called upon us and treated us with kindness, no one offering to molest or misuse us. This village is not so large as either of those before mentioned, but is quite a pretty one.

We left the steamboat then, having travelled a long distance on the prettiest river I ever saw (except our Mississippi) and took the stage. Being unaccustomed to this mode of travelling, we soon got tired and wished ourselves seated in a canoe on one of our own rivers, that we might return to our friends. We had travelled but a short distance before our carriage turned over, from which I received a slight injury, and the soldier had one arm broken. I was sorry for this accident, as the young man had behaved well.

We had a rough and mountainous country for several days, but had a good trail for our carriage. It is astonishing what labour and pains the white people have had to make this road, as it passes over several mountains, which are generally covered with rocks and timber, yet it has been made smooth and easy to travel upon.

Rough and mountainous as this country is there are many *wigwams* and small villages standing on the roadside. I could see nothing in the country to induce the people to live in it, and was astonished to find so many whites living on the hills.

I have often thought of them since my return to my own people, and am happy to think that they prefer living in their own country to coming out to ours and driving us from it, as many of the whites have already done. I think with them, that wherever the Great Spirit places his people they ought to be satisfied to remain, and be thankful for what He has given them, and not drive others from the country He has given them because it happens to be better then theirs. This is contrary to our way of thinking, and from my intercourse with the whites, I have learned that one great principle of their religion is "to do unto others as you wish them to do unto you." Those people in the mountains seem to act upon this principle, but the settlers on our frontiers and on our lands seem never to think of it, if we are to judge by their actions.

The first village of importance that we came to, after leaving the mountains, is called Hagerstown. It is a large village to be so far from a river and is very pretty. The people appear to live well and enjoy themselves much.

We passed through several small villages on the way to Fredericktown, but I have forgotten their names. This last is a large and beautiful village. The people treated us well, as they did at all other villages where we stopped,

Here we came to another road much more wonderful than that through the mountains. They call it a railroad, (the Baltimore and Ohio). I examined it carefully, but need not describe it, as the whites know all about it. It is the most astonishing sight I ever saw. The great road over the mountains will bear no comparison to it, although it has given the white people much trouble to make. I was surprised to see so much money and labour expended to make a good road for easy travelling. I prefer riding horse back, however, to any other way, but suppose these people would not have gone to so much trouble and expense to make a road if they did not prefer riding in their new fashioned carriages, which seem to run without any trouble, being propelled by steam on the same principle that boats are on the river.

They certainly deserve great praise for their industry.

On our arrival at Washington, we called to see our Great Father, the president. He looks as if he had seen as many winters as I have, and seems to be a great brave. I had very little talk with him, as he appeared to be busy and did not seem to be much disposed to talk. I think he is a good man; and although he talked but little, he treated us very well. His *wigwam* is well furnished with everything good and pretty, and is very strongly built.

He said he wished to know the cause of my going to war against his white children. I thought he ought to have known this before; and consequently said but little to him about it, as I expected he knew as well as I cold tell him.

He said he wanted us to go to Fortress Monroe and stay awhile with the war chief who commanded it. But having been so long from my people, I told him that I would rather return to my nation; that Keokuk had come here once on a visit to him, as we had done, and he had let him return again, as soon as he wished, and that I expected to be treated in the same manner. He insisted, however, on our going to Fortress Monroe; and as the interpreter then present could not understand enough of our language to interpret a speech, I concluded it was best to obey our Great Father, and say nothing contrary to his wishes.

During our stay at the city, we were called upon by many of the people, who treated us well, particularly the squaws; we visited the great council home of the Americans; the place where they keep their big guns; and all the public buildings, and then started for Fortress Monroe. The war chief met us on our arrival, and shook hands, and appeared glad to see me. He treated us with great friendship, and talked to me frequently. Previous to our leaving this fort, he made us a feast, and gave us some presents, which I intend to keep for his sake. He is a very good man and a great brave. I was sorry to leave him, although I was going to return to my people, because he had treated me like a brother, during all the time I remained with him.

Having got a new guide, a war chief (Major Garland), we started for our own country, taking a circuitous route. Our Great Father being about to pay a visit to his children in the big towns towards sunrise, and being desirous that we should have an opportunity of seeing them, had directed our guide to take us through.

On our arrival at Baltimore, we were much astonished to see so large a village; but the war chief told us we would soon see a larger one. This surprised us more. During our stay here, we visited all the public buildings and places of amusement, saw much to admire, and were well entertained by the people who crowded to see us. Our Great Father was there at the same time, and seemed to be much liked by his white children, who flocked around him, (as they had around us) to shake him by the hand. He did not remain long, having left the city before us. In an interview, while here, the president said:

> When I saw you in Washington, I told you that you had behaved very badly in going to war against the whites. Your conduct then compelled me to send my warriors against you, and your people were defeated with great loss, and several of you surrendered, to be kept until I should be satisfied that you would not try to do any more injury. I told you, too, that I would inquire whether your people wished you to return, and whether, if you did return, there would be any danger to the frontier. General Clark and General Atkinson, whom you know, have informed me that your principal chief and the rest of your people are anxious you should return, and Keokuk has asked me to send you back. Your chiefs have pledged themselves for your good conduct, and I have given directions that you should be taken to your own country.
>
> Major Garland, who is with you, will conduct you through some of our towns. You will see the strength of the white people. You will see that our young men are as numerous as the leaves in the woods. What can you do against us? You may kill a few women and children, but such a force would seen be sent against you as would destroy your whole tribe. Let the red men hunt and take care of their families. I hope they will not again raise the tomahawk against their white brethren. We do not wish to injure you. We desire your prosperity and improvement. But if you again make war against our people, I shall send a force which will severely punish you. When you go back, listen to the councils of Keokuk and the other friendly chiefs; bury the tomahawk and live in peace with the people on the frontier. And I pray the Great Spirit to give you a smooth path and a fair sky to return.

I was pleased with our Great Father's talk and thanked him. Told him that the tomahawk had been buried so deep that it would never be resurrected, and that my remaining days would be spent in peace with all my white brethren.

We left Baltimore in a steamboat, and travelled in this way to the big village, where they make medals and money, (Philadelphia.) We again expressed surprise at finding this village so much larger than the one we had left; but the war chief again told us we would see another much larger than this. I had no idea that the white people had such large villages, and so many people. They were very kind to us, showed us all their great public works, their ships and steamboats. We visited the place where they make money, (the mint) and saw the men engaged at it. They presented each of us with a number of pieces of the coin as they fell from the mint, which are very handsome.

I witnessed a militia training in this city, in which were performed a number of singular military feats. The chiefs and men were all well dressed, and exhibited quite a warlike appearance. I think our system of military parade far better than that of the whites, but as I am now done going to war I will not describe it, or say anything more about war, or the preparations necessary for it.

We next started for New York, and on our arrival near the wharf, saw a large collection of people gathered at Castle Garden. We had seen many wonderful sights in our way—large villages, the great national road over the mountains, the railroad, steam carriages, ships, steamboat, and many other things; but we were now about to witness a sight more surprising than any of these. We were told that a man was going up in the air in a balloon. We watched with anxiety to see if this could be true; and to our utter astonishment, saw him ascend in the air until the eye could no longer perceive him. Our people were all surprised and one of our young men asked the Prophet if he was going up to see the Great Spirit?

After the ascension of the balloon, we landed and got into a carriage to go to the house that had been provided for our reception. We had proceeded but a short distance before the street was so crowded that it was impossible for the carriage to pass. The war chief then directed the coachman to take another street, and stop at a different house from the one we had intended. On our arrival here we were waited upon by a number of gentlemen, who seemed much pleased to see us. We were furnished with good rooms, good provisions, and everything necessary for our comfort.

The chiefs of this big village, being desirous that all their people should have an opportunity to see us, fitted up their great council home for this purpose, where we saw an immense number of people; all of whom treated us with great friendship, and many with great generosity. One of their great chiefs, John A. Graham, waited upon us and made a very pretty talk, which appeared in the village papers, one of which I now hand you.

Mr. Graham's Speech.

Brothers: Open your ears. You are brave men. You have fought like tigers, but in a bad cause. We have conquered you. We were sorry last year that you raised the tomahawk against us; but we believe you did not know us then as you do now. We think, in time to come, you will be wise, and that we shall be friends forever. You see that we are a great people, numerous as the flowers of the field, as the shells on the sea shore, or the fishes in the sea, We put one hand on the eastern, and at the same time the other on the western ocean. We all act together. If some time our great men talk long and loud at our council fires, but shed one drop of white men's blood, our young warriors, as thick as the stars of the night, will leap aboard of our great boats, which fly on the waves and over the lakes—swift as the eagle in the air—then penetrate the woods, make the big guns thunder, and the whole heavens red with the flames of the dwellings of their enemies. Brothers, the president has made you a great talk. He has but one mouth. That one has sounded the sentiments of all the people. Listen to what he has said to you. Write it on your memories, it is good, very good.

Black Hawk, take these jewels, a pair of topaz earrings, beautifully set in gold, for your wife or daughter, as a token of friendship, keeping always in mind, that women and children are the favourites of the Great Spirit. These jewels are from an old man, whose head is whitened with the snows of seventy winters, an old man who has thrown down his bow, put off his sword, and now stands leaning on his staff, waiting the commands of the Great Spirit. Look around you, see all this mighty people, then go to your homes, open your arms to receive your families. Tell them to bury the hatchet, to make bright the chain of friendship, to love the white men, and to live in peace with them, as long as the rivers run into the sea, and the sun rises and sets. If you do so, you will be happy. You will then insure the prosperity of unborn generations of your tribes, who will go hand in hand with the sons of the white men, and all shall be blessed by the Great Spirit. Peace and happiness by the blessing of the Great

Spirit attend you. Farewell.

In reply to this fine talk, I said:

> Brother: We like your talk. We like the white people. They are very kind to us. We shall not forget it. Your council is good. We shall attend to it. Your valuable present shall go to my squaw. We shall always be friends.

The chiefs were particular in showing us everything that they thought would be pleasing or gratifying to us. We went with them to Castle Garden to see the fireworks, which was quite an agreeable entertainment, but to the whites who witnessed it, less magnificent than would have been the sight of one of our large prairies when on fire.

We visited all the public buildings and places of amusement, which, to us, were truly astonishing yet very gratifying.

Everybody treated us with friendship, and many with great liberality. The squaws presented us many handsome little presents that are said to be valuable. They were very kind, very good, and very pretty—for pale-faces.

Among the men, who treated us with marked friendship, by the presentation of many valuable presents, I cannot omit to mention the name of my old friend Crooks, of the American Fur Company. I have known him long, and have always found him to be a good chief, one who gives good advice, and treats our people right. I shall always be proud to recognize him as a friend, and glad to shake him by the hand.

Being anxious to return to our people, our guide started with us for our own country. On arriving at Albany, the people were so anxious to see us, that they crowded the streets and wharfs, where the steamboats landed, so much, that it was almost impossible for us to pass to the hotel which had been provided for our reception. We remained here but a short time, it being a comparatively small village, with only a few large public buildings. The great council home of the state is located here, and the big chief (the governor) resides here, in an old mansion. From here we went to Buffalo, thence to Detroit, where I had spent many pleasant days, and anticipated, on my arrival, to meet many of my old friends, but in this I was disappointed. What could be the cause of this? Are they all dead? Or what has become of them? I did not see our old father them, who had always given me good advice and treated me with great friendship.

After leaving Detroit it was but a few days before we landed at Prairie du Chien. The war chief at the fort treated us very kindly, as did the people generally. I called on the agent of the Winnebagoes, (General J. M. Street), to whom I had surrendered myself after the battle at Bad Axe, who received me very friendly. I told him that I had left my great medicine bag with his chiefs before I gave myself up; and now, that I was to enjoy my liberty again, I was anxious to get it, that I might head it down to my nation unsullied.

He said it was safe; he had heard his chiefs speak of it, and would get it and send it to me. I hope he will not forget his promise, as the whites generally do, because I have always heard that he was a good man, and a good father, and made no promise that he did not fulfil.

Passing down the Mississippi, I discovered a large collection of people in the mining country, on the west side of the river, and on the ground that we had given to our relation, Dubuque, a long time ago. I was surprised at this, As I had understood from our Great Father that the Mississippi was to be the dividing line between his red and white children, and he did not wish either to cross it. I was much pleased with this talk, and I knew it would be much better for both parties. I have since found the country much settled by the whites further down, and near to our people, on the west side of the river. I am very much afraid that in a few years they will begin to drive and abuse our people, as they have formerly done. I may not live to see it, but I feel certain the day is not far distant.

When we arrived at Rock Island, Keokuk and the other chiefs were sent for. They arrived the next day with a great number of their young men, and came over to see me. I was pleased to see them, and they all appeared glad to see me. Among them were some who had lost relations the year before. When we met, I perceived the tear of sorrow gush from their eyes at the recollection of their loss, yet they exhibited a smiling countenance, from the joy they felt at seeing me alive and well.

The next morning, the war chief, our guide, convened a council at Fort Armstrong. Keokuk and his party went to the fort; but, in consequence of the war chief not having called for me to accompany him, I concluded that I would wait until I was sent for. Consequently, the interpreter came and said, "they were ready, and had been waiting for me to come to the fort." I told him I was ready and would accompany him. On our arrival there the council commenced. The war chief said that the object of this council was to deliver me up to Keokuk. He then read a paper, and directed me to follow Keokuk's advice, and be governed by his counsel in all things! In this speech he said much that was mortifying to my feelings, and I made an indignant reply.

I do not know what object the war chief had in making such a speech; or whether he intended what he said; but I do know that it was uncalled for, and did not become him. I have addressed many war chiefs and listened to their speeches with pleasure, but never had my feelings of pride and honour insulted on any other occasion. But I am sorry I was so hasty in reply to this chief, because I said that which I did not intend.

In this council I met my old friend (Colonel. Wm. Davenport,) whom I had known about eighteen years. He is a good and brave chief. He always treated me well, and gave me good advice. He made me a speech on this occasion, very different from that of the other chief. It sounded like coming from a brave. He said he had known me a long time, that we had been good friends during that acquaintance, and, although he had fought against my braves, in our late war, he still extended the hand of friendship to me, and hoped that I was now satisfied, from what I had seen in my travels, that it was folly to think of going to war against the whites, and would ever remain at peace. He said he would be glad to see me at all times, and on all occasions would be happy to give me good advice.

If our Great Father were to make such men our agents he would much better subserve the interests of our people, as well as his own, than in any other way. The war chiefs all know our people, and are respected by them. If the war chiefs at the different military posts on the frontier were made agents, they could always prevent difficulties from arising among the Indians and whites; and I have no doubt, had the war chief above alluded to been our agent, we would never have had the difficulties with the whites we have had. Our agents ought always to be braves. I would, therefore, recommend to our Great Father the propriety of breaking up the present Indian establishment, and creating a new one, and make the commanding officers at the different frontier posts the agents of the government for the different nations of Indians.

I have a good opinion of the American war chiefs generally with whom I am acquainted, and my people, who had an opportunity of seeing and becoming well acquainted with the great war chief (General Winfield Scott), who made the last treaty with them, in conjunction with the great chief of Illinois (Governor Reynolds), all tell me that he is the greatest brave they ever saw, and a good man—one who fulfils his premises. Our braves spoke more highly of him than of any chief that had ever been among us, or made treaties with us. Whatever he says may be depended upon. If he had been our Great Father we never would have been compelled to join the British in the last war with America, and I have thought that as our Great Father is changed every few years, that his children would do well to put this great war chief in his place, for they cannot find a better chief for a Great Father anywhere.

I would be glad if the village criers, in all the villages I passed through, would let their people know my wishes and opinions about this great war chief.

During my travels my opinions were asked for on different subjects, but for want of a good interpreter (our regular interpreter having gone home on a different route), were seldom given. Presuming that they would be equally acceptable now, I have thought it a part of my duty to lay the most important before the public.

The subject of colonizing the negroes was introduced and my opinion asked as to the best method of getting clear of these people. I was not fully prepared at that time to answer, as I knew but little about their situation. I have since made many inquiries on the subject, and find that a number of States admit no slaves, whilst the balance hold these negroes as slaves, and are anxious, but do not know how to get clear of them. I will now give my plan, which, when understood, I hope will be adopted.

Let the free States remove all the male negroes within their limits to the slave States; then let our Great Father buy all the female negroes in the slave States between the ages of twelve and twenty, and sell them to the people of the free States, for a term of years, say those under fifteen until they are twenty-one, and those of and over fifteen, for five years, and continue to buy all the females in the slave States as soon as they arrive at the age of twelve, and take them to the free States and dispose of them in the same way as the first, and it will not be long before the country is clear of the black-skins, about which I am told they have been talking for a long time, and for which they have expended a large amount of money.

I have no doubt but our Great Father would willingly do his part in accomplishing this object for his children, as he could not lose much by it, and would make them all happy. If the free States did not want them all for servants, we would take the balance in our nation to help our women make corn.

I have not time now, nor is it necessary to enter more into detail about my travels through the United States. The white people know all about them, and my people have started to their hunting grounds and I am anxious to follow them.

Before I take leave of the public, I must contradict the story of some of the village criers, who, I have been told, accuse me of having murdered women ad children among the whites. This assertion is false! I never did, nor have I any knowledge that any of my nation ever killed a white woman or child. I make this statement of truth to satisfy the white people among whom I have been travelling, and by whom I have been treated with great kindness, that, when they shook me by the hand so cordially, they did not shake the hand that had ever been raised against any but warriors.

It has always been our custom to receive all strangers that come to our village or camps in time of peace on terms of friendship, to share with them the best provisions we have, and give them all the assistance in our power. If on a journey or lost, to put them on the right trail, and if in want of moccasins, to supply them. I feel grateful to the whites for the kind manner they treated me and my party whilst travelling among them, and from my heart I assure them that the white man will always be welcome in our village or camps, as a brother. The tomahawk is buried forever! We will forget what has passed, and may the watchword between the Americans and the Sacs and Foxes ever be—*Friendship*.

I am done now. A few more moons and I must follow my fathers to the shades. May the Great Spirit keep our people and the whites always at peace, is the sincere wish of

Black Hawk.

Starts for a New Home

After we had finished his autobiography the interpreter read it over to him carefully, and explained it thoroughly, so that he might make any needed corrections, by adding to, or taking from the narrations; but he did not desire to change it in any material matter. He said:

It contained nothing but the truth, and that it was his desire that the white people in the big villages he had visited should know how badly he had been treated, and the reason that had impelled him to act as he had done.

Arrangements having been completed for moving to his new home, he left Rock Island on the 10th of October with his family and a small portion of his band, for his old hunting grounds on Skunk River, on the west side of the Mississippi River below Shokokon. Here he had a comfortable dwelling erected, and settled down with the expectation of making it his permanent home, thus spending the evening of his days in peace and quietude.

Our next meeting with the chief was in the autumn of 1834 while on our way to the trading house of Captain William Phelps (now of Lewistown, Ills.), at Sweet Home, located on the bank of the Des Moines River. This was soon after the payment of the annuities at Rock Island, where the chiefs and head men had been assembled and received the money and divided it among their people by such rule as they saw fit to adopt; but this mode of distribution had proved very unsatisfactory to a large number of Indians who felt that they had been sorely wronged. The Sacs held a convocation at Phelps' trading house soon after our arrival, and petitioned their Great Father to change the mode of payment of their annuities. Black Hawk was a leading spirit in this movement, but thought best not to be present at the meeting.

The writer of this drew up a petition in advance of the assembling of the meeting, in accordance with the views of the Messrs. Phelps, and after a short council, in which the Indians generally participated, the interpreter read and explained to them the petition, which was a simple prayer to their Great Father, to charge the mode of payment so that each head of a family should receive and receipt for his proportion of the annuity. They were all satisfied and the entire party "touched the goose quill," and their names were thus duly attached to this important document.

The Secretary of War had long favoured this mode of payment of the annuities to the Indians, and at a meeting of the Cabinet to consider this petition the prayer of the Indians was granted, and in due time the Indian department received instructions, so that upon the payment of 1835 this rule was adopted. On his return from Rock Island, Black Hawk, with a number of his band, called on his old friend Wahwashenequa (Hawkeye), Mr. Stephen S. Phelps, to buy their necessary supplies for making a fall hunt, and to learn at what points trading houses would be established for the winter trade. During their stay the old chief had frequent interviews with the writer (his former amanuensis). He said he had a very comfortable home, a good corn field, and plenty of game, and had been well treated by the few whites who had settled in his neighbourhood. He spent several days with us and then left for home with a good winter outfit.

The change in the manner of payment of annuities would have been opposed by Keokuk and his head men, had they been let into the secret, as the annuity money when paid over was principally controlled by him, and always to the detriment of the Sacs' traders who were in opposition to the American Fur Company, the former having to rely almost entirely upon the fall and winter trade in furs and peltries to pay the credits given the Indians before leaving for their hunts.

BLACK HAWK'S LAST VISIT—

. . . . to Yellow Banks was in the fall of 1836, after the town of Oquawka had been laid out, and when told that the town had taken the Indian name, instead of its English interpretation, he was very much gratified, as he had known it as Oquawka ever since his earliest recollection and had always made it a stopping place when going out to their winter camps. He said the Skunk River country was dotted over with Cabins all the way down to the Des Moines River, and was filling up very fast by white people. A new village had been started at Shokokon (Flint Hills) by the whites, and some of its people have already built good houses, but the greater number are still living in log cabins. They should have retained its Indian name, Shokokon, as our people have spent many happy days in this village. Here too, we had our council house in which the braves of the Sac nation have many times assembled to listen to my words of counsel.

It was situated in a secluded but romantic spot in the midst of the bluffs, not far from the river, and on frequent occasions, when it became necessary to send out parties to make war on the Sioux to redress our grievances, I have assembled my braves here to give them counsel before starting on he warpath. And here, too, we have often met when starting out in the fall for our fall and winter's hunt, to counsel in regard to our several locations for the winter. In those days the Fur Company had a trading house here and their only neighbours were the resident Indians of Tama's town, located a few miles above on the river.

The Burlington *Hawk-Eye*, of a late date, in reference to this council house, says:

> A little distance above the water works, and further around the turn of the bluff is a natural amphitheatre, formed by the action of the little stream that for ages has dripped and gurgled down its deep and narrow channel to the river. It is a straight, clear cut opening in the hill side, slightly rising till at a distance of seventy-five or one hundred yards from the face of the bluff it terminates as suddenly and sharply as do the steeply sloping sides.
>
> Well back in this grassy retreat, upon a little projection of earth that elevates it above the surrounding surface, lies a huge granite boulder. In connection with the surroundings it gives to the place the appearance of a work of man, everything is so admirably arranged for a council chamber. Here, it is rumoured by tradition, the dusky warriors of the Sacs gathered to listen in attentive silence to the words of their leader, Black Hawk, who from his rocky rostrum addressed the motionless groups that strewed the hill sides; motionless under his addresses and by them aroused to deeds of darkness and crafty daring that made the name of their chief a synonym with all things terrible.

Whatever of truth this story may contain we cannot say, and it may be no one knows. Certain it is, however, that Black Hawk's early history is intimately linked and interwoven with that of our city, and in justice to a brave man and a soldier, as well as a 'first settler' and a citizen, his name and his last resting place should be rescued from the oblivion that will soon enshroud them.

Another village has been commenced by the whites on the Mississippi River, at Fort Madison, which is being built up very rapidly. The country, too, is fast settling up by farmers, and as the Sacs have made a settlement on the frontier farther west, on our old hunting grounds, he said he would have to move farther back so as to be near his people; and on bidding us farewell, said it might be the last time, as he was growing old, and the distance would be too great from the point at which he intended to build a house and open a little farm to make a visit on horseback, and as the Des Moines River is always low in the fall of the year he could not come in his canoe.

At the close of the summer of 1837 the President of the United States invited deputations from several tribes Of Indians residing on the Upper Mississippi to visit him at Washington. Among those who responded to his invitation were deputations from the Sacs and Foxes and Sioux, who had been at enmity, and between whom hostilities had been renewed, growing out of their inhuman treatment of many of the women and children of the Sacs, after they had made their escape from the Battle of Bad-Axe, at the close of the war.

Keokuk, principal chief of the Sacs and Foxes, (by the advice of his friend, Sagenash, Colonel George Davenport, of Rock Island) invited Black Hawk to join his delegation, which invitation he readily accepted, and made one of the party; whilst the Sioux were represented by several of their crafty chiefs. Several counsels were held, the object of which was to establish peace between the Sacs and Foxes and Sioux, and in order to perpetuate it, make a purchase of a portion of the country of the Sioux, which territory should be declared neutral, and on which neither party should intrude for any purpose; but the Sioux, whose domain extends far and wide, would not consent to sell any of their land; hence nothing was accomplished.

Before returning to their county the Sac and Fox delegation visited the large cities in the East, in all of which Black Hawk attracted great attention; but more particularly in Boston, as he did not visit it during his former tour. The delegation embraced Keokuk, his wife and little son, four chiefs of the nation, Black Hawk and son, and several warriors. Here they were received and welcomed by the mayor of the city, and afterwards by Governor Everett as the representative of the State. On the part of the city, after a public reception, the doors of Faneuil Hall were opened to their visitors to hold a levee for the visits of the ladies, and in a very short time the "old cradle of liberty" was jammed full.

After dinner the delegation was escorted to the State House by a military company, and on their arrival were conspicuously seated in front of the Speakers' desk, the house being filled with ladies, members of the legislature, and dignitaries of the city council.

Governor Everett then addressed the audience, giving a brief history of the Sac and Fox tribe, whose principal chiefs (including the great war chief) were then present, and then turning to them he said:

> Chiefs and warriors of the united Sacs and Foxes, you are welcome to our hall of council. Brothers, you have come a long way from your home to visit your white brethren; we rejoice to take you by the hand. Brothers, we have heard the names of your chiefs and warriors. Our brethren who have travelled in the West have told us a great deal about the Sacs and Foxes. We rejoice to see you with our own eyes.
>
> Brothers, we are called the Massachusetts. This is the name of the red men who once lived here. Their *wigwams* were scattered on yonder fields, and their council fire was kindled on this spot. They were of the same great race as the Sacs and Foxes.
>
> Brothers, when our fathers came over the great water they were a small band. The red man stood upon the rock by the seaside and saw our fathers. He might have pushed them into the water and drowned them; but he stretched out his hand to them and said: 'Welcome, white man.' Our fathers were hungry, and the red man gave them corn and venison. They were cold, and the red man wrapped them in his blanket. We are now numerous and powerful, but we remember the kindness of the red men to our fathers. Brothers, you are welcome; we are glad to see you.
>
> Brothers, our faces are pale, and your faces are dark, but our hearts are alike. The Great Spirit has made His children of different colours, but He loves them all.
>
> Brothers, you dwell between the Mississippi and Missouri. They

are mighty rivers. They have one branch far East in the Alleghanies and another far West in the Rocky Mountains, but they flow together at last into one great stream and ran down into the sea. In like manner the red man dwells in the West and the white man in the East, by the great water; but they are all one band, one family. It has many branches; but one head.

Brothers, as you entered our council house, you beheld the image of our great father, Washington. It is a cold stone; it cannot speak to you, but he was the friend of the red man, and bade his children live in friendship with their red brethren. He is gone to the world of spirits, but his words have made a very deep print in our hearts, like the step of a strong buffalo on the soft clay of the prairie.

Brother, (addressing Keokuk) I perceive your little son between your knees. May the Great Spirit preserve his life, my, brother. He grows up before you, like the tender sapling by the side of the great oak. May they flourish for a long time together; and when the mighty oak is fallen on the ground may the young tree fill its place in the forest, and spread out its branches over the tribe.

Brothers, I make you a short talk and again bid you welcome to our council hall.

Keokuk rose and made an eloquent address. Several of the other chiefs spoke, and after them the old war chief, Black Hawk, on whom the large crowd were looking with intense interest, arose and delivered a short but dignified address.

Presents were then distributed to them by the governor. Keokuk received a splendid sword and a brace of pistols, his son a nice little rifle, the other chiefs long swords, and Black Hawk a sword and brace of pistols.

After the close of ceremonies in the Capitol, the Indians gave a exhibition of the war dance, in the common in front of the Capitol, in presence of thirty thousand spectators, and then returned to their quarters.

BLACK HAWK'S REMOVAL TO THE DES MOINES RIVER.

Soon after his return from Boston he removed his family and little band farther West, on the Des Moines River, near the storehouse of an Indian trader, where he had previously erected a good house for his future home. His family embraced his wife, two sons, Nashashuk and Gamesett, and an only daughter and her husband. As he had given up the chase entirely—having sufficient means from the annuities—he now turned his attention to the improvement of his grounds, and soon had everything comfortably around him. Here he had frequent visits from the whites, who came out in large numbers to look at the country, many of whom called through curiosity to see the great war chief, but all were made welcome and treated with great hospitality.

In 1838 Fort Madison had grown to be a little village, and its inhabitants were not only enterprising and industrious, but patriotic citizens. On the 4th of July of that year they had a celebration and having known and respected Black Hawk while residing in that part of the country, invited him to join them as a guest on that occasion.

In reply to a letter of B.F. Drake, Esq., of Cincinnati, asking for such incidents in the life of Black Hawk as he knew, Hon. W. Henry Starr, of Burlington, Iowa, whom we knew for many years as a highly honourable and intelligent gentleman, gave the following account of the celebration in his reply, dated March 21, 1839:

> On the 4th of July, 1838, Black Hawk was present by special invitation, and was the most conspicuous guest of the citizens assembled in commemoration of that day. Among the toasts called forth by the occasion was the following:
>
>> Our illustrious guest, Black Hawk: May his declining years be as calm and serene as his previous life has been boisterous and full of warlike incidents. His attachment and great friendship to his white brethren, fully entitle him to a seat at our festive board.
>
> So soon as this sentiment was drank, Black Hawk arose and delivered the following speech, which was taken down at the time by two interpreted, and by them furnished for publication:
> It has pleased the Great Spirit that I am here today. I have eaten with my white friends. The earth is our mother—we are now on it— with the Great Spirit above us—it is good. I hope we are all friends here. A few summers ago I was fighting against you—I did wrong, perhaps; but that is past—it is buried—let it be forgotten.
> Rock River was a beautiful country—liked my towns, my cornfields, and the home of my people. I fought for it. It is now yours—keep it as we did—it will produce you good crops.
> I thank the Great Spirit that I am now friendly with my white

brethren—we are here together—we have eaten together—we are friends—it is his wish and mine. I thank you for your friendship.

I was once a great warrior-I am now poor. Keokuk has been the cause of my present situation—but do not attach blame to him. I am now old. I have looked upon the Mississippi since I have been a child. I love the Great River. I have dwelt upon its banks from the time I was an infant. I look upon it now. I shake hands with you, and as it is my wish, I hope you are my friends.'

In the course of the day he was prevailed upon to drink several times, and became somewhat intoxicated, an uncommon circumstance, as he was generally temperate.

In the autumn of 1837, he was at the house of an Indian trader, in the vicinity of Burlington, when I became acquainted and frequently convened with him in broken English, and through the medium of gestures and pantomime. A deep seated melancholy was apparent in his countenance, and conversation. He endeavoured to make me comprehend, on one occasion, his former greatness, and represented that he was once master of the country, east, north, and south of us—that he had been a very successful warrior-called himself, smiting his breast, 'big Captain Black Hawk,' *'nesso Kaskaskias,'* (killed the Kaskaskias,) *'nesso Sioux a heap,'* (killed a great number of Sioux). He then adverted to the ingratitude of his tribe, in permitting Keokuk to supersede him, who, he averred, excelled him in nothing but drinking whisky.

Toward Keokuk he felt the most unrelenting hatred. Keokuk was, however, beyond his influence, being recognized as chief of the tribe by the government of the United States. He unquestionably possessed talents of the first order, excelled as an orator, but his authority will probably be short-lived, on account of his dissipation and his profligacy in spending the money paid him for the benefit of his tribe, and which he squanders upon himself and a few favourites, through whose influence he seeks to maintain his authority.

You inquire if Black Hawk was at the Battle of the Thames? On one occasion I mentioned Tecumthe to him and he expressed the greatest joy that I had heard of him, and pointing away to the East, and making a feint, as if aiming a gun, said, *'Chemocoman* (white man) *nesso,'* (kill.) From which I had no doubt of his being personally acquainted with Tecumthe, and I have been since informed, on good authority, that he was in the Battle of the Thames and in several other engagements with that distinguished chief.

In September, 1838, he started with the head men of his little band to go to Rock Island, the place designated by the Agent, to receive their annuities, but was taken sick on the way and had to return to his home. He was confined to his bed about two weeks, and on the 3rd day of October, 1838, he was called away by the Great Spirit to take up his abode in the happy grounds of the future, at the age of seventy-one years. His devoted wife and family were his only and constant attendants during his last sickness, and when brought home sick, she had a premonition that he would soon be called away.

The following account of his death and burial we take from the Burlington Hawk-Eye, and as we knew the writer as a reliable gentleman, many years ago, we have no doubt of it being strictly correct.

Captain James H. Jordan, a trader among the Sacs and Foxes before Black Hawk's death, was present at his burial, and is now residing on the very spot where he died. In reply to a letter of inquiry he writes as follows:

Eldon, Iowa, July 15, 1881.
Black Hawk was buried on the northeast quarter of the southeast quarter of section 2, township 70, range 12, Davis county, Iowa, near the northeast corner of the county, on the Des Moines river bottom, about ninety rods from where he lived when he died, and the north side of the river. I have the ground on which he lived for a door yard, it being between my house and the river. The only mound over the gave was some puncheons split out and set over his grave and then sodded over with blue gross, making a ridge about four feet high. A flag-staff, some twenty feet high, was planted at the head, on which was a silk flag, which hung there until the wind wore it out. My house and his were only about four rods apart when he died.

He was sick only about fourteen days. He was buried right where he sat the year before, when in council with Iowa Indians, and was buried in a suit of military clothes, made to order and given to him when in Washington City by General Jackson, with hat, sword, gold epaulets, etc., etc.

The Annals of Iowa of 1863 and 1864 state that the old chief was buried by laying his body on a board, his feet fifteen inches below the surface of the ground, and his head raised three feet above the ground. He was dressed in a military uniform, said to have been presented to him by a member of General Jackson's cabinet, with a cap on his head ornamented with feathers. On his left side was a sword presented him by General Jackson; on his right side a cane presented to him by Henry Clay, and one given to him by a British officer, and other trophies.

Three medals hung about his neck from President Jackson, ex-President John Quincy Adams and the city of Boston, respectively. The body was covered with boards on each side, the length of the body, which formed a ridge, with an open space below; the gables being closed by boards, and the whole was covered with sod. At the head was a flag-staff thirty-five feet high which bore an American flag worn out by exposure, and near by was the usual hewn post inscribed with Indian characters representing his war-like exploits, etc. Enclosing all was a strong circular picket fence twelve feet high. His body remained here until July, 1839, when it was carried off by a certain Dr. Turner, then living at Lexington, Van Buren county, Iowa. Captain Horn says the bones were carried to Alton, Ills., to be mounted with wire. Mr. Barrows says they were taken to Warsaw, Ills.

Black Hawk's sons, when they heard of this desecration of their father's grave, were very indignant, and complained of it to Governor Lucas of Iowa Territory, and His Excellency caused the bones to be brought back to Burlington in the fall of 1839, or the spring of 1840. When the sons came to take possession of them, finding them safely stored "in a good dry place" they left them there. The bones were subsequently placed in the collection of the Burlington Geological and Historical Society, and it is certain that they perished in the fire which destroyed the building and all the society's collections in 1855; though the editor of the *Annals*, (April, 1865,) says there is good reason to believe that the bones were not destroyed by the fire, and he is "creditably informed that they are now at the residence of a former officer of said society and thus escaped that catastrophe.

Another account, however, and probably a more reliable one, states that the last remains of Black Hawk were consumed as stated, in the burning building containing the collections and properties of the Burlington Geological and Historical Society.

In closing this narrative of the life of this noble old chief it may be but just to speak briefly of his personal traits. He was an Indian, and from that standpoint we must judge him. The make-up of his character comprised those elements in a marked degree which constitutes a noble nature. In all the social relations of life he was kind and affable. In his house he was the affectionate husband and father. He was free from the many vices that others of his race had contracted from their associations with the white people, never using intoxicating beverages to excess. As a warrior he knew no fear, and on the field of battle his feats of personal prowess stamped him as the "bravest of the brave."

But it was rather as a speaker and counsellor that he was distinguished. His patriotism, his love of his country, his home, his lands and the rights of his people to their wide domain, moved his great soul to take up arms to protect the rights of his people. Revenge and conquest formed no part of his purpose. *Right* was all that he demanded, and for *that* he waged the unequal contests with the whites. With his tribe he had great personal influence and his young men received his counsel and advice, and yielded ready acquiescence in his admonitions. With other tribes he was held in high esteem, as well as by English and American soldiers, who had witnessed his prowess on the field of battle.

THE BLACK HAWK TOWER.

This favourite resort of Black Hawk, situated on the highest bank of Rock River, had been selected by his father as a lookout, at the first building up of their village. From this point they had an unobstructed view up and down Rock River for many miles, and across the prairies as far as the vision could penetrate, and since that country has been settled by the whites, for more than half a century, has been the admiration of many thousands of people.

The village of Black Hawk, including this grand "look out," was purchased from the government by Colonel George Davenport, at Black Hawk's particular request, for the reason, as he afterwards told us, that he could leave it with an abiding assurance that the graves of their people would be protected from vandal hands.

This property including hundreds of acres lying between Rock River and the Mississippi, is now owned by Hon. B. Davenport, and as it has long been a pleasure resort for picnic and other parties, he has erected an elegant pavilion on its site, with a good residence for a family, who have charge of it, which will now make it the finest pleasure resort in that part of the country. And in order to make it more easy of access, he has constructed a branch from the Rock Island and Milan railroad, leading directly to the tower. Now its many visitors in the future can sit on the veranda, and while enjoying the elegant scenery, can take ease and comfort in the cool shade. And for this high privilege the name of Davenport will receive many hearty greetings.

Fifty years ago (1832) we made, our first visit to Black Hawk's Tower with Colonel George Davenport, and listened with intense interest to his recital of scenes that had been enacted there may years before; and one year later had them all repeated, with may more, from the lips of Black Hawk himself. How changed the scene. Then it was in its rustic state, now this fine pavilion, being a long, low structure, built somewhat after the Swiss cottage plan, with broad sloping roofs, and wide, long porches on the north and south sides, the one facing the road and the other fronting the river and giving a view of a beautiful stretch of country up and down Rock River, greatly enhances its beauty and adds much to the comfort of visitors.

The following beautiful word paintings by a recent visitor to the tower, we take from the Rock Island Union:

BLACK HAWK'S WATCH TOWER.

By Jennie M. Fowler

Beautiful tower! famous in history
Rich in legend, in old-time mystery,
Graced with tales of Indian lore,
Crowned with beauty from summit to shore.

Below, winds the river, silent and still,
Nestling so calmly 'mid island and hill,
Above, like warriors, proudly and grand,
Tower the forest trees, monarchs of land.

A landmark for all to admire and wonder,
With thy history ancient, for nations to ponder,
Boldly thou liftest they head to the breeze,
Crowned with they plumes, the nodding trees.

Years are now gone—forever more fled,
Since the Indians crept, with cat-like tread,
With mocasined foot, with eagle eye—
The red men our foes in ambush lie.

The owl, still his nightly vigil keeps,
While the river, below him, peacefully sleeps,
The whip-poor-will utters his plaintive cry,
The trees still whisper, and gently sigh.

The pale moon still creeps from her daily rest,
Throwing her rays o'er the river's dark breast,
The katy-did and cricket, I trow,
In days gone by, chirruped, even as now.

Indian! thy camp-fires no longer are smouldering,
They bones 'neath the forest moss long have been mouldering,
The "Great Spirit" claims thee. He leadeth they tribe,
To new hunting-grounds not won with a bribe.

On thy Watch Tow'r the pale face his home now makes,
His dwelling, the site of the forest tree takes,
Gone are thy wigwams, the wild deer now fled,
Black Hawk, with his tribe, lie silent and dead.
Rock Island, August 18, 1882.

The Black Hawk War

On the 12th of April, 1832, soon after our arrival at Rock Island on a visit to relatives, (the family of Colonel Geo. Davenport) a steamboat came down from Galena with officers to Fort Armstrong, for the purpose of laying in supplies and medical stores for a brigade then being formed at that place. One regiment, composed principally of miners, who had abandoned their mines and came in to offer their services as soldiers in the field, were unanimous in the election of Henry Dodge as Colonel. They had long known him as a worthy, brave and accomplished gentleman, the soul of honor, and hence would be an intrepid soldier.

Among the officers on this trip was Dr. A. K. Philleo, well known to Colonel Dodge as a social gentleman, a skilled physician and an accomplished surgeon, who had accepted the position of surgeon at his urgent request, with a *proviso*: Being editor of the *Galenian*, (the only paper printed in the town) he considered the position a very important one, as it was the only paper within hundreds of miles of the seat of war, and the only one on the Mississippi above Alton, Ill.; hence he must procure a substitute or decline the appointment of surgeon. Having made his acquaintance after he had learned that we had been engaged in newspaper life, he insisted that we should take a position on the *Galenian* for a few weeks, or until the close of the war, so that he could accept the offer of Colonel Dodge, and seeing that he was a great favourite among the officers, and anxious to go to the field, we accepted the position and accompanied him to Galena the same evening.

Here we found an infantry regiment, commanded by Colonel J.M. Strode, composed principally of miners and citizens of Galena, which had been hurriedly organized for home protection, whilst that of Colonel Dodge, being well mounted, were making preparations

KEOKUK AND SON

PROPHET

to take the field. After taking charge of the *Galenian* we made the acquaintance of Colonel Strode, and found him to be a whole-souled Kentuckian, who advised us to enrol our name on the company list of Captain M. M. Maughs, and as our time would mostly be devoted to the paper, he would detail us *Printer to the Regiment,* by virtue of which appointment we would become an honorary member of his staff. We retained our position on the paper and that on the staff of the colonel throughout the war, and was made the recipient of dispatches of the regular movement of the army, its skirmishes and battles from officers of the regular army as well as that of the volunteers, from which we made our weekly report, and from these data we have made up most of our history of the war.

Fox Murderers Wanted

Early in April, 1832, Brigadier-General Atkinson, with about three hundred troops, was ordered to Fort Armstrong to prevent a threatened war between the Menominees and Fox Indians, on account of a massacre, committed by a band of the latter on a small band of drunken Menominees the previous summer at a point near Fort Crawford. To prevent bloodshed he was directed to demand the murderers of the Foxes; but on arriving at Rock Island he soon learned that there was imminent danger of a war of a different character—that Black Hawk, with his entire band, was then on his way to invade the State of Illinois and would probably be joined by the Pottowattamies and Winnebagoes. In order to ascertain the facts in the case, he called upon the Indian Agent and Colonel George Davenport, both located here, and requested them to furnish, in writing, all the information they had in relation to the movements and intentions of Black Hawk in coming to the State of Illinois. Both gentlemen replied to his inquiries immediately as follows:

Rock Island, April 12, 1832.

My opinion is that the squaws and old men have gone to the Prophet's town, on Rock River, and the warriors are now only a few miles below the mouth of Rock River, within the limits of the State of Illinois. That these Indians are hostile to the whites there is no doubt. That they have invaded the State of Illinois, to the great injury of her citizens, is equally true. Hence it is that that the public good requires that strong as well as speedy measures should be taken against Black Hawk and his followers.

Respectfully, I have the honor to be your obedient servant,
(Signed,) Andrew S. Hughes.
To Brig-General Atkinson.

Rock Island, April 13, 1832.
Dear Sir:—In reply to your inquiry of this morning, respecting the Indians, I have to state that I have been informed by the man I have wintering with the Indians that the British band of Sac Indians are determined to make war upon the frontier settlements. The British band of Sac Indians did rendezvous at old Fort Madison, and induced a great many of the young men to join them on their arrival at the Yellow Banks. They crossed about five hundred head of horses into the State of Illinois, and sent about seventy horses through the country toward Rock River. The remainder, some on horseback the others in canoes, in a fighting order, advanced up the Mississippi, and were encamped yesterday five or six miles below Rock River and will no doubt endeavour to reach their stronghold in the Rock River swamps if they are not intercepted. From every information that I have received, I am of the opinion that the intentions of the British band of Sac Indians is to commit depredations on the inhabitants of the frontier."

Respectfully, your obedient servant,
(Signed,) George Davenport.
To Brig. General Atkinson.

Being satisfied from the information thus acquired, that there was danger ahead for the small settlements of whites in the Northern portion of the State, he immediately addressed a letter to Governor Reynolds, of Illinois, from which we take the following:

Fort Armstrong, April 13, 1832.
Dear Sir:—The band of Sacs, under Black Hawk, joined by about one hundred Kickapoos and a few Pottowattomies, amounting in all to about five hundred men, have assumed a hostile attitude. They crossed the river at the Yellow, Banks on the sixth inst., and are now moving up on the east side of Rock River, towards the Prophet's village.
The regular force under my command is too small to justify me in pursuing the hostile party. To make an unsuccessful attempt to coerce them would only irritate them to acts of hostility on the frontier sooner than they probably contemplate.

Your own knowledge of the character of these Indians, with the information herewith submitted, will enable you to judge of the course proper to pursue. I think the frontier is in great danger, and will use all the means at my disposal to co-operate with you in its protection and defence. With great respect,

Your most obedient servant,

H. Atkinson,
Brigadier General of the U. S. Army,
His Excellency, Governor Reynolds, Belleville, Ills.

On receipt of General Atkinson's letter, Governor Reynolds issued his proclamation, calling out a strong detachment of militia to rendezvous at Beardstown on the 22nd of April. In obedience to this command a large number of citizens assembled and offered their services. They were met by Governor Reynolds, and after bring organized into a brigade, he appointed Brigadier General Samuel Whitesides commander. His brigade embraced 1600 horsemen and two hundred footmen—being four regiments and an odd spy battalion.

First regiment, Colonel Dewitt; second, Colonel Fry; third, Colonel Thomas; fourth, Colonel Thompson; Colonel James D. Henry, commanded the spy battalion.

The troops took up their line of march at once, under command of General Whitesides, accompanied by the commander-in-chief, Governor Reynolds. For the purpose of laying in provisions for the campaign they went to Yellow Banks, on the Mississippi River, where Major S. S. Phelps, who had been appointed quarter master, supplied them. They arrived on the 3rd of May, and left for Rock River on the 7th.

The Black Hawk War Continued

About the first of April Black Hawk's band assembled at Fort Madison for the purpose of making arrangements to ascend the Mississippi, and soon after the entire party started. The old men, women and children, with their provisions and camp equipage, in canoes, and the men all armed, came on horseback. On the sixth day of April, the braves, on horseback, made a call at Yellow Banks, one day after the canoes had passed the same point, and told Josiah Smart, Mr. Phelps' interpreter, where they were going, and the object of their visit. They said they had observed a great war chief, with a number of troops going up on a steamboat, and thought it likely that the mission of this war chief was to prevent them going up Rock River, but they were bound to go. Messrs. Phelps and Smart tried to persuade them to recross the river and return to their country, assuring them that the government would not permit them to come into Illinois in violation of the treaty they had made last year, in which they had agreed to remain on the west side of the river. But they would not listen to their advice. On the next day they took up the line of march for Rock River, and on the 10th of April, 1832, Black Hawk, with a portion of his band of Sacs, reached the mouth of Rock River a few miles below Rock Island. The old men, women and children with their provisions and camp equipage, who came up in canoes, arrived on the 9th, and the men all armed, came up on horseback, reaching the camp on the 10th.

While encamped there they were joined by the Prophet, who had previously invited them to come up to the country of the Winnebagoes and raise a crop. He called on his way at Fort Armstrong and had talks with the agent and Colonel Davenport, the trader, both of whom advised him to persuade Black Hawk and party to return to their own country, or they would be driven back by the soldiers then at Fort Armstrong, under the command of General Atkinson, who had just arrived. The Prophet would not listen to their advice, but assured Black Hawk that he had a right to go forward with his entire party to the Winnebago country; and as he expected large reinforcements to his little army as he ascended Rock River, he was determined to go forward, but had given positive orders to his band, under no circumstances, to strike a blow until they had been reinforced by warriors from the Winnebagoes and Pottowattomies.

Early next morning they broke camp and started up Rock River, but were soon overtaken by a small detachment of soldiers, who held a council with Black Hawk and communicated to him the orders of General Atkinson. These were for him to return with his band and re-cross the Mississippi. Black Hawk said, as he was not on the war path, but going on a friendly visit to the Prophet's village, he intended to go forward, and continued on his journey. On receipt of his answer, General Atkinson sent another detachment to Black Hawk with imperative orders for him to return, or he would pursue him with his entire army and drive him back. In reply, Black Hawk said the general had no right to make the order so long as his band was peaceable, and that he intended to go on to the Prophet's village.

In the meantime the forces under the command of General Whitesides had arrived, and were turned over to General Atkinson by the governor. The brigade, under the command of General Whitesides, was ordered up Rock River to Dixon's Ferry, and as soon as boats could be got ready, General Atkinson started for the same destination with 300 regulars and about the same number of Illinois militia. Black Hawk with his party had already reached a point some thirty or forty miles above Dixon's Ferry, where they were met in council by some Pottowattomies and Winnebago chiefs. They assured Black Hawk that their people would not join him in making war against the United States, and denied the Prophet's story to him. During this council Black Hawk became convinced that he had been badly imposed upon by the Prophet, and resolved at once to send a flag of truce to General Atkinson and ask permission to descend Rock River, re-cross the Mississippi and go back to their country.

STILLMAN'S DEFEAT.

About this time, General Whitesides had concentrated a large force of militia at Dixon's Ferry, and at the solicitation of Major Stillman, permitted him to take out a scouting party of nearly 300 mounted men. They went up Rock River, about thirty miles to Sycamore

Creek, and encamped within a few miles of Black Hawk's camp, but were not aware of its position at the time. Indian scouts having intercepted their coming reported at once to Black Hawk that a large army of mounted militia were coming towards his camp; and before the volunteers had entirely completed their arrangements for encampment, outside guards espied three Indians coming in with a white flag. After holding a parley with them, (one of the guards being able to talk a little with them in their own language), they were hurried into camp, and before any explanations were made, the flag bearer was shot and instantly killed, whilst his comrades made their escape during the confusion in getting the regiment ready to pursue the fleeing Indians.

These had secreted themselves in ambush as the army rushed by, helter-skelter, after another small party of Indians who had followed the flag bearers, and who, when hearing the uproar in camp made a hasty retreat. The entire regiment was soon mounted and started out in squads towards the camp of Black Hawk. The latter having learned by a scout that the army was coming, started at once with less than fifty mounted warriors, his entire force then in camp, to meet the enemy, and on arriving at a copse of timber and underbrush near Sycamore Creek, made ready to meet them.

Captain Eads' company, who were the first to start out, killed two of the five fleeing Indians. Soon after crossing Sycamore Creek they were surprised by a terrific war whoop from the Indians, who were concealed in the bushes near by, and with deadly aim commenced firing into the front ranks of the regiment, and with unearthly yells (as one of the fleeing party told us on arriving at Galena), charged upon our ranks, with tomahawks raised, ready to slaughter all who might come within their reach. Judging from the yelling of the Indians, their number was variously estimated at from one thousand to two thousand.

The entire party was thrown into such confusion that Major Stillman had no control of any of them, and, with one exception, the entire army continued their flight to Dixon's Ferry, thirty miles distant, whilst some went back to their homes.

The retreating army passed through their camping ground near Sycamore creek, where they should have halted, and under cover of the timber, could have shot down their pursuers while yet in open prairie. Black Hawk and a small portion of his command gave up the chase, and returned to his camp, while the remainder pursued the fugitives for several miles, occasionally overtaking and killing some soldiers, whose horses had given out.

Among the retreating party was a Methodist preacher, whose horse was too slow to keep out of the reach of the Indians, who adopted a novel plan to save himself and horse. On coming to a ravine he left the track of his pursuers some distance, and followed down the ravine until he found a place deep enough to shelter himself and horse from view, and remained there for two hours in safety. He had the precaution to keep a strict count of the Indians as they went forward, and waited their return. Being satisfied that all had returned and continued on the way to their camp, he quietly left his hiding place, trotted leisurely along and reached Dixon's Ferry about sunrise next morning.

He reported his mode of procedure and the strategy used to render his safety certain from the Indians who had dispersed and driven the army before them. He was interrogated into the number, and when he reported *twenty*, great indignation was manifested by some of the *brave* volunteers who had got into camp some hours before him, and reported the number at fifteen hundred to two thousand! But as he was well known to many of the volunteers and highly respected as a meek and lowly Christian gentleman, they stood by him and prevented any personal violence.

When the report of this fiasco came into Galena the next morning about 8 o'clock, on the 15th of May, our regiment was immediately called to arms, as great danger was apprehended by the citizens. The general supposition was that the Pottowattomies and Winnebagoes had joined Black Hawk, it being well known that his entire band, including women and children, that had gone up Rock River, did not exceed one thousand persons. Dwellings were vacated and most of the inhabitants repaired to the stockades for safety.

The news of Stillman's defeat "by 2,000 blood-thirsty Indian warriors" spread fast, far and wide, and the Governor of Illinois called for more volunteers; and when the news reached Washington, the Secretary of War ordered General Scott, then at New York, to take a thousand soldiers and proceed to the seat of war and take command of the army.

This violation of a flag of truce, the wanton murder of its bearers, and the attack upon a mere remnant of Black Hawk's band when suing for peace, precipitated a war that should have been avoided.

(In confirmation of the dastardly act of the volunteers in killing the bearer of a white flag, and by which the war was precipitated, we give the following letter of Mr. Elijah Kilbourn, one of the scouts connected with Stillman's command. Mr. K. is the man Black Hawk makes mention of in his narrative as having been taken captive during our last war with Great Britain, and by him adopted into the Sac tribe; and again taken prisoner by three of his braves at the battle of Sycamore creek.)

Kilbourn's Narrative
A Reminiscence of Black Hawk.
(From the Soldier's Cabinet.)

Much has been said both for and against the Indian character; but we doubt whether greater or nobler qualities have ever been exhibited in the conduct of civilized rulers or commanders than are shown in the incidents we are about to relate concerning Black Hawk, whose deeds upon the north-western frontier will render his name illustrious while history exists.

Elijah Kilbourn, the subject of the great chieftain's kindness, and to whom we are indebted for the present sketch, was a native of Pennsylvania. Just before the outbreak of the late war with Great Britain, he left the place of his birth to join the stirring scenes of adventure on the borders; and although now an old man, he still remembers, and loves to recount, the deed, and perils of his younger days, and especially those we are about to record.

Kilbourn, in whose own language the story shall be given, commenced:

> We had been scouting through the country that lay about Fort Stephenson, when early one morning one of our number came in with the intelligence that the Fort was besieged by a combined force of British and Indians. We were very soon after in our saddles, bearing down with all speed in that direction for the express purpose of joining in the fight—but on arriving, we found that the enemy had been signally repulsed by the brave little garrison under the command of Major Crogan. Our disappointment at learning this was, however, in a measure lessened, when we learned that Black Hawk, the leader of the savages, had, soon after the termination of the battle, gone with

some twenty of his warriors back to his village on Rock River, whither we instantly determined to follow him.

At sunrise the next morning we were on his trail, and followed it with great care to the banks of a stream. Here we ascertained that the savages had separated into nearly equal parties—the one keeping straight down the banks of the stream, while the other had crossed to the other side and continued on toward Rock River. A council was now held, in which the oldest members of our party gave it as their opinion that Black Hawk had changed his intention of going to his village, and had, with the greater part of his followers, pursued his way down the stream, while the rest had been sent by him for some purpose to the town. In this opinion all coincided; but still our leader, who was a very shrewd man, had some doubts on his mind concerning the movements of the chief, and therefore, to make everything sure, he detailed four of us to follow the trail across the stream, while he with the rest, some seven or eight in number, immediately took the one down the bank.

We soon after found ourselves alone and in the vicinity of Indian settlements, and we were therefore obliged to move with the utmost caution, which had the effect of rendering our progress extremely slow. During the course of the following morning we came across a great many different trails and by these we were so perplexed that we resolved to return to the main body; but from the signs we had already seen we knew that such a step would be attended with the greatest risk, and so it was at last decided that it would be far more safe for all hands to separate, and each man look out for himself.

This resolve was no sooner made than it was put into execution, and a few minutes later found me alone in the great wilderness. I had often been so before, but never before had I been placed in a situation as dangerous as the present one, for now on all sides I was surrounded by foes, who would rejoice in the shedding of my blood. But still I was not gong to give up easily, and looking well to my weapons and redoubling my caution, I struck off at an angle from the course I had first chosen, why I hardly knew.

I encountered nothing very formidable till some two hours before sunset, when, just as I emerged from a tangled thicket, I perceived an Indian on his knees at a clear, sparkling spring, from which he was slaking his thirst. Instinctively I placed my rifle to my shoulder, drew a bead upon the savage and pulled the trigger. Imagine, if you can, my feelings as the flint came down and was shivered to pieces while the priming remained unignited.

The next moment the savage was up on his feet, his piece levelled directly at me and his finger pressing the trigger. There was no escape; I had left my horse in the woods some time before. The thicket behind me was too dense to permit me to enter it again quickly, and there was no tree within reach of sufficient size to protect me from the aim of my foe, who, now finding me at his mercy, advanced, his gun still in its threatening rest, and ordered me to surrender. Resistance and escape were alike out of the question, and I accordingly delivered myself up his prisoner, hoping by some means or other to escape at some future period. He now told me, in good English, to proceed in a certain direction. I obeyed him, and had not gone a stone's throw before, just as I turned a thick clump of trees, I came suddenly upon an Indian camp, the one to which my captor undoubtedly belonged.

As we came up all the savages, some six or eight in number, rose quickly and appeared much surprised at my appearing thus suddenly amongst their number; but they offered me no harm, and they behaved with most marked respect to my captor, whom, upon a close inspection, I recognized to be Black Hawk himself.

'The White mole digs deep, but Makataimeshekiakiak (Black Hawk) flies high and can see far off,' said the chieftain is a deep, guttural tone, addressing me.

He then related to his followers the occasion of my capture, and as he did so they glared on me fiercely and handled their weapons in a threatening manner, but at the conclusion of his remarks they appeared better pleased, although I was the recipient of many a passing frown. He now informed me that he had told his young men that they were to consider me a brother, as he was going to adopt me into the tribe.

This was to me but little better than death itself, but there was no alternative and so I was obliged to submit, with the hope of making my escape at some future time. The annunciation of Black Hawk, moreover, caused me great astonishment, and after pondering the matter I was finally forced to set down as its cause one of those unaccountable whims to which the savage temperament is often subject.

The next morning my captors forced me to go with them to their village on Rock River, where, after going through a tedious ceremony, I was dressed and painted, and thus turned from a white man into an Indian.

For nearly three years ensuing it was my constant study to give my adopted brothers the slip, but during the whole of that time I was so carefully watched and guarded that I never found an opportunity to escape.

However, it is a long lane that has no turning, and so it proves in my case. Pretending to be well satisfied with my new mode of life, I at last gained upon the confidence of the savages, and one day when their vigilance was considerably relaxed, I made my escape and returned in safety to my friends, who had mourned for me as dead.

Many years after this I was a participant in the battle at Sycamore Creek, which, as you know, is a tributary of Rock River. I was employed by the government as a scout, in which capacity it was acknowledged that I had no superior; but I felt no pride in hearing myself praised, for I knew I was working against Black Hawk, who, although he was an Indian, had once spared my life, and I was one never to forget a kindness. And besides this I had taken a great liking to him, for there was something noble and generous in his nature. However, my first duty was to my country, and I did my duty at all hazards.

Now you must know that Black Hawk, after moving west of the Mississippi, had recrossed, contrary to his agreement, not, however, from any hostile motive, but to raise a crop of corn and beans with the Pottowattomies and Winnebagoes, of which his own people stood in the utmost need. With this intention he had gone some distance up Rock River, when an express from General Atkinson ordered him peremptorily to return. This order the old chief refused to obey, saying that the general had no right to issue it. A second express from Atkinson threatened Black Hawk that if he did not return peaceably, force would be resorted to. The aged warrior became incensed at this and utterly refused to obey the mandate, but at the same time sent word to the general that he would not be the first one to commence hostilities.

The movement of the renowned warrior was immediately trumpeted abroad as an invasion of the State, and with more rashness thin wisdom, Governor Reynolds ordered the Illinois militia to take the field, and these were joined by the regulars, under General Atkinson, at Rock Island. Major Stillman, having under his command two hundred and seventy-five mounted men, the chief part of whom were volunteers, while a few like myself were regular scouts, obtained leave of General Whitesides, then lying at Dixon's Ferry, to go on a scouting expedition.

I knew well what would follow; but still, as I was under orders, I was obliged to obey, and together with the rest proceeded some thirty miles up Rock River to where Sycamore creek empties into it. This brought us to within six or eight miles of the camp of Black Hawk, who, on that day—May 14th-was engaged in preparing a dog feast for the purpose of fitly celebrating a contemplated visit of some Pottawattomie chiefs.

Soon after preparing to camp we saw three Indians approach us bearing a white flag; and these, upon coming up, were made prisoners. A second deputation of five were pursued by some twenty of our mounted militia, and two of them killed, while the other three escaped. One of the party that bore the white flag was, out of the most cowardly vindictiveness, shot down while standing a prisoner in camp. The whole detachment, after these atrocities, now bore down upon the camp of Black Hawk, whose braves, with the exception of some forty or fifty, were away at a distance.

As we rode up, a galling and destructive fire was poured in upon us by the savages, who, after discharging their guns, sprung from their coverts on either side, with their usual horrible yells, and continued the attack with their tomahawks and knives. My comrades fell around me like leaves; and happening to cast my eyes behind me, I beheld the whole detachment of militia flying from the field. Some four or five of us were left unsupported in the very midst of the foe, who, renewing their yells, rushed down upon us in a body. Gideon Munson and myself were taken prisoners, while others were instantly tomahawked and scalped.

Munson, during the afternoon, seeing, as he supposed, a good opportunity to escape, recklessly attempted to do so, but was immediately shot down by his captor. And I now began to wish that they would serve me in the same manner, for I knew that if recognized by the savages, I should be put to death by the most horrible tortures. Nothing occurred, however, to give me any real uneasiness upon this point till the following morning, when Black Hawk, passing by me, turned and eyed me keenly for a moment or so. Then, stepping close to me, he said in a low tone: '*Does the mole think that Black Hawk forgets?*'

Stepping away with a dignified air, he now left me, as you may well suppose, bordering in despair, for I knew too well the Indian character to imagine for a single instant that my life would be spared under the circumstances. I had been adopted into the tribe by Black Hawk, had lived nearly three years among them, and by escaping had incurred their displeasure, which could only be appeased with my blood. Added to this, I was now taken prisoner at the very time that the passions of the savages were most highly wrought upon by the mean and cowardly conduct of the whites. I therefore gave up all hope, and doggedly determined to meet stoically my fate.

Although the Indians passed and repassed me many times during the day, often bestowing on me a buffet or a kick, yet not one of them seemed to remember me as having formerly been one of the tribe. At times this infused me with a faint hope, which was always immediately after extinguished, as I recalled to mind my recognition by Black Hawk himself.

Some two hours before sunset Black Hawk again came to where I was bound, and having loosened the cords with which I was fastened to a tree, my arms still remaining confined, bade me follow him. I immediately obeyed him, not knowing what was to be my doom, though I expected none other than death by torture. In silence we left the encampment, not one of the savages interfering with us or offering me the slightest harm or indignity. For nearly an hour we strode on through the gloomy forest, now and then starting from its retreat some wild animal that fled upon our approach. Arriving at a bend of the river my guide halted, and turning toward the sun, which was rapidly setting, he said, after a short pause:

'I am going to send you back to your chief, though I ought to kill you for running away a long time ago, after I had adopted you as a son—but Black Hawk can forgive as well as fight. When you return to your chief I want you to tell him all my words. Tell him that Black Hawk's eyes have looked upon many suns, but they shall not see many more; and that his back is no longer straight, as in his youth, but is beginning to bend with age. The Great Spirit has whispered among the tree tops in the morning and evening and says that Black Hawk's days are few, and that he is wanted in the spirit land. He is half dead, his arm shakes and is no longer strong, and his feet are slow on the war path. Tell him all this, and tell him, too,' continued the untutored hero of the forest, with trembling emotion and marked emphasis, 'that Black Hawk would have been a friend to the whites, but they would not let him, and that the hatchet was dug up by themselves and not by the Indians.

Tell your chief that Black Hawk meant no harm to the pale faces when he came across the Mississippi, but came peaceably to raise corn for his starving women and children, and that even then he would have gone back, but when he sent his white flag the braves who carried it were treated like squaws and one of them inhumanly shot. Tell him too,' he concluded with terrible force, while his eyes fairly flashed fire, '*that Black Hawk will have revenge*, and that he will never stop until the Great Spirit shall say to him, "*come away*."'

Thus saying he loosened the cord that bound my arms, and after giving me particular directions as to the best course to pursue to my own camp, bade me farewell and struck off into the trackless forest, to commence that final struggle which was decided against the Indians.

After the war was over, and the renowned Black Hawk had been taken prisoner, he was sent to Washington and the largest cities of the seaboard, that he might be convinced how utterly useless it was for him to contend against fate. It was enough, and the terrible warrior returned to the seclusion of his wilderness home, while the sceptre of his chieftainship was given to the celebrated Keokuk.

On the occasion of the ceremony by which Black Hawk was shorn of his power, and which took place on Rock Island, in the Mississippi, I shook the hand of the great chief, who appeared highly pleased to meet me once more; and upon parting with me he said with mournful dignity, as he cast above him a glance of seeming regret: 'My children think I am too old to lead them any more!'

This was the last time I ever saw him; and the next I learned of him was that he had left his old hunting grounds forever, and his spirit had gone to that bar where the balance will be rightly adjusted between the child of the forest and his pale face brethren.

Although the Winnebagoes and the Pottowattomies had resolved to take no part in the war, a few young men from each of these tribes, being emboldened by Black Hawk's victory in the engagement with Stillman's regiment, concluded to join him. As the party moved up the river, war parties were sent out, in one of which the Winnebagoes joined, whilst the Pottowattomies, some twenty-five or thirty, went alone on the war path into a settlement that had been made on Indian creek, not far from its entrance into Fox river, and killed fifteen men, women and children, and took two young ladies prisoners, the Misses Hall, whom two young Sacs, who had just rode up, took upon their horses and carried them to a Winnebago camp, with a request that they be delivered to the whites. They were returned soon after, and to the writer said they had been well treated by the Winnebagoes.

On the 19th of June a message came into Galena from Kellogg's Grove, with a report that a party of Indians had been seen in that neighbourhood and that they had stolen some horses. Captain James Stephenson, with twelve picked men from his company, started immediately in pursuit of the Indians. On seeing him approach they took to the brush, when the captain and his men dismounted. Leaving one to hold the horses, the balance entered the thicket, and two of them were killed at the first fire of the Indians, while three of the enemy were laid prostrate. For the purpose of reloading, Captain Stephenson ordered a retreat, which was a bad move, as it gave the Indians time to re-load and seek trees for safety.

Captain Stephenson and party again advanced, both parties firing simultaneously, each losing a man, when an Indian who had been secreted behind a tree rushed forward with his knife, but was suddenly checked by one of the soldiers running his bayonet through him. While in this position he seized the bayonet with both hands and had almost succeeded in pushing it out, when another soldier rushed forward, and with one stroke of his knife almost severed the head from his body. In this engagement Captain Stephenson lost three of the best men of his company and the Indians five, just one-half of their number.

✶✶✶✶✶✶

Captain Stephenson was held in high estimation as a brave and accomplished gentleman, and at the organization of Rock Island county the county commissioners honoured his name by calling the county seat Stephenson, which name it retained until after his death, when that of Rock Island was adopted.

On the return of Captain Stephenson and party the news of his loss of three men, who were well known and highly respected, soon spread over town and caused much sorrow among their many friends. After learning the mode of attack, military men generally criticized it severely.

✶✶✶✶✶✶

Battle of Pecatonica

On the 14th of June, a mall scouting party of Sacs killed five men at the Spafford farm, and on reception of the news next day, General Atkinson ordered Colonel Henry Dodge to take command of Posey's brigade, then stationed near Fort Hamilton, and while on his way from Fort Union, where his regiment was in camp, to visit the brigade, he heard the sharp crack of a rifle, and instantly looking in the direction of the sound, saw a man fall from his horse, who had been shot by Indians nearby. Instead of going forward as he set out to do, he hastily returned to his command, mustered a portion of his cavalry and went in pursuit of the Indians, and soon got on the trail of twenty-five warriors, who had commenced their retreat soon after shooting, and espying him, hastened back to the front.

The Indians crossed and recrossed the Pecatonica River several times, being closely pushed by Colonel Dodge and his men, and finding escape hopeless, made a stand. The colonel immediately dismounted his men and picked his way cautiously, with the intention of firing and then charging upon them. But the Indians, being on the lookout, watched their opportunity and got the first fire, by which a brave soldier named Apple was killed, and another by the name of Jenkins was wounded. The fight continued vigorously until the last Indian was killed, several of them having been shot while trying to escape by swimming. At the commencement of the fight, the forces on each side were nearly equal, but the Indians, in swimming the river, had got their powder wet, and although they made desperate efforts to close in on our men with knives, they were shot down in their endeavours.

Colonel Dodge, in speaking of this engagement, at Galena, after the close of the war, said he was amazed at the desperation displayed by a big, burly brave, who came towards him with gun at his shoulder and halted quickly when only a few paces from him, drew the trigger, and was sorely disappointed in his gun not going off. Quick as thought the colonel brought his rifle in position, pulled the trigger, but, owing to the dampness of the powder, it failed to go off. In the meantime the brave was coming towards him, knife in hand and desperation in his eye, and when only a few feet from him the colonel shot him down with his revolver. At the same time one of his brave boys, by the name of Beach, was engaged in a desperate encounter with the last remaining savage, in which both used knives; the Indian was killed and Beach very badly wounded.

Thus ended one of the most sanguinary engagements of the war.

Fight at Apple River Fort

Captain A.W. Snyder's Company, of Colonel Henry's Regiment, was detailed to guard the country between Galena and Fox and Rock Rivers, and was surprised on the night of the 17th of June, while encamped in the vicinity of Burr Oak Grove. His sentinels, while on duty, were fired upon by Indians, who did not deem it prudent to continue the attack, but immediately fled. As soon as it was light enough next morning to follow their trail, Captain Snyder started with his company, but on reaching their camp, found that they had fled on his approach. He redoubled his speed and continued on their trail until he overtook them. Finding that there was no escape, the Indians got into a deep gully for protection, but were soon surrounded, when Captain Snyder ordered his men to charge upon them.

The Indians fired as they approached and mortally wounded one of his men, Mr. William B. Mekemson, a brave volunteer from St. Clair county, (whose father's family afterwards settled in this, Henderson county, all of whom, except one brother, Andrew, a highly respected Christian gentleman, have, long since, gone to meet their kinsman in another world.) Mr. M. being unable to ride, a rude litter was made and men detailed to carry him back to camp, at Kellogg's Grove. The company had not proceeded far before they were attacked by about seventy-five Indians, and two men, Scott and McDaniel, killed, and a Mr. Cornelius wounded.

The company was soon formed into line by the aid of General

Whiteside, who was then acting merely as a private, and using the precaution of Indians, each man got behind a tree, and the battle waxed furiously for sometime without any serious results, until the Indian commander was seen to fall, from the well directed aim of General Whiteside's rifle. Having now no leader the Indians ingloriously fled, but for some reason were not pursued. Our reporter, however, said that most of the company refused, for the reason that the second term of their enlistment had expired, and they were anxious to be mustered out of service, although the officers were eager to pursue.

The company then commenced their march to camp, and on approaching the litter on which Mekemson lay, found that the Indians had cut off his head and rolled it down the hill. Soon after, Major Riley, with a small force of regulars, came up, and after consultation with Captain Snyder, it was deemed best not to follow the retreating Indians, as their route probably led to the main army of Black Hawk.

Apple River Fort.

On the 23rd of June scouts came into Galena, and reported at headquarters that a large body of Indians had been seen about thirty miles distant, but not being on the march, they were not able to conjecture to what point they were going. Colonel Strode immediately made all necessary preparations to receive them, should Galena be the point of attack, and dispatched an express early next morning for Dixon's Ferry. On their arrival at Apple River Fort they halted for a short time, and then proceeded on their journey, and while yet in sight, at the crack of a gun the foremost man was seen to fall from his horse and two or three Indians rushed upon him with hatchets raised ready to strike, while his comrades galloped up, and with guns pointed towards the Indians kept them at bay until the wounded man reached the Fort. But had the Indians known these guns were *not loaded*, (as afterwards reported) they could have dispatched all three of them with their tomahawks.

In a very short time after hearing the crack of the gun a large body of Indians surrounded the fort, yelling and shooting, when the inmates, under command of Captain Stone, prepared for defence, every port hole being manned by sharpshooters. One man, Mr. George Herclurode, was shot through a port hole and instantly killed, and Mr. James Nutting wounded in the same way, but not seriously; which was the only loss sustained during the engagement of more than one hour's duration. A number of Indians were wounded and carried off the field. Captain Stone had only twenty-five men, with a large number of women and children in the fort, but had providentially received a quantity of lead and provisions from Galena only an hour before the attack, and as he was short of bullets, the ladies of the fort busied themselves in melting lead and running balls as long as the battle lasted.

Black Hawk, finding the fort impregnable from assault without firing it—an act that he well knew would, in a very short time, have brought a large body of troops on his path—concluded that it would be better to return and carry with them all the flour they could, killed a number of cattle and took choice pieces of beef, and all the homes that were in the stable. One of the expressmen, not deeming the fort a place of safety, hurried back to Galena, but getting lost on the way did not get in until early next morning. On hearing the news, Colonel Strode took one hundred picked men, well mounted, and went to the relief of the fort, and was much gratified to find that its noble defenders had put to flight about one hundred and fifty Indians who had been under the command of Black Hawk himself.

Kellogg's Grove Fort.

After leaving Apple River Fort, being well supplied with provisions, the Indians moved leisurely toward the fort at Kellogg's Grove, with the intention of taking it, as scouts had come in and reported that it was not very strongly garrisoned on the day previous to their arrival on the 23rd of June. At this time the Illinois troops were rendezvoused at a place known as Fort Wilbourn on the Illinois river, at or near where now stands the city of LaSalle. What was then called the new levy, after Stillman's defeat, were assembled there, numbering about three thousand men, being formed into military organizations consisting of three brigades. The first brigade was commanded by General Alexander Posey. The second by General M. K. Alexander, and the third by General James D. Henry. Major John Dement, of Vandalia, was elected to the command of a spy battalion composed of three companies. General Atkinson, of the United States Regulars, commanding, while these organisations were progressing.

The Indians had made a raid on Bureau Creek, situated between the Illinois and Rock Rivers. John Dement had been chosen major by the members of three companies of General Posey's brigade, which was a spy battalion. The major's battalion being ready for duty when the news reached the fort of the attack upon the settles on Bureau

Creek, it was ordered to march at once to the scene of danger for protection of the settlers, and to discover and watch the movements of the Indians, if possible. The major was ordered to scour the country through to Rock River, and then to report to Colonel Zackary Taylor, who commanded a small force of United States troops at a small fortification at Dixon's Ferry on Rock River.

On the 22nd of June, 1832, Major Dement reached Colonel Taylor's command, having performed the duties to which he was assigned by General Atkinson. On his arrival Colonel Taylor informed the major that he had arrived at an opportune time, as he wished him to take his command, swim their horses across the river, and promptly occupy the country between his position and the Lead Mines at Galena, a distance of about sixty miles, with headquarters at Kellogg's Grove, thirty- seven miles in the direction of Galena and Apple River Fort. There had been stationed at the grove two companies of Regulars, commanded by Major Riley, and three companies of Volunteers that had abandoned this position the day before the arrival of Major Dement, and left the country without protection and entirely unguarded.

These troops had been engaged in two or three skirmishes with the Indians, and according to the reports of the soldiers, had been worsted in each. Major Dement's command numbered one hundred and forty men, all told, not one of whom had ever seen any military experience, but they were men to be relied upon. They were citizen soldiers, brave and intelligent, equal to any emergency, and had no superiors in the service. This being an odd battalion, Major Dement was entitled to the staff of a colonel. His staff was composed of Zadoc Casey, Paymaster; ——— Anderson, Colonel Hicks, and others. The captains of the companies, and the staff officers, were leading citizens, who had, at short warning, left their several avocations to engage in defending the country against the attacks of the Indians.

Major Dement's Battle With the Indians.

On the evening of the second day, after crossing Rock River, the major's command marched to the stockade at Kellogg's Grove and encamped. In the morning, learning that Indian traces had been seen four or five miles from the grove, twenty-five volunteers were called for to go out and reconnoitre. This number was quickly filled, nearly every one volunteering being an officer, and, as it afterward turned out, they were unfortunately accepted. These volunteers had not yet gotten out of sight of their camp, before three Indians were seen on their ponies between the fort and a small grove on the prairie, riding backward and forward. The reconnoitring party started after them in one, two and three order, according to the speed of their horses, while the Indians made straight for the small grove. Major Dement, who was watching the movements of the volunteers from his camp, and seeing the movements of the Indians, at once suspected a trap, mounted with a portion of his men, and went to their aid.

His men that had first started were a mile out upon the prairie in pursuit of those few Indians. Being well mounted, the major and his relief party soon overtook the hindermost of the little band, but several were too far in advance in their mad pursuit of the fleeing Indians for him to reach them in time. The fleeing Indians were making for a grove some three miles away, hotly pursued by the major's men. In this grove, as the commander feared, a large number of the Indians were concealed. When within four or five hundred yards of this grove he halted and dismounted his men and formed them in line. Some six or seven of his men were still in advance following the Indians toward this grove. On nearing the grove, his men who were in advance, were received with a galling fire, which killed two and wounded a third. With hideous yells the Indians emerged from the grove and rapidly approached. They were all mounted, stripped to their waists and painted for battle.

As they reached the bodies of the dead soldiers, a large number surrounded them, clubbing and stabbing their lifeless remains. A volley from the rifles of the whites killed two or three at this point, but by the time the last of the little band had reached the ridge upon which their comrades were drawn up in line, the Indians were close upon them and on both flanks. At this point three men who had been out of their camp hunting for their homes, came in sight and were massacred in sight of their friends. The main portion of the battalion had been ordered to hold themselves in readiness for any emergency, but hearing the yelling, instead of obeying the order, mounted in hot haste and started to the rescue of their companions. On discovering the force of the Indians, they retreated to the grove, and almost neck and neck with the Indians, sprang over their horses and occupied the Block House.

On the least exposed side of the fort was a work bench; over this the major threw the bridle rein of his horse, and most of the horses huddled around this as if conscious of their danger. The Indians swarmed around the Block House under cover; an ominous stillness pervaded the air, which was soon broken by the crack of the rifles of the white men. The best marksmen with the best guns were stationed at the port holes, and a lively fire was kept up by the little garrison. The Indians finding that they were making no impression, turned their attention to shooting the horses, twenty-five of which they succeeded in killing. After sharp firing for two hours they retreated, leaving nine of their men dead on the field. This was the first engagement in this war, in which the whites had held their position until reinforcements arrived, without retreating.

If the main force had remained in the grove at this Block House after the volunteers went out, without making any demonstration when the Indians came charging up and still in the open prairie, they could have been easily repulsed. This was the major's plan of action, but the men became excited by the firing, and having no commissioned officers to guide them, started without order to assist their exposed comrades in the open prairie, when they were flying for their lives to the blockhouse.

That evening General Posey came up with his brigade, and although the Indians were encamped a short distance away, he made no effort to attack them but contented himself with reporting the situation to Colonel Z. Taylor at Dixon's Ferry. General Whiteside had said to Major Dement before crossing Rock River, that he was going into the Indian rendezvous, where he could have an Indian for breakfast every morning, and he found it literally true.

It seems strange that Major Dement should have been ordered by Colonel Taylor into the enemy's country, across Rock River, with so small a force of volunteers, while a large force of Regulars and Volunteers, commanded by regular United States officers, remained securely entrenched in the rear. It was Major Dement's opinion that there were more fighting men of Black Hawk's band of warriors in the engagement at Kellogg's Grove than ever afterwards made a stand during the war. It was easy for General Posey to have moved up and attacked the Indians on his arrival at the grove, and then have dealt them a fatal blow by forcing them to battle then, but he refused to do so, and the war was not terminated until the fight at Bad Axe some two months later, in which the Illinois troops did not engage. During this engagement at the Block House, four whites and eleven Indians were killed. The whites lost a large part of their horses—the Indians shooting them from the timber, while the poor animals were huddled about the Block House.

Although in command, Black Hawk remained in the grove doing the engagement, looking on to see that his principal aid, whose voice was like a trumpet call, carried out his orders.

While reciting the incidents of this battle to the author, when writing his Autobiography, Black Hawk spoke in high praise of Major Dement as a commander, who had shown not only good military skill in coming to the rescue of his party, but in withdrawing his little party to the Fort. After Dement's engagement General Posey's brigade started for Fort Hamilton and remained there a short time. News of Dement's engagement and march of Posey's brigade having been received at Dixon's Ferry, where the two other brigades were stationed, General Alexander, with the 2nd brigade was ordered to cross Rock River and march to Plum River to intercept the Indians, as it was deemed probable that they would make for that point to cross the Mississippi.

General Atkinson, with regulars, and General Fry with his brigade, remained at Dixon waiting for news of the route taken by the Indians. Next day Captain Walker and three Pottowottamie Indians came into Dixon and reported seventy-five Pottowaottamies ready to join the army now encamped at Sycamore creek, and they were afraid that Black Hawk and his army was not far off. For their protection, and to await the coming of the balance of the second brigade, Colonel Fry, of Henry's brigade, was sent forward immediately. The next morning General Henry's brigade moved forward with General Atkinson at the head, intending to march up Rock River, to the Four Lakes, and camped at Stillwell's battle-ground the first night and joined Colonel Fry and his Pottowottamie Indians on the 29th, and continued their march. On the 30th, when going into camp, they saw signs of Sac Indians, but the sentinels were undisturbed during the night.

The next day they saw one Indian, but he was on the other side of Plum River. On the 2nd of July, Major Ewing being in front, spied a fresh trail, and soon after came upon the fresh trail of Black Hawk's entire force, at a point near Keeshkanawy Lake. Scouts from the battalion came up to Black Hawk's encampment, from which they had apparently taken their departure a few days before. Here they found five white men's scalps which had been left hung up to dry. This battalion continued to march around the lake in detachments, one of which found where there had been another encampment, but on returning to camp and comparing notes they began to despair of finding the main body of Black Hawk's army in that region.

On the 5th of July, General Atkinson with his army took a rest. During the day some scouts brought in an old Indian nearly blind and half famished with hunger, whom the Indians had left in their flight. After eating, General Atkinson questioned him closely as to the whereabouts of Black Hawk and his army, but was satisfied from his replies and helpless condition, that he did not know, but on taking up his line of march the near morning, General Atkinson did not leave him as the Indians had done, alone and without any means of subsistence, but left him an abundance of food, and as we afterwards learned, the old man recuperated and afterwards got back to his tribe.,

On the evening of the 9th the army encamped at White Water, and the next morning Indians were seen on the other side of this stream which was not fordable, one of whom shot and wounded a regular. After breaking camp, General Atkinson ordered a move up the river, and that night camped with his entire force—all having met at the same point. General Dodge's corps had taken a Winnebago prisoner and brought him into camp for the purpose of finding out if he knew where Black Hawk's forces were. He said they were encamped on an island near Burnt Village. Colonel William S. Hamilton, a brave and honoured son of Alexander Hamilton, in command of a company of Menomonees, who had joined the main army the day before, with Captain Early and his command, after scouring the island thoroughly, reported there were no Indians on the island.

Governor Reynolds, who had been on the march up Rock River with his volunteers and the main army, together with Colonel Smith, Major Sidney Breese and Colonel A. P. Field, left the army and came into Galena on the 12th, from whom we obtained our information of the movements of the army. They were firmly of the opinion that the Indians had taken to the swamps, and gotten entirely out of reach of the army, and that no farther danger need be apprehended. Colonel Field, who is an eloquent speaker, at the solicitation of Colonel Strode, although nearly worn out with hard marches, made an able and soul-stirring speech to our regiment, and a large number of the inhabitants of Galena.

At this time the army was nearly out of provisions, and Fort Winnebago, about seventy-five miles distant, the nearest point at which they could replenish. General Atkinson then ordered General Posey with his brigade, to Fort Hamilton, General Henry's and Alexander's brigade and General Dodge's squadron to Fort Winnebago for provisions; and sent General Ewing and his regiment to Dixon with

Colonel Dunn, who had been seriously wounded by one of his own sentinels, but who afterwards recovered. General Atkinson then built a fort near the camping ground, which was Fort Keeshkanong. General Alexander returned on the 15th with provisions to the fort, while Generals Dodge and Henry thought best to go with their commands to the head of Fox River, and while on the way stopped at a Winnebago village and had a talk with their head men, who assured them that Black Hawk was then at Cranberry Lake, a point higher up Rock River.

After a consultation by the generals, it was deemed best to send an express to General Atkinson at Fort Keeshkanong, to let him know of the information they had got, and their intention of moving on the enemy the next morning. Dr. Merryman, of Colonel Collins' regiment, and Major Woodbridge, Adjutant of General Dodge's corps, volunteered to go, and with Little Thunder, a Winnebago chief, as pilot, started out to perform this dangerous service, and after traveling a few miles, came on fresh Indian trails, which Little Thunder pronounced to have been made by Black Hawk's party, and fearing that they would be intercepted, insisted on returning to camp. Night was then approaching, and having no guide to lead them forward, they reluctantly followed Little Thunder back to camp. Orders were then given for an early move next morning, and at daylight the bugle sounded, and the army moved onwards. The trail was followed for two days, leading for Four Lakes.

On the second day, July 21st, scouts from General Dodge's corps came in and reported Indians, and as a confirmation of the fact, Dr. A.K. Philleo exhibited a scalp that he had taken from the head of one that he had shot. Dr. Philleo was brave as the bravest, and whenever a scouting party started out to look for Indians (unless his services were required in camp), was always in the lead, and this being his first Indian, took his scalp, and sent it to the writer, with written instructions how to preserve it. To this end we handed over both to a deaf and dumb printer in the office, who boasted somewhat of his chemical knowledge, who spent considerable time for a number of days in following the doctor's instructions.

After the killing of this Indian, some of the scouts discovered fresh signs of more Indians, and after pursuing it for some miles, Dr. Philleo and his friend Journey, equally as brave, being in the lead, espied two more Indians, when each picked his man and fired, and both fell; one of them, although badly wounded, fired as he fell, and wounded one of the scouts. The doctor's attention was now directed to his wounded companion, hence his second Indian was allowed to retain his scalp.

The scouts, finding that the trail was fresh, and the Indians were rapidly retreating, having strewed their trail with camp equipage, in order to facilitate their movements, sent an express back to camp, when the army hastily took up the line of march, with Dodge's corps and Ewing's Spy battalion in the front. By fast riding they soon came up with the Indians, whom they found already in line to receive them.

At Wisconsin Heights

Orders were at once given to dismount (leaving enough to hold the horses) and charge upon the Indians. They had scarcely time to form into line when they were met by the yelling Indians and a heavy volley from their guns.

Dodge and Ewing ordered a charge, and as they moved forward, returned the fire at close quarters, with deadly effect. The Indians then commenced a flank movement, and by securing a position in the high grass where they could in a measure conceal themselves, fought bravely, until Dodge and Ewing gave orders to charge upon them at the point of the bayonet. In this engagement Colonel Jones had his horse shot from under him, and one man killed—but at the word "*charge*," he went forward with his brave men, and all performed their duty nobly and fearlessly, and soon dislodged the Indians from their hiding place and forced them into a hasty retreat. It being then too late to pursue them, orders were given to camp on the battleground.

In this engagement Neapope had command, who was not only brave and fearless, but well skilled in strategy. Having become well acquainted with him after the war, he told the writer that he knew General Dodge personally, and had met him on the field of battle, and considered him one of the bravest men he had ever met, although in this engagement all the officers showed great skill and bravery, and thus encouraged their men to acts of noble daring to a degree that he had never before witnessed in common—not regular—soldiers. He said in this engagement, the command had been entrusted to him of this small force— about two hundred—Indians, in order to give Black Hawk and the remainder of his party, time to cross the river. He reported his loss at twenty-eight killed.

The next morning a portion of the army was ordered forward to pursue the fleeing enemy, but on reaching the river, found that they had taken to the swamps, when it was deemed prudent to return to camp without attempting to follow them.

Here the army rested for one day, and made comfortable provisions to carry the wounded, after having consigned the remains of John Short, who had been killed the day before, to mother Earth, with the honours of war.

In the meantime, General Atkinson arrived with his regulars and the brigades of Generals Posey and Alexander; and on the 28th of July, took up the line of march with General Atkinson at the head. Their route led through a mountainous country for several days, as the Indiana seemed to have selected the most difficult route they could find in order to gain time, and reach the river in advance, and then secure the best possible positions to defend themselves.

Having learned from an old Indian that had been left behind, that the enemy was only a short distance ahead, General Atkinson, on breaking camp at an early hour in the morning, gave orders for the march towards the river, with General Dodge's squadron in front; Infantry next; Second brigade, under command of General Alexander, next; General Posey's brigade next, and General Henry's in the rear.

After marching a few miles General Dodge's scouts discovered the rear guard of the enemy, when an express was sent immediately to General Atkinson, who ordered troops to proceed at double quick. In the meantime General Dodge's command pushed forward and opened a heavy fire, from which many Indians were shot down while retreating toward the Mississippi, where their main body was stationed. Dodge's squadron being in the lead, were first to open upon the main army of the Indians, whilst General Henry's brigade, that had been placed in the rear in the morning, came first to his aid.

The battle waged furiously for more than two hours, and until the last visible Indian warrior was killed. The Indians had commenced crossing before the battle opened, and a number took to their canoes and made good their escape as the battle progressed. The number killed was estimated at something over one hundred, but the Indians afterward reported their loss at seventy-eight killed and forty-two wounded. Our loss was seventeen killed and about the same number wounded.

During the engagement several squaws were killed accidentally and a number wounded, including children, who were taken prisoners. Among the latter, Dr. Philleo reported a boy with one arm badly broken, who exhibited a greater degree of stoicism during the operation of amputation, than he had ever before witnessed. Being very hungry, they gave him a piece of bread to eat, which he ravenously masticated during the entire operation, apparently manifesting no pain whatever from the work of the surgeon.

Many of the Indians who got across the river in safety were afterwards killed by the Menomonees.

Steamboat "Warrior's" Fight

On the 2nd of August, 1832, the steamboat, *Warrior*, was lying at Prairie du Chien, and word having been received at the fort that Black Hawk's main army was then at, or near the river above, at a point designated for all to meet for the purpose of crossing the river, Lieutenant Kingsbury took her in charge, and started up with one company, in order to intercept the Indians and prevent their crossing before the main army arrived, as he knew it was in close pursuit of them. The boat soon came in view of Indians on both sides of the river—Black Hawk and several lodges having already crossed over-when they were hailed by Lieutenant Kingsbury.

A white flag was hoisted by the Indians, and Black Hawk directed the Winnebago interpreter on board the *Warrior*, to say to his chief that he wanted him to send out his small boat so as he could go on board, a he desired to give himself up. The Winnebago, however, reported to the commander that they refused to bring their flag aboard. He then directed his interpreter to say that if they still refused he would open fire upon them. In reply, the interpreter said they still refused, when the lieutenant directed his six-pounder to be fired among them, and also opened a musketry fire by his company. This was returned by the Indians, and the battle continued for some time. Several Indians were killed at the first fire, after which the remainder sought protection behind trees, stumps, etc.

It was then getting late in the afternoon, and as the boat was nearly out of wood they dropped down to the fort to replenish, and started back again the next morning. On reaching an island some miles above their battle-ground of the day before, they commenced to rake it with their six-pounder, supposing the Indians had taken shelter there, and the army considering it a salute, General Atkinson returned it. Soon after the boat landed and took on board General Atkinson and the regulars and then returned to Prairie du Chien. The Illinois volunteers were ordered to Dixon, at which place they were discharged, while the troops of the lead mines were mustered out at Galena.

After the boat started down the evening before, Black Hawk and a few of his people left for the lodge of a Winnebago friend, and gave himself up. Thus ended a bloody war which had been forced upon Black Hawk by Stillman's troops violating a flag of truce, which was contrary to the rules of war of all civilized nations, and one that had always been respected by the Indians. And thus, by the treachery or ignorance of the Winnebago interpreter on board of the *Warrior*, it was bought to a close in the same ignoble way it commenced— disregarding a flag of truce—and by which Black Hawk lost more than half of his army. But in justice to Lieutenant Kingsbury, who commanded the troops on the *Warrior*, and to his credit it must be said, that Black Hawk's flag would have been respected if the Winnebago, who acted as his interpreter on the boat, had reported him correctly.

General Atkinson's Report.

Headquarters First Artillery Corps, North-Western Army, Prairie du Chiens, Aug. 25, 1832.

Sir:—I have the honor to report to you that I crossed the Ouisconsin on the 27th and 28th *ultimo*, with a select body of troops, consisting of the regulars under Colonel Taylor, four hundred in number, part of Henry's, Posey's and Alexander's brigades, amounting in all to 1,300 men, and immediately fell upon the trail of the enemy, and pursued it by a forced march, through a mountainous and difficult country, till the morning of the 2nd inst., when we came up with his main body on the left bank of the Mississippi, nearly opposite the mouth of the Ioway, which we attacked, defeated and dispensed, with a loss on his part of about a hundred and fifty men killed, thirty men, women and children taken prisoners—the precise number could not be ascertained, as the greater potion was slain after being forced into the river.

Our loss in killed and wounded, which is stated below, is very small in comparison with the enemy, which may be attributed to the enemy's being forced from his position by a rapid charge the commencement, and throughout the engagement the remnant of the enemy, cut up and disheartened, crossed to the opposite side of the river, and had fled into the interior, with a view, it is supposed, of joining Keokuk and Wapello's bands of Sacs and Foxes.

The horses of the volunteer troops being exhausted by long marches, and the regular troops without shoes, it was not

KEOKUK AND SON

thought advisable to continue the pursuit; indeed, a stop to the further effusion of blood seemed to be called for, till it might he ascertained if the enemy would surrender.

It is ascertained from our prisoners that the enemy lost in the battle of the Ouisconsin sixty-eight killed and a very large number wounded; his whole loss does not fall short of three hundred. After the battle on the Ouisconsin, those of the enemy's women and children, and some who were dismounted, attempted to make their escape by descending that river, but judicious measures being taken by Captain Loomis and Lieutenant Street, Indian Agent, thirty-two women and children and four men have been captured, and some fifteen men killed by the detachment under Lieutenant Ritner.

The day after the battle on the river, I fell down with the regular troops to this place by water, and the wounded men will join us today. It is now my purpose to direct, Keokuk to demand a surrender of the remaining principal men of the hostile party, which, from the large number of women and children we hold prisoners, I have every reason to believe will be compiled with. Should it not, they should be pursued and subdued, a step Major-General Scott will take upon his arrival.

I cannot speak too highly of the brave conduct of the regular and volunteer forces engaged in the last battle, and the fatiguing march that preceded it, and as soon as the reports of officers of the brigades and corps are handed in, they shall be submitted with further remarks:

5 killed, 6 wounded, 6th inft.
2 wounded, 5th inft.
1 Captain, 5 privates, Dodge's Bat., mounted.
1 Lieutenant, 6 privates, Henry's Bat.
1 private wounded, Alexander's.
1 private wounded Posey's.

I have the great honor to be, with great respect,

    Your obedient servant,

                        H. Atkinson, Brevet
                        Brig. General U.S.A.

Major General Macomb, Com. in Chief, Washington.

Appendix

AT YELLOW BANKS.

Among the many hundreds of troops that came to Yellow Bank—Oquawka— on their way to the sea of war, Major S. S. Phelps always spoke in high terms of their good discipline and gentlemanly conduct, except in one instance—that of a few persons in a company from McDonough county, who came over at a time when old chief Tama and his wife, who was noted for being the white man's friend, came over to get provisions for his little band. On seeing an Indian some of these soldiers, who had been using their canteens rather frequently, were eager to slay him, and not only threatened him but Major P. also, for harbouring him. The officers seemed to have no control of these men—and just at a time when their threats were loudest of what they intended to do at the close of three minutes, Major P. and one of his clerks, Mr. Joseph Smart, were standing with their rifles cocked ready to make the first shot, a cry came from outside of the building, by one of the more peaceable soldiers, "Here comes another company, Captain Peter Butler's, from Monmouth," when these would-be braves instantly retreated.

We are assured by one of Captain B.'s company, Mr. James Ryason, that the foregoing is literally true, and that Major P. and Mr. Smart, afterwards, amid the threats of these same soldiers, escorted Tama and wife to the river bank to take their canoe to cross the river, and stood there with their guns, ready to protect the Indians until they got out of reach of gunshot—Smart threatening all the time to put a ball though the first man that attempted to shoot.

In order to appease the wrath of these soldiers and prevent some of them being killed, Captain B. advised Major P. not to give Tama any provisions; but on the way down, Mr. Ryason says, Smart (who talked their language equal to a native born) told them to meet them at a certain point after night and they would be supplied; and that for the purpose of assisting Mr. Smart in taking supplies to Tama, he got leave of absence from the captain until next morning.

Messrs. James Ryason and Gabriel Shot, both honourable and highly respected Christian gentlemen, are the only survivors of that company now residing in this county, (as at time of first publication).

Tama's village, located on South Henderson, half a mile below the farm of Mr. John T. Cook, at Gladstone, was always noted as being the abode of friendly Indians. In the fall of 1829, some white men came in and made improvements on the land in the vicinity, and at the advice of Mr. Phelps, Tama crossed the river and made a new town at the mouth of Flint river on the Mississippi, and at the time of Black Hawk's raid into Illinois, it was the rendezvous of many young men who had been persuaded by Tama not to join Black Hawk. But when the news reached them of the indignities offered to their good old chief, they secretly determined to go upon the war path, and soon after four young Foxes started to cross the river and avenge the insult. On going up Henderson Creek they espied Mr. William Martin while in the act of mowing, at a point near Little York, whom they shot and killed, and for fear of detection, immediately took to the brush. It being late when they got through the woods, they made a fire and camped just at the edge of the prairie.

Some time after the shooting, friends of Mr. Martin discovered his lifeless body and after removing it to the home, started on the trail of his murderers, and followed it some distance through the underbrush, but wisely concluded, as it was growing late, to return and give the alarm. An express was sent to Captain Butler during the night, who started out with his company early in the morning, and on emerging into the prairie discovered the camp fire of the Indians, and followed their trail to a slough in the Mississippi two miles below Keithsburgh. Here the Indians embarked in their canoes and were probably on the other side of the river by this time. A demand was immediately made upon Keokuk for the murderers, as they belonged to his band of Foxes, who surrendered two men to the commanding officer at Rock Island.

These Indians soon afterwards made their escape, and before the time fixed for their trial, Keokuk delivered four young men to Major Phelps, then sheriff of Warren county, to be tried for the offence. Major P. and his deputy, Mr. James Ryason, took them to Monmouth jail, where the following proceedings were had before the Circuit Court (for a copy of which we are indebted to George C. Rankin, Esq., now Circuit Clerk):

WARREN COUNTY CIRCUIT COURT.

William Martin was shot and scalped by two Indians, near Little York, Warren County, August 9th, 1832. In their report at the October term of the Warren Circuit Court, the grand jurors say:

> Six or seven Indians of Keokuk's band of Sac and Fox Indians who were not included in the war path under Black Hawk and other chiefs of the Sac and Fox Nation, came over from the western bank of the Mississippi River to the inhabited parts of Warren County, in said State. and unlawfully and feloniously murdered the said William Martin in the most barbarous manner. That the names of the said Indians are unknown to the Grand Jury. That two of the said Indians have been heretofore given up by the chiefs of said Indians, that they were confined in the Fort at Rock Island for some time but have made their escape, and are now at large in their own country. That the Grand jury cannot now find an indictment because the names of the said Indiana are unknown to said jury. But they recommend that the governor of the State be furnished with a copy of this presentment, and that he be desired to request of the President of the United States that the whole of the said Indians concerned in the said murder may be demanded of the said Sac and Fox nation that they may be indicted and punished for murder under the authority of the laws of this State.

In compliance with the demand of the president, the chiefs surrendered four Indians, namely, with their interpretations;

Sa-sa-pi-ma (he that troubleth).
Ka-ke-mo (he that speaks with something in his mouth).
I-o-nah (stay here).
Wa-pa-sha-kon (the white string).
Concerning which, the Grand jury at the June term 1833 say:

> From an examination made by this Grand Jury they we now able to state that the four Indians lately surrendered by the chiefs at the request of the President of the United States, are not the real murderers of Martin. The chiefs represent that at the time the demand was made the real offenders had escaped from the territory and power of their nation. That the prison-

ers now in custody volunteered themselves to be surrendered in place of those who escaped, and that from custom amongst Indians, they supposed this would be a sufficient compliance with the requisition of the president. The Grand Jury will not positively say that the chiefs have prevaricated, but they do say that the demand already made has been eluded.

By a writ of *habeas corpus,* the four Indians above named were brought before the judge, presiding, Hon. Richard M. Young, June 14th, 1833, and released.

Indictment was returned against the real murderers, Shash-quo-washi, Muck-que-che-qua, Muck-qua-pal-ashah, and Was-a-wau-a-quot, who, "not having the fear of God before their eyes, but being moved and seduced by the instigations of the devil," killed Wm. Martin. The indictment was drawn by Thomas Ford, States Attorney, and recites that William Martin was shot a little below the shoulder blade. Among the witnesses named were Keokuk and Stabbing Chief. The guilty parties were never arrested, and a *nolle prosequi* was entered at the October term at court, 1835.

GENERAL SCOTT ARRIVES AT CHICAGO.

General Scott, with a full regiment of regulars, came up the lake and landed at Chicago about the 10th of July—the cholera in the meantime having broken out among his troops, from which several had died. While encamped at that point, it continued its virulence to such an extent, and in a number of cases fatally, that he deemed it best to much out on the high land, and soon after continued his journey, by slow marches, to Rock Island. On reaching Rock River, where Milan is now situated, the cholera had disappeared, and he went into camp with his entire regiment. The clear water of this beautiful stream was a Godsend to the many tired men, for the ablution of their bodies and the cleansing of their apparel, tents, etc., and seemed to have a general invigorating effect upon the entire regiment.

General Scott then went over to Rock Island with two companies to garrison Fort Armstrong, and there learned the situation of affairs in the army, and the great reduction made in the ranks of Black Hawk's band of Indians, so that a final close of the war was daily expected.

A few days after their arrival at Fort Armstrong, symptoms of cholera again appeared among the troops of the company, and the physician in charge tried every known remedy to check it, but failed in every instance, and after running its course, which was usually about twenty-four hours, the patient died. During the first three or four days of its ravages, about one-half of that company had been consigned to their last resting place in the soldiers' cemetery.

Being on a visit to Rock Island at the time the cholera was raging, the writer, at the request of Colonel Wm. Berry, (who had also come down from Galena to pay his respects to General Scott,) accompanied him to the fort and introduced him to the general. It was a very warm, but beautiful Sabbath, when we were admitted to the general's quarters, about 10 o'clock in the morning, and after the introduction of our friend and the usual salutations of the day, the general, after expressing his doubts of the propriety of admitting us into the fort, forcibly and touchingly detailed the ravages that the cholera was making in his ranks. Medicine, in the hands of a skilful physician, seemed to have no effect to stay its progress, and he was just on the eve of trying a different remedy as we came in, and if we would join him in a glass of brandy and water, he would proceed at once to put it into execution. He said he was satisfied that brandy was a good antidote to cholera, and by its use many of his soldiers were still well.

THE GENERAL'S REMEDY.

The general pulled off his coat, rolled up his sleeves, and directed an orderly to tear off strips of red flannel, fill a bucket with brandy and carry them to the hospital. On arriving at the bedside of a patient he directed him to be stripped, and then with flannel soaked in brandy he rubbed his chest thoroughly, in order to bring on a reaction, in the meantime administering a little brandy with a spoon. In the course of half an hour he returned and reported progress. He said he left his patient free from pain, and directed a small portion of the brandy to be given occasionally.

The well soldiers, seeing that their general was not afraid of cholera, nor too proud to act as nurse to a sick soldier, took courage and insisted on his retiring, so that they could fill his place. Seeing that new life had been infused among the well soldiers, and a gleam of hope seeming to inspire the sick, he gave directions for them to continue, as he had commenced, and then retired.

On returning to his quarters he washed his hands, rolled down his sleeves, put on his uniform, and then invited us to take a little brandy. After listening to his mode of treatment, we casually remarked that it looked feasible, but at the same time reprehensible in the general of the army exposing himself in the performance of a duty that could be done as well by a common soldier. He gave us a look, and kept his eyes upon us as his giant form raised up, and, with a sweep of his sword arm, said in majestic tones:

> Sir, it is the duty of a general to take care of his army; should he fall another can take his place; but, without an army his occupation is gone!

The general's treatment was continued right along, and the result was that many of those attacked got well.

Soon after the close of the war, which terminated with the Battle of Bad Axe, on the second day of August, 1832, he came to Galena, and, in conference with Governor John Reynolds, ordered the chiefs head men and warriors of the Winnebago Nation to meet them at Fort Armstrong, Rock Island, on the 15th day of September, 1832, for the purpose of holding a treaty.

At the time fixed by the commissioners they were met by the chiefs, head men and warriors of the Winnebago Nation, with whom a treaty was made and concluded, by which the Winnebagoes ceded to the United States all the lands claimed by them lying to the south and east of Wisconsin River and the Fox River of Green Bay. The consideration of this cession on the part of the United States, to be a grant to the Winnebago Nation of a tract on the west side of the Mississippi River known as the neutral ground and annual annuities for twenty-seven years of $10,000 in specie and a further sum, not to exceed $3,000 annually, for the purposes of maintaining a farm and a school for the education of Winnebago children during the same period of twenty-seven years.

Treaty With Sacs and Foxes.

After concluding the treaty with the Winnebagoes, and for the purpose of making a lasting peace with the Sacs and Foxes, these commissioners held a treaty at the same place, and a week later, on the 21st day of September, with chiefs, head men and warriors of that confederate tribe. The commissioners demanded, partly as indemnity for expenses incurred in the late war with Black Hawk's band and to secure future tranquillity, a cession of a large portion of their country bordering on the frontiers. In consideration thereof the United States agree to pay to said confederate tribes annually, for thirty years, $20,000 in specie; also, to pay Messrs. Farnham and Davenport, Indian traders at Rock Island, the sum of $40,000, to be receipted for in full of all demands against said Indians. And, further, at the special request of said confederate tribes, the United States agree to grant, by letters patent, to their particular friend, Antoine LeClair, interpreter, one section of land opposite Rock Island and one section at the head of the rapids of the Mississippi River.

THE CITY OF DAVENPORT, IOWA.

This beautiful city now covers that "Section of land opposite Rock Island" that was donated by treaty to Antoine LeClair by the Sacs and Foxes, and also three or four more sections. At that time it was wholly uninhabited, the Foxes having removed their village from that point some three years before. As a town site it was regarded by strangers and travellers on steamboats as the most beautiful west of the Mississippi between St. Louis and St. Paul, and now, with its twenty-three thousand inhabitants, elegant residences, magnificent public buildings, fine churches, schoolhouses, extensive manufactories, and large business blocks, it Stands unrivalled as a beautiful city. It has ten miles of street railroads, affording easy access to all parts of the city. It has two daily papers, the *Gazette* and *Democrat*, (morning and evening) both ably conducted; and also a German daily and two weeklies. The river is spanned by an elegant bridge that was built at the cost of nearly a million dollars, which is used by the various railroads from East to West, and has a roadway for teams and pedestrians.

THE CITY OF ROCK ISLAND—

..... is located on the bank of the river in Illinois, immediately opposite to Davenport, and is a large and flourishing city, with a population of about twelve thousand inhabitants. It has fine public buildings, elegant churches and residences, substantial business blocks, extensive manufactories and elegant water works. The city is lighted by electric lights, from high towers, that cast their refulgent rays over the entire city, which makes it the finest lighted city in the west. There are two daily papers, (morning and evening) *The Union* and *The Argus*, both enjoying the privilege of Press dispatches, and both issue weeklies. *The Rock Islander* is also published weekly, and all have the appearance of great prosperity.

The professions are represented by men of fine ability, including some of wide reputation. The banking business is done principally by two National Banks, that have a deservedly high reputation, and are doing a large business. There are two first-class hotels—the Harper

House and Rock Island House—and several of less pretentions. The city has large coal fields, in close proximity, with railroads running daily to and from the banks, by which the three cities are supplied.

The City of Moline—

..... is located two miles up the river from Rock Island, but connected with it by street railways. It has a population of over 8,000 inhabitants, and is extensively known from its many manufacturing establishments, which are supplied with water power from a dam across the river from the island.

Fifty Years Ago,

When the writer first visited this most beautiful Island in the Mississippi River, then and now known as Rock Island, the ground on which the triplet cities of Davenport, Rock Island, and Moline now stands, was covered with prairie grass, and apparently a sterile waste as regards to the two former, whilst the latter was principally covered with timber. Now how changed! Then the site of Davenport was claimed to be the most beautiful on the west bank of the Mississippi, between St. Paul and St. Louis by Black Hawk and his confreres, who had travelled up and down the river in canoes, whilst his judgment was confirmed by thousands of passengers who viewed it from steamboats in after years. Now—

The Triple Cities—

.... are widely known as the leading manufacturing cities of the great west, with railroads stretching out from ocean to ocean, and although the Mississippi makes a dividing line, they are united by a magnificent bridge, which makes their intercourse easier than over paved streets.

Rock Island, at that time, was excluded from settlement by the orders of Government, as it had been reserved, on the recommendation of Hon. Lewis Cass, whilst he was in the Senate and Cabinet, as a site for a United States Arsenal and Armoury. Fort Armstrong was situated on the lower end of the island, and was then in command of Colonel William Davenport. The Sac and Fox agency (Major Davenport, agent,) stood on the bank of the river about half a mile above the fort; next came the residence and office of Antoine Le Clair, United States Interpreter for the Sam and Foxes, and a little higher up, the residence, storehouse and out buildings of Colonel George Davenport, who had by an act of Congress, pre-empted a claim of two hundred acres of land running across the Island from bank to bank of the river.

The island is about two miles long, and being at the foot of the rapids has the best water power on the river, capable of running a much greater amount of machinery than is at present in operation. The entire island is now owned and occupied by the government, (the heirs of Colonel Davenport having sold and deeded their interest), and is now used as an—

Armoury and Arsenal,—

..... which are destined to be in the near future, the most extensive works of the kind probably in the world. Indeed, army officers who have travelled extensively in the Old World, say they have never seen anything to compare with it, in elegant grounds, water power and buildings, and with such facilities for moving anything to and from the arsenal. These works were commenced under the supervision of General Rodman, the inventor of the Rodman gun, and since the death of the General, D. W. Flagler, Lieutenant Colonel of Ordinance, has been in command, and a more efficient and better qualified officer for the place could not have been found in the army.

There are already completed ten massive stone buildings, which are used for workshops, storage, etc., officers' quarters, both durable and comfortable, and many other buildings. The former residence of Colonel George Davenport, (the house in which he as killed for money many years ago) built in 1831, of solid hewed timber, and afterwards weather-boarded, still stands unoccupied.

The island is mostly covered with trees of different varieties, which are kept neatly trimmed, and is laid out like a park, with wide avenues extending its whole length, which makes the most elegant drives and shady walks for the thousands of visitors who flock to the Island to feast their eyes upon its magnificence.

The City of Keokuk, Iowa—

.... is located at the foot of the Lower Rapids, 139 miles from Rock Island, and bears the name of the distinguished chief of the Sacs and Foxes. At our first visit there, in 1832, there was a long row of one-story buildings fronting on the river, that were used by Colonel Farnham, agent of the American Fur Company, as a store and warehouse— this being the principal depot for trade with the Sacs and Foxes, who were then the sole proprietors of the country and its principal inhabitants, with the exception of a few individuals who had got permission to put up shanties for occupation during the low-water season, while they were engaged in lighting steamers passing up and down the river, but unable to cross the rapids while loaded.

At that day the old chief, Keokuk, boasted of having the handsomest site for a big village that could be found on the river, and since that day it has grown to be a large and elegant city, with wide streets, fine public buildings, nice churches, school-houses, elegant residences, extensive business houses, wholesale and retail stores, manufactories, and a flourishing Medical University with elegant buildings, which has been in successful operation for more than twenty years. The United States District Court for Southern Iowa is also located here. The city is well provided with good hotels. The Patterson House, an immense building, five stories high, being chief, which has always ranked as first-class-with a number of hotels of smaller dimensions, but well kept—affording ample accommodation for the thousands of travellers that frequently congregate at this place. The various professions are represented by men of fine ability—some of them of wide reputation. They have two daily papers, *The Gale City*, and *The Constitution*, which are ably conducted.

A fine canal, running the entire length of the rapids, from Montrose to Keokuk, has been built by the United States, through which steamboats can now pass at any stage of water—but designed more particularly for low water—so that there is no longer any detention to lighten steamboats over the rapids.

THE CITY OF MUSCATINE, IOWA.

Muscatine was first settled as a wood yard by Colonel John Vanater, in July, 1834, and was laid out as a town by him in 1836, and called Bloomington. The county was organized in 1837, under the name of Muscatine, and Bloomington made the county seat. The name of the town was changed to correspond with that of the county in 1851. Its population at the last census was 8,294; present population not less than 10,000. Besides being the centre of a large trade in agricultural products, it is extensively engaged in manufacturing lumber, sash, doors and blinds, and possesses numerous large manufactories, oat-meal mills, and the finest marble works in the State. It is also the centring point of a very large wholesale and retail trade. It is situated at the head of the rich Muscatine Island, the garden spot of the Northwest, and is the shipping point for millions of melons and sweet potatoes annually.

Muscatine is a good town, with a good business and good newspapers. The *Journal* and *Tribune* are published daily, semi-weekly and weekly. Hon. John Mahin has been the editor of the *Journal* since 1852, and there is no editor in the State whose service dates further back than his.

THE CITY OF DUBUQUE.

Soon after the close of the war and the discharge of the volunteer army, the writer, with some twenty others who had served through the war, formed a company for the purpose of laying out the town of Dubuque. One of their number, Captain James Craig, being a surveyor, he was selected to survey the lines and lay out the town. About the middle of September, 1832, he started out from Galena with his chain-carriers, stake-drivers, etc., (stakes having been previously sawed and split on an island opposite, all ready for use), and in due time completed the survey. Blocks fronting the river on three or four streets back were completed, each lot receiving its stakes, whilst those farther back were staked as blocks, and not subdivided.

A few of the original proprietors built and took possession at once. Among them were the Messrs. Langworthy, enterprising and energetic young gentlemen, who commenced business as grocers in a small way, with supplies for miners. Their faith was strong that adventurers would come in, and that the time was not far distant when the town would take a start, and in a few years become a populous city. Miners and prospectors soon took possession of claims in the immediate vicinity, and in one instance a claim was made and ore struck within the limits of our survey.

It was well known that the Indians had been in the habit, for many years, of visiting this portion of their country, for the purpose of getting their supplies of lead; hence the supposition of miners, who had long been engaged in prospecting for lead-mining, that lead would be found on this side of the river and in the vicinity of Dubuque. This caused a great rush to the new fields, of hundreds, who expected to strike it rich with less labour and expense. All were aware, however, that under the treaty just made with the Sacs and Foxes by General Scott and Governor Reynolds, they had no right to enter upon these lands, and stood in daily fear of being ordered off by United States troops. But their numbers steadily increased.

At length the long expected order came. Major Davenport, Indian Agent at Rock Island, was ordered to go forward, and, with one company of infantry in two Mackinaw boats, commanded by Lieutenant Beach, they landed near the mouth of Fever river (Galena) about the first of October. The major came up to Galena with a letter from Colonel George Davenport to the writer, to assist him in the discharge of his delicate duty. Word was sent to Lieutenant Beach not to proceed up the river until the afternoon of the next day, as the sight of troops by the miners might make them hard to manage; otherwise, I assured the major, he would have no trouble.

We proceeded at once to a point opposite Dubuque, where we found a comfortable stopping place with the ferryman, and he being a man of considerable influence, I suggested to him the propriety of going over to Dubuque to send men to all the mining camps, requesting a meeting the next morning, at nine o'clock, of all the miners, with the agent, to hear what he had to say, and to assure them at the same time that his mission was a peaceable one, and that there should be no objection manifested to disobey the orders of the government.

After the departure of our messenger we took a private room to talk over the programme for the meeting, when we suggested that, on assembling, the major should make a little speech explanatory of his visit, in which he should express sorrow for the hardships it would be to leave their claims, with the hope that the time was not distant when all might lawfully return, etc. The major said he was not a speech-maker, or a very good talker, but would read the orders sent to him to dispossess them, and see that they crossed the river.

After some discussion, the writer, at his request, wrote out a short address for the major, and on going over the next morning, we met some four or five hundred miners at the grocery store, who had assembled to listen to the orders sent for their removal. There being no boards or boxes into which to improvise a stand for the speaker, a whisky-barrel was introduced, from the head of which, after apologizing to the miners for the disagreeable duty that had been placed upon the major, and in consequence of his suffering from a bad cold, we had taken the stand to read to them his short address, and as most of them had spent the summer in the service of the government as soldiers in the field, and had been honourably discharged, the major felt satisfied that there would be no objection manifested by any one in the large crowd before us to disobey an order from the government.

After the close of the major's address, the question was put to vote by raising of hands. There was a general upraising of hands, which was declared to be unanimous for immediate removal. Owing to the good treatment received by the major, he proposed to treat the entire party, and, to facilitate the matter, buckets of whisky with tin cups were passed around, and after all had partaken they shook hands with the major and commenced Crossing over in flatboats.

At three o'clock in the afternoon we crossed over on the last boat, and took our departure for Galena. During the evening the major's report of how his peaceable removal of a large body of intruders from the west to the east bank of the Mississippi had been accomplished, was made out and mailed. But the further fact that all those miners had recrossed the river, and were then in their mining camps, was not recorded, for the reason that the major had not been posted as to their intentions.

Owing to the provisions of the treaty, it was a long time before Congress passed an act for the sale of these lands, and confirmation to the titles of town sites, hence, many of those who had laid out the town of Dubuque had left the county, and at the time of proving up their claims failed to put in an appearance—the writer being one of them—whilst those who remained, with the Messrs. Langworthy, became sole proprietors—the latter having lived to see the town rise in importance, and at this time become one of the most populous cities on the west side of the Mississippi.

Wakefield's History of the Black Hawk War

BLACK HAWK

Contents

John Allen Wakefield	167
Preface	173
The Winnebagoes Attack Captain Lindsey's Keel Boats in 1827	177
The Sac and Fox Indians Cross Over the Mississippi to the State of Illinois, in a Warlike Manner	190
March to Fox River	202
Attack on Apple River Fort	214
Narrative of the Imprisonment of the Two Miss Halls	240
We Defeat the Enemy	254
General Engagement	267
March Down to Prairie du Chien	281
Description of Black Hawk and the Prophet	290
Appendix A	304
Appendix B	334

John Allen Wakefield

John Allen Wakefield, second son of William and Diana (Varner) Wakefield, was born February 22, 1797, at Pendleton, South Carolina. The father was a native of North Carolina, of Scotch-Irish ancestry. The mother (who died at Quincy, Illinois, at the age of nearly 107 years) was a native of South Carolina, of Scotch-Irish and French Huguenot ancestry. The father, William, a man of education, spent most of his manhood as a teacher.

John Allen received his name in honour of Major-General John Allen of Virginia, who was a cousin to Diana Varner Wakefield.

When he was seven years old, John's parents moved to middle Tennessee, where they remained but a short time, and then pushed on to Barren County, Kentucky. In 1808, the family removed to Illinois Territory, settling where Lebanon, St. Clair County, is now located.

During the first two years of life in Illinois, and while the family was "forted," owing to the hostility of the Indians, privations without number were endured. The war of 1812-14, which followed, was particularly aggressive and sanguinary in Illinois. Militia companies, organised for campaign and scouting duties, constantly patrolled the state.

Wakefield, though but sixteen years of age, manifested an unusual aptitude for scouting service, and to gratify a passion for that service, he enlisted in the company of Captain Jacob Short, in which he served from February 27 to June 9, 1813. Afterward he served as special scout for General Howard, earning the highest praises from that faithful officer, particularly as the bearer of dispatches, later called "expresses." One of his trips was fraught with such peril that his father applied for a writ of *habeas corpus* to take him from it; but learning of the issuance of the writ, he stole away in the night and crossed the Mississippi in a canoe, swimming his horse behind. The trip was made in answer to a call from General Russell, then at St. Louis, for a volunteer to carry dispatches to Vincennes (called in the vernacular of the day *Post Vinsan*), through a trackless wilderness of 175 miles, swarming with hostile Indians. It proved as perilous as had been anticipated, but he made it safely, returning by another route. One night he camped in a sink hole. The following morning was foggy. A war party of unusual size was heard approaching. His horse became nervous and liable at any moment to attract attention; but he hastily threw a blanket over its head, and the party passed within a few feet of the sink-hole, without detecting him. The dangers and struggles of the Illinois frontiersman during those perilous days cannot be magnified, and Wakefield had his full share of them.

At the close of the war he went to Cincinnati, where he studied medicine diligently for a considerable period, afterward going to St. Louis to finish his studies. But it seems that once in possession of his diploma, he decided medicine did not offer him the field anticipated, and at once turned to studying for the bar, to which he was admitted when in his twenty-first year. His examination was conducted at Vandalia, where he settled and remained until 1837, during the last three years of which time he saw much of Abraham Lincoln. As an outgrowth of an intimacy formed in the Black Hawk campaign, Mr. Lincoln, while a member of the legislature, lived with Mr. Wakefield in Vandalia.

In 1818 Wakefield was married to Eliza Thompson, a native of Bourbon County, Kentucky, daughter of Abram Thompson and Elizabeth (Brown) Thompson.

One of the most important services rendered by Wakefield, and one which should command the respect of every Illinoisan, was his determined stand against the introduction of slavery in the State of Illinois, attempted during the administration of Governor Edward Coles. The legislature which convened at Vandalia, December 2, 1822, and adjourned February 18, 1823, passed a resolution by infamous means, calling for a constitutional convention, at which an amendment was expected to be framed which would permit slavery in the State. For sixteen months the young State was a battleground, during which the anti-convention men were made targets for every manner of insult and assault. Wakefield, being a ready speaker and writer, plunged into the campaign with great vigour, paying his own expenses while canvassing the State, and had the satisfaction of witnessing the rout of the slavery or convention men by a decisive victory.

JOHN ALLEN WAKEFIELD

For his services during that campaign, he was elected a member of the next (fourth) House of Representatives, which sat from November 15, 1824, to January 18, 1825, and from January 2 to January 18, 1826.

From *The Vandalia Whig* of July 3, 1834, I notice that he was a candidate for Representative against Robert Blackwell and Colonel Samuel Houston, but Mr. Blackwell was elected.

When Governor Reynolds called for volunteers to drive out Black Hawk in 1832, Wakefield enlisted in the company of Captain John Dement. It was mustered into service April 20th, but with the entire army was mustered out May 28th, after the unfortunate Stillman's battle. Neither Wakefield nor Captain Dement's company participated in Stillman's battle. When a new levy of troops reached Dixon's Ferry, Wakefield was found enlisted in the company of Captain William L. D. Ewing. Ewing, being elected Major of a spy battalion, served as captain but a day or so, and Captain Samuel Huston (or Houston) succeeded in command.

First appointed surgeon, by reason of his medical knowledge, Wakefield was speedily transferred to the scouting service, in which he continued to the end of the war. For his efficient work he was promoted to the rank of Major. At the Bad Axe battle, fought at the mouth of the Bad Axe River, he received a slight wound. As that engagement finished the war and the fighting career of Black Hawk, the army marched over land to Dixon's Ferry, where Wakefield was discharged by Lieutenant Robert Anderson, August 16, 1832.

The following year, Major Wakefield wrote the history of that war, which is hereafter set forth. Written when fresh in his memory, and from his daily journal kept without interruption from its beginning to its end, this first history of the war must be accorded accuracy as well as general interest. Inasmuch as the records of the War Department do not disclose the names of many of the officers, the value of the record which Wakefield's book supplied is inconceivable.

The Black Hawk War having made the people of southern Illinois acquainted with the fertility and richness of the northern part of the State and the southern part of Wisconsin, a series of northward migrations set in. In 1837 Major Wakefield joined in the hegira, and settled in Jo Daviess County, where he remained, with the exception of the years 1839 and 1840, spent in Carroll County, until 1846, when he crossed over into Iowa County, Wisconsin, and there remained until the spring of 1849. In that year he removed to St. Paul, Minnesota, and was elected its first city judge.

The winters of Minnesota were so severe that he moved again southward to Allamakee County, Iowa, in 1851, where he lived until 1854. Then he went to Kansas to enjoy its milder climate, and settled at the point which subsequently became Lawrence, whence not more than half a dozen families had preceded him. Becoming a landholder, he remained at that place until the day of his death, June 18, 1873.

Upon the history of Kansas Wakefield left an indelible imprint. There the question of slavery had to be fought as he had fought it in Illinois thirty years before. In his new home the struggle was much longer, and he suffered the loss of much of the considerable wealth which he had accumulated in Minnesota and Iowa. But his fortunes improving, he became a strong factor in moulding Kansas into a rich commonwealth, and his declining years were prosperous.

In the struggle in Kansas with the slavery element, he was made the first free-state candidate for delegate to Congress, for which office he received three fourths of the legal votes cast at the election. But it will be remembered, that following the hint of Senator Atchison of Missouri, "When you reside within one day of the Territory, you can send five hundred of your young men who will vote in favour of your institutions," voters were poured into Kansas from Missouri, and the candidate of the slave-holding interests was elected by an enormous majority. Indeed, he received eleven hundred votes more than the number of legal voters in the Territory three months afterward.

Wakefield was elected State Treasurer under the Topeka constitution which he had helped to frame, and as chairman of the judiciary committee of the first and many succeeding legislatures, was largely responsible for the State's excellent code of laws. Lawrence was the storm-centre of those perilous times. During the fierce " border troubles," when the Territory was constantly invaded by large bodies of armed men from Missouri, Wakefield was constantly the leader of the free-state settlers, and for his courage and pertinacity in opposing the slavery forces was made the principal target for their attacks. Just west of Lawrence he had built a large house and many substantial outbuildings, but the invaders, on the night of September 1, 1856, fired and burned every building on the place. The fine library in the house and two manuscripts ready for publication, together with 140 acres of wheat and oats in the stack, were destroyed. That disaster involved a loss of $10,000. The attack was so sudden and unexpected, that the escape of the family was nothing short of miraculous.

Judge Wakefield, as he was called the latter years of his life, died at

Lawrence June 18, 1873, in his seventy-seventh year.

To conclude, it should be added that his wife Eliza died in 1871. From the union twelve children were born, eight of whom reached middle age or more. Lysander and Alvin, first and second sons respectively, died at Vandalia in childhood. George Washington, the third son, lost his life by an accident in California when about 45 years of age. Mrs. Mary A. Willard, eldest daughter, died December 7, 1903, in Los Angeles, California, at the age of 82. Martha Ann Wakefield died near Lawrence in 1855. Mrs. Emily Terry, third daughter, resides at present in the city of Chicago. Mrs. Eliza J. Snyder, fourth daughter, died at Lawrence, December 7, 1902. William H. T. Wakefield, fourth son, to whom I am under obligation for the facts herein stated, is a resident of Mound City, Kansas. John Allen, Jr., died July 31, 1865, aged 29 years. Thomas J., the youngest, was accidentally killed at Denver, Colorado, November 1, 1890, by the fall of a derrick. Two daughters, Sarah and Diana, died in infancy.

Frank Everett Stevens.

Preface

In presenting this small volume to the world, the author is aware that he is exposing his name to the public calumny, by those who are ready at all times to find fault; but he hopes the candid, who will reflect a moment on the many difficulties attending the compiling such a work, will be as charitable towards him, as the nature of the case will admit. They must reflect that the many actors in the late war have not all the same views of things that took place—as it is the nature of man to differ in opinions, and those that were eye witnesses of the events recorded in this narrative, (or history,) to have different opinions from each other.

The writer who traces events at a remote period from the time they transpired, stands on more favourable ground, because they are not fresh in every one's memory, and men are not disposed to find so much fault.

But it has been the aim of the author to track as near the truth, as his knowledge of the different actors, and all that were in any way concerned in the war, would permit. If he is found in error, it will be an error of the head and not of the heart.

But he is aware that he has not done this subject that justice which its importance deserves. But, as he has already observed, he hopes an honourable and patriotic people will exercise all the charity that characterizes the American people, and, more especially, to one that never attempted before to write for the inspection of an enlightened republic.

For a history of the expedition against the Indians, the author has to depend upon public record, and such other information as is well authenticated by men that can be confided in; but in the last two campaigns, the author was an eye witness to almost all that he has here written.

In order to give a full detail of all the transactions and relationship between those Indians and the United States, the author has thought it would be more satisfactory to give all the treaties that ever were held with them, which commenced in eighteen hundred and four.

Many false reports have gone abroad respecting the lands of those Indians, representing that the government has not done strict justice.

In giving an account of the frontier massacres by the Indians, the author has to depend on newspaper information; but it is his opinion that all that have been found upon record, which were published in this state, are literally true, and may be relied upon as facts.

But, it is not in the power of the author to give an account of all the massacres that the Indians have committed on the frontier, as many were committed that have not been recorded; or, if they were, the author has not been fortunate enough to get possession of them.

In giving the different treaties, the author principally confines himself to the Sac and Fox nations:—But, in the last treaty which has lately been made, he will be able to give the substance, or the whole of the treaty with the Winnebagoes.

He would be glad to enter into a history of the hostilities that took place between the Winnebagoes and the United States, in 1827, but he has not such documents before him as would justify a review of it. And he is also well aware that some more able hand will, in due time, give the whole of the transactions of those Indians a thorough investigation; and that the public will not suffer by the author's passing over the particulars of that expedition against those Indians.

The author deems it necessary to confine himself to facts, and without some public documents, more than his own knowledge, he could not with any propriety, enter into a full history of the transactions between the United States and those Indians, more than simply to state, that they made an attack on some keel boats that were running on the Mississippi, and commanded by Captain Allen Lindsey, and the general outline of the transactions afterward, in bringing them to a treaty.

This was the first difference, of any importance, that took place between the United States and those Indians, since the war with Great Britain.

The author, in order to show the cause of difference between the United States and the Sac and Fox Indians, thinks it best to lay before the reader many interesting documents, consisting of letters and a number of depositions, to show the necessity of the executive in calling upon the militia of the state of Illinois, to protect its citizens:—And he flatters himself that, after the perusal of those letters and depositions, none will have the hardihood to say, that Governor Reynolds did wrong in the course he pursued to subdue those Indians.

The author takes more pains, and troubles the reader with those documents more than he would have done, if he had not seen with regret, that misrepresentations have gone abroad respecting those Indians.

He flatters himself that, after a perusal of the different treaties entered into by the United States and the Sac and Fox Indians, and the many violations of those treaties by those Indians, all will justify the course taken to bring them to subjection, and restore peace to our country,—which is the case at this time:—and that it could not be done in any other way than a resort to arms, as all other means were tried, both by General Clark, and the different Indian Agents; and that with a great degree of forbearance on the part of the General Government, which the reader will plainly see when he takes a full view of the many outrages and depredations committed by those lawless savages, who did everything except murder, before there was a call for men to volunteer in defence of their country.

The author wishes further to observe, that he has taken all the pains that lay in his power, to place the different officers to their proper command, and to detail the part they acted in the war: But he at the same time is well aware that there may be some officers whom he may not mention, that are deserving well of their country; on account of not having it in his power to get a complete list of all the mounted volunteers, that turned out in defence of their country; for many of them were stationed on the frontier, and did not march with the main army, but performed important services in defence of the northern frontiers; as many of the citizens would have certainly been destroyed by the Indians, whose known mode of warfare, is to steal upon the helpless part of (the) community, at the dead hour of night, when there is no chance of defence.

So, I consider that those rangers who were placed on the frontier, performed a high and important ser vice, in ranging those frontiers, and protecting the lawful settler in quietness at his own fireside, and (saving) his wife and children from becoming a prey to the savage barbarity of the tomahawk and scalping knife.

The Author.

Vandalia, Illinois, 1833.

Chapter 1

The Winnebagoes Attack Captain Lindsey's Keel Boats in 1827

The author, in giving a history of the late war between the United States and the Sac and Fox nations of Indians, thinks it would be doing the subject injustice, not to give an outline of the difficulties that took place between the United States and the Winnebagoes, in the year eighteen hundred and twenty-seven, which he has observed in his preface, was the first disturbance of any kind that took place between the Government of the United States and the Winnebagoes since the last war with Great Britain. But the author, in giving a small outline of this disturbance, has to depend upon his memory alone; as, at that time, it had never entered his head that he would be the biographer of this small disturbance that took place between the government and those Indians.

But, in attempting to give the public the causes and particulars of the war betwixt the government and the Sac and Fox nations of Indians, he thinks that it would not be amiss to take a passing notice of the transactions that took place on this occasion.

Captain Allen Lindsey, a gentleman of the first respectability in our country, was running a couple of keel boats on the Upper Mississippi, in the summer of eighteen hundred and twenty-seven; when within a few miles of Prairie du Chien, was visited by a number of Winnebago Indians, some of them came aboard of his boats and showed signs of hostility to him, such as preyed upon his mind so much that, before he returned, he provided himself with a few firearms, so that, in case of an attack by them, he might be able to defend himself.

✴✴✴✴✴✴

Stevens's *The Black Hawk War.* Movements of the militia from eastern Illinois are mentioned fully in the paper by Hon. H. W. Beckwith, number ten, Fergus Historical Series. From Sangamon and Morgan Counties in Illinois, a regiment of mounted volunteers, under command of Colonel Thomas M. Neale of Springfield, marched to Galena; but when that point had been reached, Red Bird, the moving spirit in the uprising, had surrendered and the regiment saw no service. Its movements, however, are to be found in an article written by Hon. William Thomas of Jacksonville, and published in the Jacksonville Journal of August 17, 1871. The reason for the Winnebago War, so frequently attributed to brutality to certain squaws, by the whites, has not a shadow of foundation in fact.

✶✶✶✶✶✶

He was at this time on his way up to St. Peters. He made his trip, and accordingly on his return, when within a few miles of Prairie du Chien, he was again visited by those same Indians. He had to pass down the river close to their towns and habitation for several miles; for that is the way these wretched beings live, in small bark *wigwams*, along some water course, where they can paddle their canoes.

But agreeably to Captain Lindsey's expectations, he was not permitted to pass by their dwellings in peace.—Very late in the evening, a number of those bloodthirsty savages made their appearance to him in a menacing manner, by opening a heavy fire upon his boats; and by the help of their canoes attempted to board them. But Captain Lindsey, had fortunately for him, anticipated that they did not intend to let him pass without firing him a salute of this description. He was prepared for them, although he had but few men aboard of his boats, but what he had proved to be soldiers

The Indians opened a heavy fire upon him, which was returned by him and his boat's crew with double interest. There were a large number of Indians, who charged upon him in their canoes, thinking to board his boats, but he prevented them by the hardest kind of fighting. They came so near boarding him, that, a number of them lashed their canoes to his boats; but he gave them a quietus in the act, and they bequeathed their canoes to him in return, and became bait for the fish of the Mississippi. At this, each one made shift for himself. The Indians paddled their canoes in one direction, and Captain Lindsey rowed his boats the other.

Captain Lindsey lost two fine men in the action, and a number wounded, (the losses were two whites killed and four wounded, two mortally and two slightly. Reports of losses by the Indians vary from seven to twelve killed, and many wounded); but how many I do not recollect at this time. If this officer had not anticipated mischief from those wretched beings, there is no doubt but that he and his whole crew would have been massacred by those inhuman barbarians; for it is generally supposed that it was plunder, or, in other words, the cargo that the boats contained, they were after.

Captain Lindsey ran his boats down as soon as possible, to Galena, a small town on Fever River, six miles above where it empties itself into the Mississippi, which is now the county seat of Jo Daviess County, in the north-west corner of the State of Illinois.

When Captain Lindsey arrived at that point, and gave the news, it created great fear and alarm; to such a degree, that expresses were sent in different directions to inform the citizens of the mines to move into Galena, and prepare for war. The people of the mines took the alarm, so that in two days' time there were not less than three thousand men, women and children, who fled to this place for safety. Those Indians had made many threats against the miners, and had at different times ordered them off, and told them to quit the diggings, saying that the ground they were digging on was theirs. This news, coming at this time, when they were apprehensive of mischief, gave them an alarm, and caused them to fly to Galena for safety. They forsook their rude habitations, and assembled at that place, in order to assist in defending each other. There were a few forts built in the more thickly settled parts of the mines, and some of the most fearless citizens occupied them.

There was a committee of safety appointed in Galena, who corresponded with all parts of the mines, and adopted measures for the safety and preservation of all; and in the meantime had some strong blockhouses built at Galena. The people likewise, who were able and willing to bear arms, volunteered and formed themselves into companies, and chose their own officers; ranged the country, and kept a good lookout, for fear the Indians would steal upon them, and take them by surprise.

Governor Cass, in the meantime, was not inactive, but corresponded with Governor Edwards, then Governor of Illinois. Governor Edwards immediately raised one regiment of mounted volunteers in the northern counties, and sent them on to the relief of the mining country, and to go against those Indians. They elected Thomas M. Neale their commander. The people of the mines formed themselves into another corps, and elected General Dodge their commander a man well qualified to command, and who had some experience in the same.

Colonel Neale marched his regiment to the mines, but no further. General Dodge, assisted by Governor Cass, (Governor Cass was not present as intimated), marched on a force of near one thousand men, to the portage of the Wisconsin and Fox Rivers, where the Indians sued for peace.

★★★★★★

The number of men employed in the expedition was 600 regulars under General Henry Atkinson and about 130 militia from the lead mines under Captain Henry Dodge. Samuel Whiteside, who was present at Galena at the time of the trouble, took command of another company of about the same strength as Dodge's company, and marched or ranged through the country to the north, emerging at Prairie du Chien. A dispute had arisen as to whether Whiteside or Dodge should be given command of the militia, which was settled by giving each a company. James M. Strode was captain of a company which remained at Galena doing guard duty.

★★★★★

A treaty was then made with them. They gave up their commander, who had been the principal cause of the war, whom they called the Red Bird. He was put in prison at Prairie du Chien, and was to have been kept as a hostage for the good behaviour of the rest of his nation, but he soon died.

After this treaty, the forts were again forsaken, and the citizens returned to their respective habitations, and peace and safety seemed to be felt by all, until the hostile movement of the Sacs and Foxes, in the spring of eighteen hundred and thirty-one; when they invaded the State of Illinois, by leaving their own side of the Mississippi, crossing over, and attempting to claim the land they had sold to the General Government, in the neighbourhood of Rock Island. Here this terrible and warlike nation of Indians committed all kinds of out rage on the citizens near this place. The citizens had purchased the land they lived upon from the General Government, and had opened good farms, built houses, and had been living in peace and quietness for nearly three years, when these wretched monsters in human shape attempted to drive them from their homes, and take possession of them themselves; which in fact they did. (Appendix A 1) But this was not all those savage monsters did. They turned their horses into their wheat fields, killed their stock, and laid waste whole farms.

It was time now for those citizens to ask for assistance from their countrymen. They did so. Petition after petition was sent to the Governor of Illinois, laying before him their grievances, (Appendix A 2), Governor Reynolds hesitated not a moment, but addressed the proper officers on this important subject. He addressed letters to Generals Clark and Gaines on this subject, and tried every means that lay in his power to dissuade those unhappy people to desist from their designs, and return back to their own side of the Mississippi to their own land. But to this they turned a deaf ear too, as well as to all kind of entreaty that could be made through their agents, or General Gaines or any other person. They bid defiance to General Gaines, and bantered him to fight them with his regulars. This was enough. General Gaines saw now that there was no way of settling this business, only by a resort to arms. He accordingly made a call upon Governor Reynolds for seven hundred mounted volunteers to co-operate with him in driving them from the State. (Appendix A 3.)

Governor Reynolds immediately obeyed the call, and issued his proclamation to the citizens of the northern counties of Illinois, who turned out to the number of fifteen hundred strong, and rendezvoused at Beardstown, on the Illinois River; and between the first and tenth days of June were organised into a brigade, under the command of General Joseph Duncan.

This brigade was officered in the following manner, *viz*: James D. Henry, of Sangamon county, Colonel of the first regiment; Jacob Fry, Lieutenant Colonel; John T. Stuart, Major; Thomas Collins, Adjutant; Edward Jones, Quarter Master; and Thomas M. Neale, Paymaster. The Captains were as follows: Adam Smith, William F. Elkin, A. Morris, Thomas Carlin, Samuel Smith, John Lorton, and Samuel C. Pierce.

The second Regiment was commanded by Colonel Daniel Leib, of Morgan County; —— ———, Lieutenant Colonel; Nathaniel Butler, Major; Captains H .Mathews, John Haines, George Bristow, William Gilham, (Hiram) Kincade, Alexander Wells, William Weatherford, and W. Jordan, Quartermaster.

There was one odd battalion, which was officered in the following manner: Nathaniel Buckmaster, (see note at end of chapter), Major; James Semple, Adjutant; Joseph Gillespie, Paymaster; (David Wright,) Quarter Master; Richard Roman, Surgeon; Captains William Moore, John Loramie, Loraine) and Solomon Miller. (Charles Higbee was Surgeon and Roman was Mate.—Original Ed.)

The spy battalion, next, was officered in the following manner: Samuel Whiteside, (see note at end of chapter), Major; Samuel F. Kendle, Adjutant; John S. Greathouse, Quartermaster; P. H. Winchester, Pay Master; Captains Erastus Wheeler, William B. Whiteside, William Miller, and Solomon Prewitt. (The orthography of foregoing names is incorrect in many instances.)

Those were the officers that composed the brigade under General Joseph Duncan, with a few exceptions. The name of the lieutenant colonel in Colonel Leib's regiment, I have not been fortunate enough to get in possession of, and I have not been able to get all the staff officers belonging to it; for I have no public record to resort to. Therefore, I hope no gentleman will think hard of me, or feel himself slighted in not having his name inserted in this history. (Governor Reynolds's aids were James D. Henry and M. K. Alexander. Upon Henry's resignation, for active service John Dement was appointed. Enoch C. March was made Quartermaster General, and William Thomas Brigade Quartermaster.) General Duncan, after his brigade was organised, took the line of march for the seat of war, or where the savage rebels were assembled and bidding defiance to General Gaines and his regulars, at or near Rock Island.

When General Duncan arrived at Rock River, he had to cross this stream near an island; and for fear of an ambuscade, General Gaines had it raked with a six pounder, so that if the enemy were concealed in this hiding place, he might drive them from it until his men could cross.—He fired his six pounder a number of times into this island, but the enemy had taken the alarm, and crossed over the Mississippi; but still kept embodied for action. (The Indians had returned to the west side of the Mississippi River during the previous night instead of during the action, as might be inferred herein.) They did not much like the sound of the six pounder.

Some of them afterwards came over to Rock Island, where General Duncan had arrived with his men, and joined General Gaines, who took command of all the forces then in the field. They held a white flag in their hands. They now sued for peace. The Black Hawk was not one of the company. General Gaines demanded of them to bring him. They at first refused, but he told them that he would march his forces across the river and cut them off, if they did not produce him. They then returned and brought the wretched Hawk, who had caused so much trouble to them and our own government.

They then entered into capitulations of a treaty, (see Appendix

A 4, also General Gaines's Report to President U. S., Appendix A 5); the articles of which they violated in a few weeks after wards by the most daring outrage. It was stipulated in the articles, that they were to remain on the west side of the Mississippi, and never to cross the river, and come into the State of Illinois, without the per mission of the President of the United States or the Governor of Illinois. But they soon forgot this agreement. They crossed over in a few weeks, went within a few hundred yards of Prairie du Chien, in the dead hour of night, fell upon a camp of Menominie Indians, slaughtered and killed twenty-five of them; and that too, within gun-shot of a garrison of regulars.

Those Menominie Indians never have been at war with the Government of the United States. They have ever looked to it for protection.—They had been that day in an Indian frolic, and were nearly all drunk. It is a well known thing, that, when Indians get into one of those drunken frolics, they are dangerous, one to another, and the squaws invariably make it a rule to hide their arms until they get sober. This was the case at this time. Those Menominies had just been gorging with this hydra monster of all evil, and were lying in their *wigwams*, lost in sleep; never dreaming or thinking that there was the least danger of being butchered by those hideous monsters, that were of the same species of human beings with themselves. But the deadly tomahawk and spear were buried in them when in their helpless situation.

The Menominies, it is said, succeeded in killing four of these savage monsters, who deserved to die the worst of deaths.

✶✶✶✶✶✶

This affair is fully related in correspondence between General Joseph M. Street, the agent at Prairie du Chien, and General William Clark of St. Louis, to be found in report of Secretary of War made shortly after the affair was reported to him. Twenty-five Menominies were killed outright in the attack, while many others were wounded.

✶✶✶✶✶✶

The Menominies immediately informed General Street of the massacre. He repaired immediately to the battleground. They appeared to be in great distress for the loss of their friends. They had killed a number of squaws and children. The Menominies made heavy complaints to General Street, saying, you have told us that you would protect us, and see that the Sacs and Foxes would let us alone. General Street told them that they would be punished for what they had done. He accordingly sent a communication to Governor Reynolds, informing him of their movements, and the slaughter of the Menominies; and at the same time, took measures to demand the murderers; the particulars of which I am not able to lay before the public.

But instead of the Sacs and Foxes delivering up the murderers, they, early in the spring following, crossed over to the State of Illinois, armed and equipped for war, and passed by, almost in sight of Fort Armstrong, bidding defiance to General Atkinson, the commander of the fort. General Atkinson then communicated to Governor Reynolds, by express, their movements. Governor Reynolds then lost no time in issuing his proclamation to the citizens of Illinois, calling for volunteers.

******

Note:—Major Nathaniel Buckmaster, youngest child of a family of eight children, son of Nathaniel and Ann (Ward) Buckmaster, was born May 1, 1787, in Calvert County, Maryland, on a plantation owned by his parents, that extended to the shores of the Chesapeake Bay.

In 1796 the family moved to Frederick County, Virginia, on a farm about 30 miles from Charlestown.

In the year 1803 Nathaniel, then 16 years old, went to a place seven miles from Harper's Ferry, to live with his sister, Catherine Anderson, where he learned the trade of brick and stone mason.

In the spring of the year 1818, clad in knee-breeches, ruffled shirt, high stock, with shoes ornamented with great silver buckles, Nathaniel Buckmaster came to Edwardsville, Illinois, to seek his fortune, and verily, fortune seemed to be awaiting his arrival, for he was elected to represent Madison County in the Second General Assembly, which met at Vandalia, December 4, 1820.

In the year 1823 we find him Sheriff of Madison County, which office he held for so long (in 1838 he was still in office) that finding no other means open to them to get him out of the office, the Whigs pushed through a constitutional amendment prohibiting a tenure of more than one term.

In 1832 he married, in Edwardsville, Miss Harriet Bartling, from which marriage four children were born, Virginia, Henry, Catherine, and Ellen.

The Black Hawk War coming on in April of that year, he enlisted early, and was second in command of the army, with the title Brigade Major. His record as major of a spy battalion in the campaign of 1831 against the same Indian had much to do with his advanced rank in this second campaign, and in his various books the "Old Ranger Governor" was fond of referring to "Buck," as he called him, as one of the few men who stuck to his colours from the first day of the first campaign to the last day of the last campaign. At the mouth of Fox River when the first levy of troops was mustered out, it was he who performed the function with the aid of Lieutenant Robert Anderson, of Fort Sumter memory, and he was the first to reenlist.

As the departure of the troops for their homes left the frontiers entirely unprotected, he was made major of a battalion of spies, and, stationed at Fort Payne (now Naperville, Illinois), he cleared the country of every hostile Indian between Chicago and Ottawa.

In 1839-40 we find him Postmaster of Alton, and soon after he was made warden of the penitentiary there, then a position of high importance. He remained at Alton to the end of his life.

In the same year, 1840, his wife died at Alton, on the spot where stands the present depot of the C. & A. R. R. Co., and it is recorded of him as a remarkable incident for those days, that he never remarried.

In 1844, having for a long time interested himself in public transportation problems and ventures, he obtained the franchise for operating the "upper ferry," which he held during his lifetime, and after death it passed to his heirs.

On June 4, 1855, he died at his home, and was buried beside his wife in the Upper Alton cemetery. Major Buckmaster was essentially a business man. Transportation problems engaged most of his attention, either as the owner of ferries or builder of turnpikes and railroads, and for his enterprise, the State of Illinois is under lasting obligation.

We find him an incorporator of The Alton and Shawneetown Railroad Company, The Madison Railroad Company, and The Illinois and Pacific Railroad Company, in which Lyman Trumbull cooperated. He was president of The Alton Marine and Fire Insurance Company, as well as of the company which built the first plank road in Madison County.

As a builder he was famous, as many of the old-time Edwards County buildings, public and private, testify to this day. The old first brick jail and the hotel at Alton are of the number.

As sheriff of his county, he showed the goodness of his nature.

A part of his duty was to sell the lands of his county for delinquent taxes, which many persons who lost their money in the panic of 1837 were unable to pay. To them he opened his purse, saving their farms at an inconvenience almost calamitous to his own business interests. This explains, to a large degree, the inability of the Whigs to get him out of office.

In personal appearance he was an unusually handsome man, well dressed, with a fine physique and carriage, six feet tall, and to his last days active.

In politics he was a Jackson Democrat. In religion he was reared a Methodist, and during his business activities, he was never so busy as to be unable to pursue a close study of the bible.

Brigadier General Samuel Whiteside. The Whiteside family, a very numerous one, was among the first to settle permanently on Illinois soil. In the year 1793, William and John, brothers, and both soldiers in the Revolutionary War, settled in what is now Monroe County, on the road between Cahokia and Kaskaskia, about halfway between the present towns of Waterloo and Columbia. There William built a log fort, which became widely known as Whiteside's station.

In the year 1802 John, the father of Samuel Whiteside, moved to the Goshen settlement in Madison County and settled near Samuel Judy, whose wife was a sister to Samuel Whiteside. The latter, with his brother Joel, afterward settled in the north east part of the present township of Collinsville, and there Samuel made the first improvements on the Ridge prairie.

Samuel Whiteside was born in the State of North Carolina in the year 1783, and there remained with his rather until the latter came to Illinois ten years later.

According to his grandson, J. D. Henderson, Samuel Whiteside married Nancy Miller just before moving to Madison County, which must have been in his twentieth year if true. But early marriages were characteristic of the young pioneer of those days, who so much needed a helpmeet to begin work at his "clearing." In Madison County, Samuel Whiteside lived until the last of his children had married, and his wife died in March, 1854. At that time, with his daughter Mrs. Henderson and her husband, he moved to a farm in Christian County, near Mt. Auburn, and there lived until his death, in June, 1866. He is buried in what is known as the "Old Hunter Cemetery."

During the Indian troubles of 1810, Samuel Whiteside, in command of a company of rangers, was almost constantly in the saddle. During that period, it was a common occurrence when tidings of a murder were received, to rendezvous at the nearest fort, organise a company and start in hasty pursuit of the murderers. It was customary to elect a captain and subordinate officers, and when the offenders had been brought to justice or escaped to other states, to disband. Hence it is that we see the name of Samuel Whiteside so many times in the early annals as captain of a company. By common consent, he became the leader in every important Indian pursuit or fight.

Thus the War of 1812 with England coming closely upon the heels of the continued Indian disturbances, Samuel Whiteside was almost the first man to be appointed captain of a company of militia by Governor Edwards. In Campbell's notable battle just oft Campbell's Island, near the present city of Moline, the company of Captain Samuel Whiteside took conspicuous part. The battle, which was fought from keel boats by the militia against the overwhelming land forces of British and Indians, among which Black Hawk was a conspicuous figure, was a bloody one, and well worth study by the student of Illinois history.

When peaceful times were restored, Samuel Whiteside turned to peaceful pursuits, and though nominally a farmer, much of his time was occupied with surveying large areas, two instances being the boundaries of the states of Illinois and Missouri.

When, in 1831, it became necessary for Governor Reynolds to send troops to the mouth of Rock River to drive Black Hawk and his band across the Mississippi River, General Whiteside was appointed major of a spy battalion.

That campaign was so successful, that when it became necessary in the following year for Governor Reynolds to pursue the wily Sac again and with larger forces, attention was naturally attracted to Samuel Whiteside, and the governor appointed him Brigadier General and commander of all the state forces.

Though but five feet tall, it has been said of him that he contained more "fight" than a battalion of the average raw militia. He knew not fear or danger. At the village of Kapas, the Pottawattomie Indian, where the duty was put upon him to decide whether the troops should be mustered out or forced to continue the pursuit of Black Hawk up into Wisconsin, he mounted a whisky-barrel and declared that with one hundred men he would fight and whip Black Hawk; but with an army of cowards he would have nothing whatever to do, and he voted to send the levy of troops back home again. In his harangue, which has been only partially preserved, Colonel Zachary Taylor ably seconded him, from the head of the same whisky-barrel.

General Whiteside knew nothing of politics, and for that reason never secured office or aspired to it.

When at the mouth of Fox River, the troops had been mustered out

Fort Armstrong

by Major Buckmaster and Lieutenant Robert Anderson, it was considered necessary to protect the frontier with an emergency regiment. Such a regiment was recruited from the ranks of the few who were willing to remain, and General Whiteside enlisted as a private in the company of Captain Adam W. Snyder. In Snyder's battle at Kellogg's Grove, a bullet from General Whiteside's rifle killed the leader of the Indians and terminated the fight decisively in favour of the whites. He was a dead shot. It may be added that Abraham Lincoln, who had been a captain in the first campaign, re-enlisted as a private in the company of Elijah Iles in the same emergency regiment.

Whiteside County, Illinois, was named in honour of Gen. Samuel Whiteside.

Chapter 2

The Sac and Fox Indians Cross Over the Mississippi to the State of Illinois, in a Warlike Manner

Extract of a letter from General Hughes, sub Indian Agent, to General Atkinson, dated,

Rock Island, April 13th, 1832.
My opinion is, that the squaws and old men have gone to the Prophet's town, on Rock River and the warriors are now only a few miles below the mouth of Rock River, within the limits of the State of Illinois. That those Indians are hostile to the whites there is no doubt. That they have invaded the State of Illinois, to the great injury of her citizens, is equally true. Hence it is, that the public good requires that strong as well as speedy measures should be taken against Black Hawk and his followers.
Respectfully I have, the honour to be,
Your obedient servant.
(Signed.) Andrew S. Hughes.
To Brig. General Atkinson.

Extract of a letter from George Davenport, Esq. to Brigadier General Atkinson, dated,

Rock Island, April 13th, 1832.
Dear Sir: In reply to your enquiries of this morning, respecting the Indians, I have to state, that I have been informed by the man I have wintering with the Indians, that the British band of Sac Indians are determined to make war upon the frontier settlements. The British band of Sac Indians did rendezvous at

old fort Madison, and induced a great many of the young men to join them on their arrival at the Yellow Banks. They crossed about five hundred head of horses into the State of Illinois, and sent about seventy horses through the country toward Rock River. The remainder, some on horseback, the others in canoes, in a fighting order, advanced up the Mississippi, and were encamped yesterday five or six miles below Rock River, and will no doubt endeavour to reach their strong hold in the Rock River swamps, if they are not intercepted. From every information that I have received, I am of opinion, that the intention of the British band of Sac Indians, is to commit depredations on the inhabitants of the frontier.

    Respectfully your obedient servant.
 (Signed.)   Geo. Davenport.
To Brig. General Atkinson.

Extract of a letter from General Atkinson to his Excellency, Governor Reynolds, dated,

        Fort Armstrong, April 13th, 1832.
Dear Sir: The band of Sacs under Black Hawk, joined by about one hundred Kickapoos, and a few Pottawatamies, amounting in all to about five hundred men, have assumed a hostile attitude. They crossed the river at the Yellow Banks, on the sixth instant, and are now moving up on the east side of Rock River towards the Prophet's village.

      ****

The regular force under my command, is too small to justify me in pursuing the hostile party. To make an unsuccessful attempt to coerce them, would only irritate them to acts of hostility on the frontier, sooner than they probably contemplate. Your own knowledge of the character of these Indians, with the information herewith submitted, will enable you to judge of the course proper to be pursued. I think the frontier is in great danger, and will use all the means at my disposal to co-operate with you, in its protection and defence.

With great respect,
    Your most obedient servant.
           H. Atkinson, Brigadier
           General of the U. S. Army.
His Excellency, Governor Reynolds, Belleville, Ill.

I will next give the reader Governor Reynolds's proclamation to the militia of Illinois, and his concluding remarks; and of the necessity of those that were able to bear arms, turning out in defence of their country's rights.

>To the Militia of the North-western section of Illinois:
>Fellow Citizens: Your country requires your services. The Indians have assumed a hostile attitude, and have invaded the State, in violation of the treaty of last summer.
>The British band of Sacs, and other hostile Indians, headed by the Black Hawk, are in possession of the Rock River country, to the great terror of the frontier inhabitants.
>I consider the settlers on the frontiers in imminent danger. I am in possession of the above information from gentlemen of respectable standing, and from General Atkinson, whose character stands so high in all classes.
>In possession of the foregoing facts and information, I hesitate not as to the course I should pursue. No citizen ought to remain quiet when his country is invaded, and the helpless part of the community is in danger. I have called out a strong detachment of militia, to rendezvous at Beardstown, on the 22nd instant; provision for the men, and corn for the horses will be furnished in abundance. I hope my countrymen will realize my expectations, and offer their services, as heretofore, with promptitude and cheerfulness, in defence of their country.
>
>>John Reynolds,
>>Commander in Chief.

I will next refer the reader to a visit made to the hostile Indians by Henry Gratiot, Esq.

On the 16th day of April, Mr. Gratiot, Indian Agent for the Rock River band of Winnebagoes, received a letter from General Atkinson, informing him of the movements of Black Hawk's band of hostile Indians, and requesting him, if possible, to ascertain the disposition of them. On the receipt of this information, Mr. Gratiot proceeded down Rock River, and on the 19th arrived at the Turtle Village, (now Beloit, Wisconsin), of Winnebagoes found them at the exercise of their religious ceremonies, and consequently could not have a hearing with them until the 22nd. He then held a talk with them, and learned from them that the Sacs had, at three different times, sent them the *wampum*, and that the last was painted red, thereby indicating war. (Black

COLONEL HENRY GRATIOT

Hawk in his autobiography was insistent that he was going to the Winnebago country by invitation, and for the sole purpose of "making corn.") The last *wampum* was not returned. They also informed Mr. Gratiot, that it was their determination not to join the hostile Sacs that there were some Winnebagoes living at the Prophet's village who were friendly to the whites—and that they requested them to leave it and come to their village to reside until all the difficulties were settled.

In order to accomplish this object, Mr. Gratiot took twenty four men of the Turtle Village to accompany him to the Prophet's Town, at which place they arrived on the 25th, and hoisted his flag of truce. He was received with much attention by the Winnebagoes, who made him a large lodge, eighty feet long, for himself and their visiting brethren. In this village he found between two and three hundred men, women and children, belonging to the Prophet's band. These Indians manifested no hostile disposition, but severally remonstrated against the conduct of the Prophet, who was at that time with the hostile band of Sacs, a few miles below, leading them on to his village. Mr. Gratiot advised these Indians to go up Rock River on their own lands, and make a village, where they might rest in peace. This they promised to do.

On the 26th, Mr. Gratiot saw at a distance, about two miles down Rock River, the army of the celebrated Black Hawk, consisting of about five hundred Sacs, well armed, and mounted on fine horses, moving in a line of battle.—Their appearance was terrible in the extreme. (The author states numbers accurately, but magnifies their ferocity.) Their bodies were painted with white clay, with an occasional impression of their hands about their bodies, coloured black. Around their ankles and bodies they wore wreaths of straw, which always indicate a disposition for blood. They moved on with great regularity, performing many evolutions; wheeling every few minutes, and firing towards Fort Armstrong; turning, flanking, and then forming into solid columns, from which they would form their line of march. In that way they marched to the beating of a drum till they came to the village.

They marched up to Gratiot's lodge, where was flying the neutral flag; formed a circle around it; took down his flag, and tauntingly hoisted the British colours in its place. They then fired into the air toward his lodge, sounded the war-whoop around it, and made several motions toward attacking Mr. Gratiot and the friendly Winnebagoes. They afterward dismounted, entered his lodge, shook hands with Mr.

Gratiot and Mr. Cubbage, a gentleman who accompanied him. They then formed a circle within his lodge, holding their spears and other implements of war, and evincing, by their actions and countenances, an unfriendly feeling. After holding a consultation among themselves, a friendly Winnebago chief, ("White Crow,") who went with Mr. Gratiot from the Turtle Village, arose, went to his blanket, took out two plugs of tobacco, and gave them to the war-chief of the hostile band; after which the war party left the lodge leaving only Black Hawk.

This chief (Black Hawk) then told Mr. Gratiot that he had received a letter from General Atkinson, but refused to let him read it at the time, but said that he would show it to him when he got to the end of his march, which was about sixty miles above.

******

Black Hawk was not a chief. He was simply a brave and leader of the band known as "the British Band"; so called by reason of its adhesion to British interests. It may be said that its hatred of everything American was more to the point than love of British interest, because so late as July 12, 1821, Captain T. G. Anderson, British Indian Agent, rebuked Black Hawk severely for his fault-finding.

******

Mr. Gratiot replied, that he was not going that way; but he was answered by Black Hawk, that he would let him know about it on the next day. So it appeared that Mr. Gratiot was then considered their prisoner of war, (it was Black Hawk's boast that he never violated a neutral or flag of truce, this is one instance of violation); which the development of other facts that after wards occurred, conclusively proved. Black Hawk shortly afterwards left Mr. Gratiot, under a promise to visit him again the next morning.

The hostile band were all night engaged in holding a council among themselves. On the following morning, the Prophet, at the head of about forty warriors, came into Mr. Gratiot's lodge, presented General Atkinson's letter, and told him, he might take the letter back to General Atkinson. Mr. Gratiot insisted on reading the letter to them; upon which request, Black Hawk and Na-a-pope were sent for, and the letter read. (This name is generally spelled Ne-a-pope, and is pronounced Naw-pope). The substance of which was, to advise the hostile chiefs to desist from their evil designs—recross the Mississippi River, settle down in peace, and plant their corn etc. In reply to

BRIGADIER-GENERAL SAMUEL WHITESIDE.

which, they requested Mr. Gratiot to hand back the letter, and inform General Atkinson, that their hearts were bad, (another admission that the mission of the band was not of peace), and that they would not return; but to the contrary, that if he brought his troops among them they would fight them. Mr. Gratiot immediately went to Rock Island and delivered the message.

Thus, reader, these documents go to show the great necessity that Governor Reynolds had, for making the call for mounted volunteers, to defend the rights of our country, and drive from our State those merciless savages, that wished to imbrue their hands in the blood of its citizens.

Agreeably to his proclamation, the citizens of Illinois, quit their peaceful firesides and homes, and volunteered to defend our dear and sacred rights, which had been purchased for us by our ancestors, at the price of much blood. There was a sufficient number turned out without drafting; the people at once saw the great danger our frontier was in; and their patriotic feelings would not suffer them to stay at home, when they knew their services were wanted in the field. Accordingly, at the appointed time, the mounted volunteers from the different counties, that were called upon, rendezvoused at Beardstown, on the Illinois River, where we were met by Governor Reynolds.

Upon our being organised into a brigade, Governor Reynolds appointed Brigadier General Samuel Whiteside commander of the brigade, who, for his courage and bravery, as an officer in the last war with Great Britain, stood pre-eminent.—He at that time had the command of a company of rangers, and was by all acknowledged to be an excellent Indian fighter.

The brigade consisted of about sixteen hundred horsemen and two hundred footmen, who were organised into four regiments, and an odd spy battalion.

Colonel Dewitt, commanded the first regiment, (Abraham B. De-Witt, of Morgan County., but DeWitt commanded the Third Regiment); Colonel Fry, (Jacob Fry), the second; Colonel Thomas, the third, (John Thomas of St. Clair County, but Thomas commanded the First Regiment); and Colonel Thompson, the fourth. Colonel James D. Henry, of Sangamon County, commanded the spy battalion.

On the twenty-seventh day of April, the troops got in motion, and took up the line of march, under the command of General Whiteside, accompanied by Governor Reynolds, the commander-in-chief. After crossing the Illinois River, we directed our course to the Yellow Banks,

(Oquawka, Illinois), on the Mississippi River, at which place, we arrived on the third day of May. Nothing very interesting occurred on our march to the Yellow Banks.

In crossing Henderson's River, we lost several head of horses, the river being very high, and not having any ferry boat to cross in; but very fortunately the men all got over safe. We had to take the point of the Yellow Banks, in order to draw provision, as a steamboat with supplies was to meet us there. It is worthy of remark, that when we got to this place, we found the citizens quietly remaining at their homes, and not in the least alarmed.

The next day after we arrived at this place, the old principal chief (Ke-o-kuck,) crossed the river, with fifty or sixty of his warriors, and a few squaws, to our encampment, held a war dance, and stated, that it was not their intention to raise arms against the United States, at the same time signifying a willingness to assist in fighting the Black Hawk.

On the third day after our arrival at the Yellow Banks, the steam boat arrived with a sufficient supply of provision, which enabled us to take the line of march for Rock River, at which place we arrived on the following day (the seventh.) On the May 8th we were mustered into the service of the United States by Brigadier General Atkinson.

******

For many years it was contended that the volunteers, a company of which was commanded by Captain Abraham Lincoln, were sworn into the United States service at Dixon's Ferry, now Dixon, Illinois, by Lieutenant Jefferson Davis, then a Lieutenant in the regular establishment serving under Lieutenant Colonel Zachary Taylor. But Wakefield is right as to the place. The editor owns a letter written by Major Nathaniel Buckmaster on May 9, 1832, at the mouth of Rock River, wherein it is specifically stated that General Atkinson swore the troops into the service at that point

******

On the evening after having been received by General Atkinson, Colonel John Ewing and myself were sent by Governor Reynolds as secret spies, with directions to keep in front of the army; he also sent a gentleman by the name of Kinney with us as a pilot. Our instructions were, to proceed as near the direction as we could, according to our judgment, form, of the course Black Hawk and his army had taken; and if possible, for us to ascertain where the encampment of the enemy was. According to our instructions, we proceeded up Rock River, as near the direction that Black Hawk had taken, as our pilot judged to be the course. On the second day after we started, we discovered several signs of Indians, who appeared to be going different directions, which led us to suppose, that they were sent by Black Hawk to ascertain whether or not we were following them.

On that night, we encamped in sight of the old Prophet's village, (the whites burned the village on their march up Rock River); next morning we went through the town, and saw where Black Hawk had encamped with his whole army. His encampment was laid off in a manner showing great skill in warfare. No American general could have laid it out in a more military style; from the appearance of the encampment, we were induced to believe that they remained there a week; from which place we proceeded, confining ourselves to Rock River, which we were going up. We had not proceeded more than five miles from this place, before we discovered two Indians coming in the direction to meet us.

Colonel Ewing and myself made up to them in great haste; on our meeting them, we demanded of them to know their business there; on their not being able to understand us, we directed Mr. Kinney to enquire of them what they were doing there? Their answer was, that they had lost their horses, and were hunting them; that they belonged to Ke-o-kuck's band. We directed the interpreter to ask them, if they knew where Black Hawk was? They signified that they did not know, and appeared to be much alarmed.

I observed in the course of the conversation, that we ought to take them as prisoners—to which Colonel Ewing made no reply, but appeared to be reflecting on the course to take, until they started and had got a short distance from us; he then came to the conclusion to take them; we immediately gave chase, they had four horses that appeared to be fresh and good, on account of which they gained distance on us, shaping their course for the river. During the chase, we discovered another Indian on our left, after consulting for a moment, we concluded to endeavour to take him prisoner; accordingly we all pursued him, until we came up with him; he told us he was a Pottawattomie; he had two horses; we directed Mr. Kinney to take his gun; he appeared unwilling to surrender it, and showed a disposition to shoot him.

Upon which Colonel Ewing drew his rifle to his face, to make ready to fire on him, if he did not give it up: upon which he gave it to Mr. Kinney. We directed Mr. Kinney to mount his horse, and take the rope that was around the neck of the Indian's horse, and lead him;

the Indian made signs to us, that there were some of his people close by, and wished to see them, and then he would go with us; to which proposition, we had no desire to accede, but forced him on. We travelled at a rapid rate.

As we were in the midst of Indians, we concluded that it was our better policy, to make our way back to the camp as quick as possible. We at this time had been three days from the army, and could not know what distance we had separated ourselves from it. We calculated that we would not be able to reach it until the following day; but we were very agreeably disappointed, as we met the army after going about ten miles; it had taken the line of march the next day after we left it, and marched a much higher way than our pilot took us. We delivered up our prisoner, who underwent an examination through an interpreter better acquainted with the Indian language than Mr. Kinney; he was found to be a Pottawattomie,—and stated that Black Hawk with his army was at the Pawpaw Grove, two days' march up the river.

******

Paw Paw Grove was in the southwest township of DeKalb County and the southeast township of Lee County as now defined, named respectively Paw Paw and Wyoming townships, and not up on the river as indicated. Near Paw Paw Grove was Sha-bo-na's village; in the grove of that name, now within the township of Shabbona in DeKalb County. The fact that Black Hawk was recruiting from the Pottawattomies at Paw Paw Grove, and that Sha-bo-na had consented to a parley at the mouth of Old Man's Creek in Ogle County, brought about this confusion in Wakefield's mind.

******

We were now close to the old Prophet's town, where General Atkinson had ordered General Whiteside to await the arrival of his boats and regulars, (as that was the way General Atkinson, with his regulars, and two hundred foot volunteers were marching;) unless General Whiteside, thought upon his arrival at the Prophet's Village, (within the present boundaries of Whiteside County., it would be actually necessary to pursue, in order to prevent the Indians from making their escape; accordingly General Whiteside ordered a forced march that evening. The country we had to pass through was an almost continual swamp,—no alternative being left for us, we put our horses to it, sometimes wading ourselves up to our waist, and not infrequently getting mired; but by great exertions and perseverance, we succeeded in getting through without losing any men in the swamps.—We this day marched until dark—a number of the men did not get up until late in the night, and some of the baggage waggons not until next morning. This day (May 12th) we got to Dixon's Ferry, (Dixon, Illinois), on Rock River, where the great road crosses going to the Lead Mines. (Kellogg' s Trail, running from Peoria to Galena and Gratiot's Grove, made by O.W. Kellogg in 1827.)

Chapter 3

March to Fox River

On our arrival here (Dixon's Ferry) we found Major Stillman with a battalion of two hundred and seventy-five men awaiting our arrival: they had been there two days with a sufficient supply of ammunition and provisions; our provisions at this time being nearly exhausted.

Major Stillman considered that he had a kind of independent corps, and did not wish to be attached to General Whiteside's brigade. He, the major, on the next morning made a request of the governor, that he might be permitted to take his corps, go out as a scouting party, and see if possible whether any discoveries could be made as to the situation of the enemy.

Accordingly, on the 12th day of May, Major Stillman and Major Bailey, (Isaiah Stillman and David Bailey), received orders from the commander in chief, to march with their respective battalions to the neighbourhood of Old Man's Creek. (Now Stillman's Run in Ogle County.) So called from the "run" subsequently made by the cowardly volunteers to ascertain, if possible, the movements of the enemy. On the morning of the 13th, Major Stillman's battalion took up their line of march. Major Bailey followed in a short time after; and after having marched eight or ten miles, both battalions encamped. The day had been rainy, and other circumstances beyond the control of officers or men, had a tendency to retard their movements.

The battalions had no connection with each other whatever, previous to their meeting on their march to Dixon's, on Rock River. There they received orders to march, before they were organised into a regiment—each battalion being independent of the other—commanded by its own officers—and three of those claiming the command of both and perhaps with equal justice.

In the result, however, the command for that expedition was conferred on Major Stillman, the choice of officers to be referred to the men on their return.

On the morning of the 14th, under the temporary organisation of the corps, the march was continued in the line, secured by strong advance and flank guards. On this day's march several fresh trails were discovered during the forenoon; and at 12 o'clock the commanding officer, was informed, that several Indian dogs had been seen by one of the flank guards, and shortly afterwards two Indians were seen.

With some difficulty occasioned by the almost impassable mires of the creeks which the corps had to cross, the march was continued until nearly sunset, when Colonel Strode, (Colonel James M. Strode of Galena, Illinois), of the advanced guard, who had volunteered his services on this occasion, returned to the battalion with information of a suitable place for encampment, and conducted the corps to the point.

A large fresh trail was discovered, which directed its course to a point of timber, a short distance to the left of the encampment. Shortly after the battalion halted, and while busily engaged in preparing supper, several horsemen were discovered on a hill about half a mile in front. They were at first sight taken for a part of the enemy's advance guard. Some of the men mounted their horses, and rode toward them. They were discovered to be Indians, and two of them came to the camp, professing to be Pottawattomies and friends, but on the approach of our advance the Indians gave a whoop, unfurled a red flag and fell back at full speed.—Our horsemen followed, and after a chase of four miles and a half, overtook them in a low marshy piece of ground, where a sharp firing took place. Three Indians were left dead, and several were dismounted; one of our men was wounded in a personal combat, and two were dismounted and lost their horses.

The Indians were driven into their encampment, where they rallied to the number of six or eight hundred, and cautiously awaited the approach of our main body. Our advance fell back, and joined the battalion on the margin of the low ground, where the firing first commenced.

An Indian approached and proposed a "talk" to an officer who was in advance. Major Stillman, with the field and staff officers together with Captain Eads, (Captain Abner Eads, then of Peoria, later of Galena), as an interpreter, went forward while the troops were advancing by heads of companies through the marsh. Captain Eads, who had been in front, suddenly wheeled and exclaimed that the line of Indians extended for more than a mile.

Major Stillman now discovered that the proposed "talk" was an expedient to obtain time, the more completely to execute their plan; for the enemy were now seen flanking him right and left in great numbers. He immediately gave orders to countermarch and form on the high ground. But instead of countermarching, the men wheeled about in their places, which threw the officers all in the rear, and fell back. The foremost of them on reaching the hard ground first, were able to proceed with much greater rapidity than those who were yet in the swamp, and by the time the officers reached the solid ground the front was out of hearing. The order to halt and form was only heard by a part of each company, who immediately formed. But the enemy knew all the passes, and had already opened a heavy fire on both flanks, which was returned with spirit by those who had formed.

It was now found necessary to retire to prevent the enemy from entirely surrounding our men, which had now become practicable. The retreat was then kept up with occasional halting and firing, until our men reached the camp. There an attempt was made to maintain our ground. Captain Barnes, (Captain David W. Barnes of Fulton County), had nearly succeeded in forming his company, when orders were given to cross the creek in rear of the camp. This order was effected by sixty or seventy men, but not before the enemy had got possession of the camp. The enemy then set up a tremendous yell, which was returned by a volley of musquetry from those who had formed in the rear of the camp,—this silenced the war-whoop in that quarter, but in a moment more two large parties of the enemy, who had crossed the creek above and below, attacked both flanks and the rear. The line was broken, and each man took his own course. One party broke off to the right where fell some of those who had formed at the creek. Another party took off to the left, where others fell, the flanking parties of the enemy pursuing them. Those of the men who took the middle course, escaped with the loss of two killed, and one wounded.

The enemy kept up the pursuit for twelve or fourteen miles. The men arrived at Dixon's Ferry in detached squads, from one o'clock a. m. until the roll call at sunrise, when it was found that fifty-two were missing: these continued to arrive for the two succeeding days, until the number missing was reduced to eleven, which were afterward found most shockingly mangled.

Captain Adams evinced the most undaunted bravery; he vehemently urged the men to maintain the ground. But the line was broken and he himself was slain.

Several personal rencounters took place. In one of them Joseph Farris and his brother David, were attacked and surrounded. David was mounted, and Joseph whose horse failed or was killed, urged him to save himself; but this he refused, until he saw him fall, fighting, and himself struck from his horse by a blow from the breech of a gun. He returned the blow which stiffened the savage on the ground, and then broke for a point of timber; he was nearly overtaken, when he called for assistance from the timber, which led the pursuers to fear that a force was then awaiting their approach. It was this presence of mind which saved his life; for the enemy immediately wheeled and retreated.

Mr. Samuel Hackelton had pursued an uniformed Indian, until he had outstripped his comrades, and had discharged his gun with effect, upon one who was dismounted immediately before him. When in the act of reloading, he saw a horseman pass, by the name of Maxfield, who discharged his piece, tumbled an Indian from his pony, and kept on without reloading. He entered the marsh where it was with difficulty that his horse could proceed—an Indian charged upon him. Hackelton seeing this, flew to his relief, and by a blow from his gun parried the spear, just as it was on the point of entering his (Maxfield's) back. The red warrior wheeled to plunge the spear into the breast of Hackelton, which he avoided by springing from his horse, who passed from between him and his antagonist, when he again met the spear by darting at his enemy, which caused it to pass between his left arm and side, wounding his hand as he attempted to parry the blow.

He then seized the spear, both held, eyeing each other for a moment, when the Indian being in the act of seizing his tomahawk, Hackelton grasped him by the throat and belt (the blanket being thrown from the Indian's shoulder) and now a deadly struggle ensued. The Indian was large and muscular, but after a severe struggle, fell before his more active foe, and broke his hold to regain his feet. Hackelton improved the movement to draw his steel, which he plunged into the breast of the savage,—and again they fell locked in deadly embrace. Maxfield, whose horse had taken fright at the yell of the Indian, ran for a considerable distance, nearly throwing his rider, readily returned to repay that service which had so generously and timely been rendered him, and with his bayonet pinned the bleeding savage to the ground.

Hackelton having lost his horse, it was with much difficulty that he halted a horseman to take him from the ground; indeed he rode with him but a few rods, whilst in leaping a pool or branch, the horse fell, and Hackelton, who was wounded in both hands, was thrown into the water;—and there the horseman left him to shift for himself. He effected his escape by running two or three miles, when he was relieved by Doctor Donaldson, who generously lent him his horse, whilst he went on foot, for the distance of two miles further, where Hackelton succeeded in getting a pony, on which he arrived in camp without further injury.

Major Stillman was unfortunate in this action; he lost some of his most choice men. Captain Adams, who commanded a company from Tazewell county; Major Isaac Perkins, ("Major" was a nickname only. Isaac Perkins was a private in the company of Captain John G. Adams); John Walters; Cyrus Childs, (Tyrus M. Childs was his name; not Cyrus. He was a private in Captain Barnes's company); Joseph Farris; Bird Ellis and James Doty, were among the slain in this battle. There were four others, but I have not got in possession of their names. They were all respectable men.

When this squadron of men got into camp, or part of them, for they came in by twos, threes and fours, and so on, all night, each company thought the rest were all killed, and reported it as being the case.

We were all immediately to our arms, not knowing but that Black Hawk and all his band were in close pursuit.

Things were represented in their worst colours. Some of the men seemed to think that there were at least two thousand Indians. Others thought there were not more than one thousand, and none would fall below five hundred; but scarcely any two of them could agree upon any one statement.

******

The author, who was not present at the fight, has adopted to a considerable extent the version given in a St. Louis paper by Stillman soon after it occurred. The encampment was just north of the present village of Stillman Valley, in Ogle County, while the thick of the fight was on the slope and at the top of the hill about half a mile to the south, upon whose summit the dead were buried. It was upon this eminence, now in the midst of the village, that Captain John G. Adams made his heroic stand, and there the State of Illinois has recently erected a handsome monument costing $5,000. The strength of the Indians was in reality much under 100 men, which when known made the retreat of the whites appear much more cowardly.

★★★★★★

It was a complete rout, and of course each one had to shift for himself; and it was natural for them to have different views when they were in such frightful condition. Next morning, at roll call, there were fifty-two men missing. It was then thought there was no doubt but they had all been slain in the action; but to the great joy of the friends of the missing, they all got in, in the course of three days, to some settlement or other, except the eleven already mentioned. It appears that they were so much alarmed, that they took different directions, and some went a contrary direction from the army. A number of them, it is said, came very near starving with hunger before they got to any settlement.

General Whiteside, when the news of the defeat reached camp, made preparations to march with the main army as soon as it was light; accordingly there were two men sent from each company to bring in our horses. The governor immediately went to making out despatches for more troops, so soon as it was light. General Whiteside had a few beeves killed to take along, with some other meat; but bread was out of the question, as we had then been without this necessary article for two days.

★★★★★★

When Reynolds and Whiteside, just above the Prophet's town, deter mined to make a forced march to Dixon's Ferry, the wagons and provisions were stacked together and left behind, after a limited supply of rations was issued to the troops. Small as the issue may have been, the famine which appeared later would have been avoided had it been providently conserved; but with profound contempt for everything orderly or systematic, the provisions were wantonly wasted, and but for the sacrifice by John Dixon of his milch cows, Reynolds never could have held the men together until Atkinson arrived.

★★★★★★

About seven o'clock on the 15th of May, General Whiteside took up the line of march at the head of about fourteen hundred effective men to the late battleground.

Here I have to leave the main army for a while. Colonel John Ewing, Robert Blackwell, Esq., and my self, were sent as express bearers for more troops, and the Rev. Mr. Horn, (Rev. Reddick Horn of Cass County), who was chaplain to the army, to St. Louis for a supply of provisions. Colonel Ewing was sent to the counties bordering on the

Ohio River; Esq. Blackwell to the counties on the Wabash, on the east side of the State; and the writer to the southern counties bordering on the Kaskaskia River.

The governor made a call for two thousand more troops, besides those already in the field. His order was for them to rendezvous at Beardstown and Hennepin, both on the Illinois River—those at Beardstown to meet on the 3rd of June, and those at Hennepin on the 10th. The volunteers from the counties I went to, were to meet at Beardstown; and those from the counties to which Messrs. Ewing and Blackwell went, at Hennepin. We started on the 15th of May, and rode with all the celerity we possibly could. When our horses gave out we pressed others. I arrived at Kaskaskia on the 22nd, a distance of about three hundred and forty miles, in seven days. We well knew the danger our frontier settlements were in.

Many of our fellow citizens had been slain in battle, who were in the field for the defence of our country; and our unsuspecting frontier was then exposed to the ruthless tomahawk and scalping knife of those demons in human shape. We knew their mode of warfare was to steal upon the fearful settler, in the shades and stillness of night, and there imbrue their hands in human blood, paying no attention to age or sex. So no obstacle stopped us on our way.

I must here relate a small anecdote, which occurred between a good old woman and myself. On the night of the 31st of May I staid at Covington. I think I never heard such a night's rain in all my life. The next morning, Esq. Bradsby, the gentleman with whom I staid all night, informed me that I would have several creeks to swim on the way from thence to Kaskaskia, and it still continued raining. I replied that I would try it at all events. I had not travelled more than four miles before I found his words verified; but to my great satisfaction, I found that the horse I rode was an excellent swimmer—so I stopped for none of the creeks. The weather being very cold for the time of year, I called at a house to empty the water out of my shoes, and to wring my socks.

An elderly looking lady, seeing me wet all over, and hearing me say I had swam all the creeks between that place and Covington, and that I had come from there that morning, looked on me (as I thought,) with an eye of suspicion, and immediately began to make some inquiries about my embassy, that I should not have relished quite so well had they come from any other source, than a good old simple woman. I soon found that she was not to be put off, but must have the whole history of my business,—and what it was that made me swim the creeks. So that while I was trying to get some of the water out of my socks, I informed her that I was the bearer of an express for more men to go against the Indians; this roused the good old dame's curiosity to the highest pitch. I then gave her the particulars in as brief a manner as I could. When I was done, she asked, if I did not get a great bounty for my services?

"Yes," I replied, "I do."—She then wanted to know how much? I replied "the honour of serving my country."

Says she "my friend, I think you are in poor business, and if that is all you get I think you had best go back home."

But I did not take the old lady's advice. I got to Kaskaskia that night. The people had got the news by way of steamboat that was at St. Louis when the Rev. Mr. Horn arrived there after provision.

Colonel Stephens, commandant in Randolph County, despatched Mr. Briggs (who afterwards became Captain Briggs) at 9 o'clock in the evening, with orders for the men to meet on the 24th, and volunteer to the number of one hundred from this county, and that it they were not enough that would volunteer, he would be obliged to cause a draft to be made. But it was here as it was in every other part of the State, there were plenty of men who saw that their country needed their services; and they very willingly forsook their homes, wives and children, and turned out to defend the rights of their brethren and fellow citizens that were threatened to be trampled on by the merciless savages.

I here must return to General Whiteside and the volunteers, that marched on the morning of the 15th to the battle ground to bury the dead that had been slain in battle; they got there that evening, found the bodies of eleven of our citizens scalped and mangled in the most barbarous manner—the heads of some were cut off, and others with their hearts cut out, legs and arms generally cut off. General Whiteside had their remains consigned to their mother earth in as decent a manner as could be expected in a wilderness country. The next day General Whiteside had to return with the army back to Dixon's on Rock River, on account of his scarcity of provisions, where General Atkinson met them with a supply.

On Saturday the 19th, the army, amounting to about twenty-four hundred men, regulars and militia, started up Rock River, in pursuit of the Indians. But owing to a variety of causes, which I am not able to lay before the public, the army became dissatisfied, and wished to be discharged from the service,—so nothing was effected on this campaign.

******

The army reached a Pottawattomie village on Sycamore Creek, now the left fork of the Kishwaukee River, the site of which subsequently became known as Coltonville, in DeKalb County. It was once the county seat, but was abandoned and is now part of a farm about a mile and a half southwest of Sycamore. There a crisis arose. The troops were still murmuring as they had been doing almost from the day they were sworn into service, and demanded their discharge, though but half of their time of enlistment had expired.

To the north lay the path to Black Hawk, to the south their homes. Colonel Zachary Taylor vigorously demanded that they continue northward, while Governor Reynolds pleaded, but to no purpose. A vote on the question by the captains, as to whether or net the army should disband, resulted in a tie, which was decided affirmatively by Whiteside, who declared he would no longer lead cowards. There upon he ordered the march resumed to the mouth of Fox River, where the men were mustered out of service. Along the line of march, the troops lawlessly robbed Indian villages, including Sha-bo-na's, and otherwise disgraced themselves.

******

The general cry with the men was, that they wished to return home. This was too at a time when their services were most needed, for the war now had begun in all its horrid shape.

Immediately after Stillman's defeat, the Indians commenced their well known practice of warfare. They went about the 20th of May to the houses of Messrs. Hall, Daviess and Pennigrew, (Davis and Pettigrew), and there killed fifteen men, women and children, and scalped them all. But even this was not enough to satisfy those bloodthirsty demons; they mutilated them in the most inhuman and indecent manner that ever was witnessed. It is enough to make the blood chill in a person's veins, to think how those merciless hell hounds served those that were not in the slightest degree able to help them selves. After every indecency that could be practised on their persons, the women were hung up by their feet. The helpless children literally chopped to pieces. The houses were burned, the furniture all destroyed, the stock killed, even the barnyard fowls.—The work of destruction and devastation had now begun, the blood of helpless women and children had been spilt.

Two young and beautiful women were taken prisoners by these monsters in human shape—for it appeared that all the bodies of the missing were found, except these two young women, who were the daughters of the unfortunate family of Hall, who, with his wife and children, had become an easy prey to these barbarians, save two boys who were in the field at work.

Mr. Hall and Mr. Daviess both had large families. Mr. Pennigrew, his companion, and children, shared the same fate.

This threw the country into the most perfect state of alarm and dismay. This horrid act was done on Indian Creek, which empties into Fox River. The families lived about fifteen miles north of Ottawa.

General Whiteside and his brigade witnessed this horrid sight soon after it was perpetrated, and helped to consign them to their mother earth, which is the last duty that we can pay to human beings in this world. (This is a mistake. A detachment from Fort Dearborn marched to Fort Beggs, Plainfield, Will County, thence to Indian Creek, and there buried the victims.) Still, his brigade cried out, "Our term of service is nearly expired, and we wish to be discharged."

Accordingly, Governor Reynolds, on the 27th and 28th, discharged all the volunteers that were then in the field, at Ottawa, within fifteen miles of the place where the Indians had just slain fifteen of our citizens, and treated them in the manner already described. This was enough to rend the hearts of the neighbourhood in this part of the frontier; but the hearts of a few could not think of leaving so many valuable citizens to perish by the scalping knife and tomahawk. They turned out a second time to guard the frontier, until the new levy of troops could arrive to their protection. I am sorry that I could not with propriety give you the names of all those who volunteered a second time; but it is due to those who did so, to say it was the love of country alone that influenced them to do so.

General Samuel Whiteside was one who saw that his country still needed his services. He here was not above shouldering his rifle, and stepping into the ranks to defend this beautiful country, where there had just perished some of its choice citizens by those merciless savages. The brave and patriotic Henry, Fry, Snyder, James of Bond County, and many others whom I cannot mention, were influenced by the same feeling. They at once saw that the devastating hand of the savage had begun the works of death and destruction in this region of the country, and well knew that if those frontiers were not guarded, its helpless citizens would become an easy prey to those demons that

CAPTAIN ADAM W. SNYDER

know no bounds to their cruelty. The smoke of the cabins of those that were slain, was scarcely out of sight, and to leave those that were still living to share the same fate, was more than they could think of doing.

Accordingly, this little band of patriots was formed into a regiment, under the command of our noble Fry, who never has disgraced his country, nor himself as a commander. Our much beloved James D. Henry was elected Lieutenant Colonel, and Mr. John Thomas, Major. There were six companies composing this regiment. The following named gentlemen were the officers and staff. The captains I will set down agreeably to their rank.

A, W. Snyder; McFadden; Smith; Benjamin James; Elijah Iles; and James Rolls, were the six captains of this regiment. (William C. Ralls from Schuyler County. Abraham Lincoln re-enlisted as a private in the company of Captain Elijah Iles. Before this re-enlistment he was captain of a company in the Fourth, Col. Thompson's Regiment.) The lieutenants were as follows: James (Jesse) M. Harrison, 1st, and Henry Roberts, 2nd Lieutenant in Captain Iles's company; Calvert Roberts, 1st Lieutenant in Captain James's company; James Scott, G. F. (Radford M.) Wyatt, W. Shirley, Jacob Waggoner, Oliver Bangs, and (W. F.) Walker. I cannot place the last lieutenants to their proper places.

Chapter 4

Attack on Apple River Fort

This band of patriots continued here and guarded the country, until the new levy of troops could arrive and be organised. And many of them still continued until the end of the last campaign.

It will be recollected that I stated in a preceding page that A. W. Snyder was elected captain of one of the six companies, who volunteered a second time to defend the northern frontier. Captain Snyder was constantly on the march with his men, between Galena, and Fox and Rock Rivers, guarding the frontiers from being taken by surprise by the Indians, as it was well known that they were prowling about through the country, as they had done considerable mischief upon the northern frontier, and particularly in the mining country, and on the road leading from Fort Clark to Galena.

Captain Snyder thought that it would be best to range between Galena and Rock and Fox Rivers; as those settlements were so exposed as easily to become a prey to their barbarity, should they be suffered to make an attack upon them.

On the night of the 17th of June, (error June 15th not 17th), Captain Snyder, (see note at end of chapter), and his company were encamped about thirty-five miles east of Galena, and not far distant from the Burr Oak Grove. On that night his sentinels were fired upon by the Indians; but the cowardly wretches did not stand to fight. They fired and retreated immediately. Next morning Captain Snyder took his company and went in pursuit of them with all possible speed. He pursued them to their camp. But they first discovered his approach, and took to flight, but he was not to be dodged. It was now day, and he had the light of the sun to see how to trail in pursuit of them. His men were mounted on horseback; and the word was—"not to spare them." They were put to the whip and spur; and in a very short time Captain

Snyder overtook them. But they sought refuge in a ditch, or hole in the ground to fight from, in order to sell their lives as dear as possible.

As it appears there were but four of them, they in all probability were out as spies from the main body of Indians. After they took shelter in this hole, or gully, there was but a very slight prospect of killing, except by a charge upon them; so Captain Snyder surrounded the hole and ordered his men to charge upon them,—which order was promptly obeyed. The Indians fired upon them as they charged, and wounded one man mortally. Colonel Semple was one of the number who charged upon them in this dangerous place, and killed one with his pistol. They killed them all in this place of supposed security, except one, and him they killed within a few steps of it, after he had got out. The wounded man was by the name of Macomson. They now had to make a litter to carry him on, as it was impossible for him to ride; accordingly Captain Snyder had one made, and eight men detailed to carry it; that being the only way they could take him along, for it was perceived that he could survive but a short time.

Captain Snyder thought that it would be best to take up the line of march toward the camp, where he had been stationed occasionally, at Kellogg's Grove, in order that if Macomson died, he might have a chance to pay the last duty that man can pay to his fellow men upon earth;—or if there was any prospect of his recovery, that there might be no means left untried to save his life:—but this was not destined to be the case. They proceeded on until the men became very much fatigued, and thirsty for want of water; likewise they thought he was dying: so they stopped to see what would be his fate; also to search round, and if possible get some water, as they were by this time very thirsty, having been in the chase ever since it was clearly light. In their eagerness to obtain this indispensable article to sustain life, they scattered in different directions in search of it; not dreaming or apprehending the slightest danger of being taken by surprise. But in this they were mistaken.

They were fired upon by about seventy or eighty Indians. Two gentlemen, one by the name of Scott, the other McDaniel, (names in full are: William B. Mecomson, Benjamin Scott, and Benjamin McDaniel), together with their horses, were killed the first fire, and a gentleman by the name of Cornelius badly wounded. The men being surprised so suddenly, became very much alarmed, and some of them commenced a retreat. Captain Snyder perceiving it, ordered a halt and endeavoured to form them for action. Some of them so panic struck, were still for taking to flight. Captain Snyder then requested General Samuel Whiteside, who was then in his company in the capacity of a private, to try and assist him, to bring the men to a stand. General Whiteside then cried aloud that he would shoot the first man that attempted to retreat. They then formed, and the battle became warm on both sides, which lasted a considerable time, both the Indians and our men taking the advantage of trees.

General Whiteside being an excellent marksman, took a cool and deliberate aim at the Indian Commander, who had been yelling and hallooing all the time of the action. As soon as his gun fired, the Indian was heard no more; and his horse was immediately seen without the rider. The Indians now began to retreat, which told us plainly that General Whiteside had killed their commander. The panic had still fast hold of a part of our company. They refused to pursue them further. Captain Snyder, General Whiteside and Colonel Semple, with some others endeavoured to persuade the men to pursue them, but it was impossible to get a part of them to consent; they peremptorily refused. When Captain Snyder perceived that it was impossible to effect anything with a part of his small band; he ordered a march back to their camp. They did not march far before they met Major Riley, with a detachment of regulars.

After a consultation between Riley and Snyder, they came to the conclusion that it was then too late to follow the Indians that night. They all then returned to their encampment and abandoned the idea of further pursuit.

They did not know but that Black Hawk and his whole army were close by, and if so small a band would fall in with them, they might fall an easy prey to their vengeance, for at that time it would have been almost impossible to have made good their retreat, for they had then been about sixty days almost constantly on the march, and their horses a greater part of them without corn, or any food except grass. This was a prudent step.

Captain Snyder immediately marched his men to headquarters, which was Fort Wilbourn, where the new levy of troops had all assembled, and had been organised into three brigades; under officers hereafter to be mentioned.

Captain Snyder made a report of his battle to General Atkinson, and having been much worn out by fatigue, and this his second term of service having expired, he and his company were discharged, and they all retired once more to their respective homes to embrace their wives and children, and enjoy the happiness of sitting by their own firesides, without the fear of being disturbed by the shrieks and yell of the savage;

and those who had fought, no doubt, felt happy that they had borne a part of the hardships of war, in defence of their country's rights. But men who will not fight in such a cause, hardly can be said to have good and noble feelings. All honourable men are generally brave, but a dishonourable man has nothing to stimulate him to be brave.

I am in possession of the names of some of those who did not do their duty in this battle,—but I will forbear mentioning any of their names; for it may be that they may have respectable fathers and mothers, or wives and children, that might be seriously injured by the exposure. So I will forbear saying anything that would tend to injure the feelings of an honourable and dutiful son, or cause a pang to reach the heart of an affectionate wife, father or mother. But it never is wrong, or does any harm to eulogize those who act honourably and brave. There were some such spirits, by all accounts, who acted that part in this little band, that were engaged in the battle, of which I have just been informing the reader about. Amongst them were General Samuel Whiteside, Colonel Semple and Captain Snyder himself. It is stated by all that they acted with bravery and fearlessness; and some others that I am not able to name at this time.

The number of Indians that were killed in this engagement could not be ascertained. As their number was so far superior to that of the company of Captain Snyder, it was thought expedient to desist, and not stay to hunt them up. But from every account we could get, there were a number, besides their commander that I have already mentioned. The men on our part that were killed, were choice citizens, and all had families, but one. The man who was wounded in the first skirmish had to share the same fate of the rest who were killed. It was out of the power of men or officers to save him from becoming a prey to their vengeance.

I shall have to dismiss this campaign for the present, and take up the second levy of troops.

Those counties, that I as an express bearer was sent to, to raise more troops, were ordered to have them ready for marching in due time so as to be at Beardstown, the place of rendezvous, on the third day of June. Accordingly in compliance with said order, the following companies rendezvoused at that place, *viz*: From Clinton County, a company of the number of sixty-eight, commanded by Captain A. Bankson;—from Washington county, a company containing fifty-three, commanded by Captain Burnes;—from Randolph, two companies, containing each fifty men, commanded by Captains Feaman and Briggs. The companies after their arrival, organised themselves into a squadron, and for their officers elected Theophilus W. Smith, of the county of Madison, their Lieutenant Colonel; and Sidney Breese, of the county of Randolph, Major. (Theophilus W. Smith, then a Judge of the Supreme Court, was appointed to the general staff, on which occasion Major Breese, later United States Senator and Judge of the Supreme Court, was made Lieutenant Colonel, and John D. Wood, Major.

On the fifth day of June, the commandant (Colonel Smith,) appointed the following persons to form his staff, *viz*: John Omelvany, Adjutant; Benjamin Bond, Paymaster; William H. Terrell, Surgeon; J. B. Logan, (Father of General John A. Logan), Surgeon's mate; C. V. Halstead, Quartermaster; John Hawthorn, Hospital Steward.

Colonel Smith after procuring provision, and waggons to transport them, took up a line of march (6th May,) for General Atkinson's headquarters at Fort Wilbourn—a small fort erected by Rev. Mr. Horn, (Rev. Reddick Horn), as a place to secure provision he had procured at St. Louis;—at which place the troops from the different parts of the State assembled, also some from the State of Indiana. Although General Atkinson could not receive them on account of there having been a sufficient number from our own State, and the scarcity of provision. Yet she certainly deserves great applause for her patriotism in sending to our assistance.

Here all the volunteers were organised into three brigades, which being the 15th May. Doctor Alexander Posey was elected Brigadier General, of the first Brigade; Willis Hargrave, Colonel, of the first regiment; William J. Gatewood, Lieutenant Colonel; and James Hampton, (Huston) Major; all from the county of Gallatin: Colonel John Ewing, from Franklin County, was elected Colonel, of the second regiment; —— Storm, Lieutenant Colonel; and Johnson Wren, Major; the third regiment under the command of Colonel Samuel Leach; Lieutenant, Colonel Campbell; and Major (Joseph) Shelton. John Dement, (see note at end of chapter), of Vandalia was elected to the command of the spy battalion.

General Posey appointed Major Alexander P. Hall and B. A. Clark as his *aides-de-camp*, and Major (John) Raum, Brigade Inspector.

The second brigade from the eastern side of the State commanded by Brigadier General M. K. Alexander; Major Wm. B. Archer, was appointed by the general his *aide-de-camp*; and Major Sheledy, Brigade Inspector. It also consisted of three regiments, and a battalion of spies.

The first regiment under the command of Colonel J. M. Blackburn; Lieutenant Colonel, Wm. Wyatt; and Major Jas. S. Jones. The second under the command of Colonel Samuel Adams; Lieutenant Colonel J. W. Barlow; and Major George Bowers. The third under the command of Colonel Moses (Hosea) Pierce; Lieutenant Colonel C. Jones; Major William Eubanks. The battalion of spies under the command of Major William McHenry.

The third brigade from the western side of the State commanded by Brigadier General James D. Henry; who appointed Major Alexander P. Field, his *aide-de c*amp; Major Murray McConnel, Brigade Inspector. This brigade had four regiments and a spy battalion. The first regiment under command of Colonel S. T. Mathews; Lieutenant Colonel James Gillham; and Major James Evans. The second, commanded by Colonel Jacob Fry; Lieutenant Colonel J. Smith; and Major Benjamin James. The third under command of Colonel Gabriel Jones; Lieutenant Colonel Theophilus W. Smith; and Major Sidney Breese. (Lieutenant Colonel Theophilus W. Smith was later appointed Adjutant General by Governor Reynolds, Major Breese succeeding him, as above stated. The fourth under command of Colonel James Collins; Lieutenant Colonel P. H. Sharp; and Major William Miller. The battalion of spies under the command of Major W. L. D. Ewing.

The aggregate strength of the three brigades being about three thousand two hundred, besides three companies of Rangers, (an independent company of spies, commanded by Captain Jacob M. Early, was organised also, in that company Abraham Lincoln served as a private until it was mustered out July 10th), that were left to protect the settlements west of the Illinois River, and the public stores at such points as it was necessary to leave provisions. This force, with the volunteers from the mining country, together with the regulars, made about four thousand effective men.

About this time the Indians attacked a fort in the mining country, known by the name of Apple River Fort.

★★★★★★

Captain Clack Stone commanded Apple River Fort during the fight and during the campaign. The place is now Elizabeth, Jo Daviess County. From correspondence with Mr. N. B. Craig of Hanover, Illinois, who as a boy served in the company of his father, Captain James Craig of Jo Daviess County, it is concluded that the Flack referred to above was private John Flack, of Captain Craig's company. Ezekiel Rawlins, father of General

John A. Rawlins, was a member of Captain Stone's company.

******

(In this attack the citizens suffered great loss by the Indians killing their stock and destroying property; which the following letter from Captain Flack will more fully show, as he was in the fort during the engagement. It is in the following words, to wit:

Mr. John A. Wakefield:

Sir:—In reply to your request, I proceed to give an account of the attack of the Indians on Apple River Fort. Apple River Fort is situated about fourteen miles east of Galena. It was on the 24th of June, when harmony and peace appeared to reign through the fort, the day before a waggon had been despatched to Galena for the purpose of bringing a supply of lead and meat, which had run short in the afternoon on Sunday, the waggon arrived with a supply of meat and lead. About the time the team was removed from the waggon, the ladies of the fort had assembled to go to the river to hunt goose-berries; after starting they discovered coming from towards Galena three men, and being anxious to hear the news from there, they concluded to wait, expecting to hear something about the Indians.

When they arrived they proved to be men on an express from Galena going to Dixon's Ferry on Rock River; one of the men was a Mr. F. Dixon, the other two I have no recollection of their names. They were all intoxicated; after coming up they recollected that their guns were empty; one of the men dismounted and charged his piece, the other two would not; the man, after loading his gun, mounted his horse and they all rode off in full speed, whooping and hallooing towards Dixon's Ferry. When they had got to the distance of about three hundred yards, the one that carried the loaded gun was some fifty or sixty yards ahead of the other two, when a large number of Indians, being in ambush; arose and fired upon him; when he fell from his horse, shot through the thigh; his horse fled and left him; he arose and fired at the Indians at about the distance of fifteen steps, but his fire took no effect as was ever ascertained.

The Indians made towards him with their hatchets, when the other two coming up to his relief with their empty guns, they presented their guns, which caused the Indians to halt till the wounded man had got between them and the fort, they kept giving back with their guns presented till the wounded man gained the fort. The firing of the guns gave the alarm just in time for the people to make their retreat to the fort.

Apple River Fort had once been an extensive smelting establishment, and had become a considerable village, the fort being small, families lived in these houses in daytime, and everyone had his own to himself, but at night all repaired to the fort for safety.

The Indians pursued these men within firing distance of the fort, all on horseback, they rode up, dismounted and hitched their horses, and I think in about three minutes the fort was surrounded by about one hundred and fifty Indians, with all the savage ferocity and awful appearance, that those monsters could possibly appear in. The inhabitants had all reached the fort in time to defend themselves, which appeared to have been a providential thing, for if it had not been for the firing of the Indians on the express bearers, the fort would have certainly been taken, as the people would have been taken upon a surprise when they were not apprehending the least kind of danger from those savage barbarians.

There was a very heavy fire kept up for the space of one hour on both sides. Early in the engagement a Mr. George Herclurode was shot in the neck, and never spoke afterwards, he being at a port hole trying to defend himself and the helpless inmates of the fort; a Mr. James Nuting was also shot at the same time in the head, but not mortally. There appeared to be no dismay in the fort.

Such bravery and heroism amongst women has scarcely ever been surpassed in any country. Women and children were all actively engaged in the defence of the fort. Girls, eight years old, were busily engaged in running balls and making cartridges, and women loading guns.

The Indians got into those houses before spoken of, and knocked out the chinking and kept up their fire until they got discouraged. They then commenced plundering the houses, chopped, split and tore up a quantity of fine furniture. There was scarcely a man or woman that was left with a second suit of clothing. They went into my father's house; there was a large bureau full of fine clothes, they took six fine cloth coats and a number of fine ruffle shirts, with their tomahawks they split the drawers and took the contents. They ripped open the bedticks, emptied the feathers, took all the bedclothing, and broke all the *delft* in the cupboards.

Some of the outhouses were kept for the purpose of storing away provisions; they got into those houses where a number of flour barrels were stowed away; they would lie down on their faces and roll a barrel after them until they would get into a ravine, where they were out of danger; they then would empty the barrels of flour, after they had destroyed this necessary article, and when they found they could not succeed in taking the fort as they expected, they then commenced the warfare upon the stock; they killed all the cattle that were near the fort and took a number of fine horses to the number of about twenty, which were never got again by the owners. The horse that lost his rider in the first onset ran to the fort, which the Indians did not get.

Mr. Dixon on his retreat never stopped at the fort, thinking from the large number of Indians the fort would be taken, he made for Galena, and not being acquainted with the country he missed his road, and went to the house of Mr. John McDonald, who had a very large farm, of which Apple River formed a part of the fence. When he got to the house he found a large number of Indians at that place, and in a few minutes found himself completely surrounded; he lit from his horse, let down a pair of draw-bars, and made his escape across the river to Galena.

At the time the Indians commenced the fire upon the express bearers, the people of the fort started an express to Galena for assistance, which never came until about eleven o'clock the next day. Colonel Strode who had the command at Galena, marched to their assistance with about one hundred men. But this little band of men, women and children, had bravely stood their ground and kept the field, in spite of the Black Hawk and his ferocious savage brothers, with all their frightful yells and war-whoops.

But it was not without some suffering that this small handful did it. There was no water in the fort, and being taken upon a surprise, the people had not time to lay any in after the attack was first made upon the express bearers, and the weather being very warm, the men and women became so fatigued and

Major James W. Stephenson

exhausted in time of the engagement that they were compelled to drink dish water, to quench their thirst.

This fort was commanded by Captain Stone, and there were twenty-five men besides women and children. This small force stood their ground before the great and mighty chief called Black Hawk, and upwards of one hundred and fifty of those hideous monsters, that take so much delight in their savage warfare; as it was afterwards ascertained that Black Hawk commanded in person at this engagement.

It was supposed that the Indians lost several of their number in this skirmish, as they were seen putting several Indians on their horses and packing them off during the engagement, and after it was over there was a quantity of blood discovered on the ground.

The Indians in killing the cattle would skin and take out of a beef such pieces as they seemed to like best, leaving the balance on the ground.

Apple River Fort is about sixteen miles from Kellogg's Grove, and it is believed by all that this was the war party of Indians that attacked Major Dement's spy battalion on the next day at this grove.

Sir, this is an outline of the transactions of this skirmish, and agreeably to my memory is a correct one, &c.

Yours respectfully, with sentiments of the highest esteem.

Flack.

In and about this time, perhaps a day or two before, another scouting party of Indians came within a quarter of a mile of Fort Hamilton, on the waters of the Pickatoleca, (Pecatonica.) Three men had just left the fort, and gone to the farm of a Mr. Spafford. They made an attack on them and killed two, (5 were killed on Spafford's farm: Spafford, Searles, Spencer, McIlwaine, and an Englishman nicknamed "John Bull"), the third fled, an Indian seeing he had got away without falling as the other two, pursued him in order to despatch him like wise, but in this the savage had made a bad calculation, the white man was not hurt, and in place of the Indian killing him he killed the Indian, and made shift to hide from the vigilant eye of the rest; after staying in his place of concealment for some time he ventured to sally forth to go to the fort, but about that time Colonel William S. Hamilton, (son of Alexander Hamilton), arrived at the fort with a large number

Dixon's Ferry

of Menominie Indians who had volunteered to go against the Sac and Fox nations, in order to assist in subduing the common enemy of both them and the whites.

The frightened man who had run so narrow a risk of being killed by them in the attack they had made upon him and his companions, seeing those friendly and harmless Menominies pouring into the fort, retreated back to his place of concealment where it is said he kept himself secreted for six or eight days, living upon nothing but the vegetation that grew out of the earth. But at last he was obliged to yield to the pangs of hunger and venture forth and risk all consequences, for he found it was as well to die by the sword as famine, when to his great joy he found his mistake.

One of the men killed in the attack was by the name of Appleton, (Henry Appel), but the other I do not recollect, neither do I know the name of the brave fellow that made his escape and so manfully gave the Indian that pursued him a quietus. Which in the sequel the reader will find the others of this party all shared the same fate on that day.

Those cowardly wretches as soon as they had killed the two men, took to flight which is their general practice, especially scouting parties. But General Dodge, who happened to arrive at the fort soon after those daring wretches had committed this depredation, with about twenty men, pursued with all possible speed, and in about six or eight miles overtook them. When they saw they were pursued they made for the Picketoleca, (Pecatonica), and got under the bank of the creek. General Dodge stopped not for the advantage they had got of him, by being under the bank, but rushed up within a few feet of them and killed the whole band of them, consisting of eleven in number as was supposed at that time, report says since that the Indians give an account of two of them getting away.

General Dodge in this skirmish had four men wounded, three of which proved mortal, Samuel Black, was one; he lived ten days; Samuel Wells, was another who lived twenty-two days; and Montaville, (Montraville), Morris who lived twenty-four days. Thomas Jenkins was shot through the hip, but not mortal.

It appears that there was about this time a number of those scouting parties prowling about the mines in order to take scalps, and steal horses.

Captain James W. Stephenson about this time, perhaps the same day, fell in with another party of those miserable beings, between Apple River Fort and Kellogg's Grove; when they discovered him and his

MAJOR JOHN DEMENT

men they took to flight. And the captain and men gave them chase, he pursued them something like five miles before he was able to overtake them. They succeeded in reaching a large thicket, here they had every advantage of him, they lay concealed in the bushes and were completely hid from him, he had no other way to get at them than to charge upon them in their hiding place; which he did, and opened a brisk fire upon them, in a very few feet of where they were laying.

But the enemy having all advantage of him, he was compelled to fall back with the loss of some of his men, but the captain and men not willing to give up the contest, charged a second and third time upon them. On the third charge the captain received a wound in his breast, which was thought to have been mortal at that time, also three of his men were killed dead on the ground. One by the name of Howard, one by the name of Ames, and a Mr. Fowler. (Those killed were Charles Eames, Michael Lovell, and Stephen P. Howard.) The men now seeing that the Indians had every advantage of them, thought it was best not to put the lives of good men in stake against the lives of those filthy savages.

It could not be ascertained in this skirmish how much execution was done to the Indians, as the men had to retreat and give the field to the enemy. As Captain Stephenson had but a small detachment of his company, and three of them lay dead on the ground, and himself wounded.

I will now return to the army at Fort Wilbourn. The first brigade, marched on the twentieth day of June. The second on the twenty-first. And the third on the twenty-second, (twenty-third.) All ordered to concentrate at Dixon's.

Major Dement who commanded the spy battalion of the first brigade was ordered on ahead, in order if possible to overtake a band of Sacs who had been doing mischief at Bureau River. He proceeded on with his battalion in front of the brigade, until he came to a grove that is generally known by the name of Kellogg's Grove.

On the 25th day of June, about two hours before day, an express arrived from Gratiot's Grove informing Major Dement that traces of Indians had been seen the day previous leading south-westward, supposed to have been about five hundred in number. The distant from Kellogg's Grove.

At daylight Major Dement, with twenty-five men, made preparations for leaving the fort on an excursion towards where the Indians had passed, about five miles from the fort, but previous to his leaving gave orders to those who remained to saddle their horses and hold themselves in readiness to act as circumstances might render necessary.

During this time the party who were to accompany Major Dement, (Colonel John Dement, subsequently of Dixon, Illinois), to examine the Indian trail had advanced about three hundred yards from the main body when they discovered seven Indian spies, and immediately pursued them—some of them however returned to the camp and informed Major Dement of this circumstance, who fearing that they might be led into an ambuscade, (first endeavouring to quell excitement which the appearance of Indians had occasioned at the fort, and requiring the prompt execution of his order, to put themselves in readiness for any emergency) started out in haste to prevent further pursuit of the Indian spies; and advancing in the direction of the Indians about one mile from the camp for that purpose, he succeeded in retaining twelve or fourteen—the remainder still further ahead.

Meantime Major Dement apprehensive that an attack might be made by a large body of Indians whom he suspected to be concealed in the grove, and observing that a number of his men had followed him out from the fort, determined on the expediency of forming his men in the prairie, then about one mile from the fort, in order to cover the retreat of those who had pursued the Indian spies.

While Major Dement was taking the necessary steps to put this determination into execution, the Indians amounting to between two and three hundred, rushed from the grove, raised a yell and commenced firing. About twenty-five men who were within hearing, formed in a body to resist the attack, and to cover the retreat of the party who had pursued the Indian spies to the grove, the remainder of those who came out from the fort immediately returning. The small company thus hastily formed, bravely stood their ground until they were in danger of being surrounded by superior numbers. Major Dement then ordered his men to retire to the fort closely pursued by the Indians. On their retreat they overtook three men on foot, who were making towards the fort, but not being able to reach it were cut off by the enemy.

The Indians kept up a brisk fire on the stockade for nearly an hour; but finding themselves unable to stand against the steady aim of the brave riflemen within, gave up all hopes of carrying it, and withdrew to the woods.

About three hours after the Indians had left the ground, General Posey arrived with a reinforcement, with which he had started from

CHIEF SHA-BO-NA

the encampment immediately after the arrival of the express from Major Dement.

The Indians remained in sight of the fort till within an hour or two of General Posey's arrival.

Next day General Posey marched to the north, in the direction in which the Indians had last been seen, crossed their trail, returned to Kellogg's Grove, where he encamped to await the arrival of the baggage waggons.

The loss of our troops were five killed, and three wounded; that of the enemy nine killed that were found on the ground, and it is supposed five others fell in the engagement, as that number of the enemy's horses came into the camp without their riders.

There were some choice spirits in this action, or the superior number of Indians would certainly have cut off this small band of men, as the place of refuge they were in was very little better than the open field.

In this small band of soldiers was our much beloved and respected Lieutenant Governor Zadock Casey; he was one of the number who formed to cover the retreat of those that had advanced in pursuit of the enemy.

It is natural always for honourable men to be brave, there is something in their breasts that always stimulates them to noble acts, and on our cool reflection they would court death before dishonour.

This, in my opinion, is what stimulates men to act bravely and patriotic. They are not only acting for the good of their country but they believe it to be an imperative duty for them to do so.

General Posey marched his whole brigade from this place to Fort Hamilton, where he remained for some days. Here Major Dement resigned his command.

I must here dismiss General Posey for the present, and return back to Dixon's, where the second and third brigades had arrived when the express came stating that Major Dement had had a battle. General Alexander, who commanded the second brigade, was despatched with his brigade with all speed across Rock River, and ordered to march his troops toward Plum River, a stream running into the Mississippi, there to intercept the Indians on their retreat, if they should attempt to cross the Mississippi. General Atkinson remained at Dixon's with the infantry, and General Henry with his brigade of volunteers for two days, in order if possible to ascertain what direction the Indians were taking; where he ascertained that the Indians had retreated back up

Rock River, and that it was only a war party of about one hundred and fifty. He came to the conclusion to pursue his intended route up Rock River on the east side of the Four Lakes; where it was stated that Black Hawk had fortified himself with his whole army, and intended to give General Atkinson a general fight.

On the evening of the 26th of June, Captain George Walker and three Pottawattomies from Chicago, came into the camp at Dixon's, and stated that there were seventy-five Pottawattomies awaiting to join the whole army at Sycamore Creek, that they had been there several days awaiting our arrival, and that they had become suspicious that they were in great danger as it was their opinion that the Sacs were not far away. Next morning General Henry sent on Colonel Fry with his regiment, with orders to reach there as soon as possible, and await our arrival. Colonel Fry always strictly doing his duty, moved on with all possible celerity, with Captain Walker as his pilot, to where these children of the forest were awaiting to join in the chase against Black Hawk and his band, with Mr. Caldwell who acts as their principal chief in council. They had also their war chief Shabbaney (Sha-bo-na) along.

Mr. Caldwell has been an interpreter to the Indian Agent for some years. He is a man of fine education and general information. His father was a British officer and his mother was a Pottawattomie squaw. But for a half breed he is very fair skinned.

The whole of the third Brigade under command of General Henry, with General Atkinson at our head, took up the line of march from Dixon's on the 27th of June, directing our course up Rock River, towards the Four Lakes. We lay on the night of the 28th, at Major Stillman's battle ground. On the 29th, we overtook Colonel Fry, with the seventy-five Pottawattomie Indians with him.

The Indians appeared to be highly pleased to think they were honoured so far as to take a hand with us against the Sacs. They were well armed, with both guns and spears.

The 30th, we passed through the Turtle village, which is a considerable Winnebago town, but it was deserted. We marched on about one mile, and en camped in the open prairie near enough to Rock River to get water from it. We here saw very fresh signs of the Sac Indians, where they had been apparently fishing on that day. General Atkinson believed we were close to them, and apprehended an attack that night. The sentinels fired several times, and we were as often paraded, and prepared to receive the enemy, but they never came. But from what the sentinels gave into the officers of the day, there was no doubt that Indians had been prowling about the camp. July first, we had not marched but two or three miles before an Indian was seen across Rock River at some distance off in a very high prairie, which no doubt was a spy, and likely was one that had been prowling about our encampment the night before. We proceeded a few miles further and came to the place where the Indians who had taken the two Miss Halls prisoners had stayed several days. It was a strong position, where they could have withstood a very powerful force, which we afterwards discovered they always encamped in such places.

We had not marched but a few miles from this place, before one of our front scouts came back meeting the army in great haste, and stated that they had discovered a fresh trail of Indians where they had just gone along in front of us. Major Ewing, who was in front of the main army some distance, immediately formed his men in line of battle and marched in that order in advance of the main army about three quarters of a mile. We had a very thick wood to march through, where the undergrowth stood very high and thick; the sign looked very fresh and we expected every step to be fired upon from the thickets. We marched in abreast in this order about two miles, not stopping for the unevenness of the ground or any thing else, but keeping in a line of battle all the time, until we found the Indians had scattered, then we resumed our common line of march, which was in three divisions.

Soon after we had formed into three divisions, the friendly Indians that were with us raised an alarm by seven or eight of them shooting at a deer some little in advance of the army. The whole army here formed for action; but it was soon ascertained that these children of the forest, had been at what their whole race seems to have been born for, tradesmen to shooting at the beasts of the forest. We here camped by a small lake this night and had to drink the water which was very bad, but it was all that could be found. Here this night a very bad accident happened.

One of the sentinels mistaking another that was on post with a blanket wrapped around him, for an Indian, he shot him just below the groin in the thick of the thigh. At first the wound was thought mortal. I understood before I left the army, the man was nearly well. Here General Atkinson had on this night breastworks thrown up which was easy done; as we were encamped in thick heavy timber; this was a precaution which he was always after famous for, which went to show that he set a great deal by the lives of his men, and by no means was any marks of cowardice;—for generalship consists more in good management than anything else.

July 2nd. We started this morning at the usual time, but went but a few miles, before Major Ewing, who was still in front with his battalion, espied a very fresh trail, making off at about a left angle. He dispatched ten men from the battalion, in company with Captain George Walker, and a few Indians, to pursue it and see if possible where it went to. He moved on in front of his battalion a small distance further, when he came on the main Sac trail of Black Hawk's whole army; which appeared to be about two days old. Captain Early, who commanded a volunteer independent company, and had got in advance this morning, called a halt, so did Major Ewing with his battalion. (Upon the discharge of Captain Iles's company after its twenty days of service, Abraham Lincoln, who had been a private therein, re-enlisted in the independent company of Captain Jacob M. Early and was engaged in scouting duty. The company was mustered out finally at Lake Koshkonong July 10, 1832.)

Then Major Ewing sent back one of his staff officers for the main army to call a halt a few minutes. He with Major Anderson of the infantry, Captain Early, and Jonathan H. Pugh, Esquire, went a little in advance, where Major Anderson, with a telescope, took a view across the lake, as we had now got to Lake Koshkonong. (Subsequently General Robert Anderson of Fort Sumter fame. Thus it will be observed that a remarkably large number of great Americans served together in the Black Hawk campaigns.) They then discovered three Indians, apparently in their canoes. Major Ewing went himself and informed General Atkinson what discovery was made, and requested General Atkinson to let him take his battalion round through a narrow defile that was between two of those lakes, where we supposed the Indians were. By this time our scouts, who had taken the trail that led off on our left, returned, bringing with them five white men's scalps. They followed the Indian trail until it took them to a large Indian encampment that they had left a few days before. They reached it; the scalps were sticking up against some of their wigwams;—some of them were identified, but I do not recollect the names of any, except one, which was said to be an old gentleman by the name of (William) Hale.

Major Ewing then marched his battalion about one mile, where the pass on the side of the lake appeared so narrow, that he dismounted his men, and had the horses all tied, and a few men left to guard them, and the rest of us marched on foot about one mile through a narrow defile on the bank of Koshkonong Lake. This was considered a dangerous procedure, but Colonel Ewing, who was in front with Major Anderson, would have been first in danger. We now found that we were getting too far in advance of our horses; so Major Ewing sent a part of the men back for them. When we mounted our horses, we were joined by Captain Early and his independent corps. We then marched some distance around the lake, and went in between two of them, in a narrow defile, until we found another deserted encampment. We now saw clearly that the Indians were gone from the Koshkonong lake. So the next thing to be done was to find which direction they had steered their course.

July 4th. Major Ewing and his spy battalion, with Colonel Collins and Colonel Jones, were sent up the river in the way the trail of the Indians seemed to be making, to see what discoveries could be made. They at last saw that they were still making up the river on the east side. We returned to the camp late in the evening. On the evening before, General Alexander had come up with us. He stated that he had been to the Mississippi, and had explored the country on Plum River, and had made no discoveries of the Indians making their escape.

July 5th. General Atkinson lay by this day with the main army; but Colonel Fry, who was always a man that wished to be actively engaged for the welfare of his country, marched across Rock River on this day, to see if there was any sign of the enemy passing up on the west side. Colonel Fry did not return until late in the evening. He reported, he had seen another Indian trail on the opposite side from us, and that he had followed it until it went into a tremendous thicket, such as his horses could not penetrate.

On the 4th of July, some of our scouts had taken an old Sac Indian a prisoner, which in their flight, the rest of the Indians had run off and left. He was nearly starved to death, and literally blind. After feeding him. General Atkinson had him examined, telling him at the same time that if he caught him in a lie he would have him put to death. The old fellow told all he knew, which was not very much. He stated that Black Hawk had passed on up the river, on the east side, the same that they were then on. He stated that he was so old that they never thought it worth while to tell him anything about their movements; that in marching, he frequently did not get up to their camp till late in the night, and sometimes not until the next morning.

So our prisoner was not of much benefit to us. He had but few days to live, and to shorten his days we concluded the best plan would be to give him plenty to eat, and leave him to kill himself in that pleasant way. But we learnt afterwards that he was denied this satisfaction, for some of General Posey's men came upon him, and he soon became an easy prey to their deadly rifles.

July 6th. General Atkinson on this day took up the line of march, still up Rock River, on the east side. We this day reached a Winnebago village called the Burnt Village, on White Water, a small stream running into Rock River, but one that was almost impassable, as it was a perfect swamp on each bank, and very deep in the middle of the channel. Next morning, on the 7th of July, one of the regulars went to this stream, which was not more than one hundred and twenty yards from our encampment, to fish. While fishing, three Indians fired on him from the opposite side of the river and wounded him very badly with two balls. This was a hard case, for the enemy to come within one hundred and twenty yards of our encampment, and wound one of our men, and we not able to help ourselves, for this dismal stream. The night we got here, (to White Water) General Posey's brigade, in company with Colonel Dodge's squadron, came up to us. They were out of provisions, and in a state of suffering, and were compelled to push on to where we were to get something to sustain nature.

Colonel John Ewing and his regiment did not reach us that night, and encamped about one mile and a half off from the main army. Here an awful accident happened. Colonel Dunn, who was a captain of a company, was here what is generally called the officer of the day, whose duty it is to visit the sentinels once or more through the course of the night. Captain Dunn in performing this duty, just before day in the morning, was fired upon by one of the sentinels, and severely wounded; he was shot in the groin, a place that generally proves fatal. When he was examined, his surgeons pronounced it mortal, which threw all his friends into mourning; for he was a man much beloved by all that knew him.

But here I must stop. It won't do to write his epitaph yet, for he is still a living man, (as at time of first publication), and is young and in the bloom of life. He still may be a useful member of society, and a friend and public servant to his country, which he has already been for several years, holding some of the most important offices in the gift of the legislature,—such as Canal Commissioner, which he still holds, and many more. So, if he had died, the State would have sustained a great loss, in losing so good a citizen.

Soon after the Indians shot the regular, General Atkinson took up the line of march, still up the river, and made shift to cross one branch of this dismal stream, White Water; but it was with much difficulty, as many a horse mired down, and threw his rider into the water, where he and his gun were literally buried in mud and water; but all made shift to get out. Here we expected to have been fired upon by the enemy. Major Ewing, still in advance of the main army some distance, got over first. He then formed his men in battle order, and stood as a front guard, until the main army could cross this dismal stream; which they had to bridge with grass, as they afterwards had to do many more the same way.

In this swampy country the grass grows very high, the ground being very rich. There were plenty of scythes, and men to use them; so it was an easy job to make a temporary bridge with this substitute, such as the heaviest kind of baggage waggons could pass with safety. We marched on this day about fifteen miles up the river. On this evening the whole forces got together, and camped together for the first time. Our forces looked like they were able to whip all the Indians in the north western territories.

At this place the old blind chief, a Winnebago Indian, came with General Dodge's corps. General Atkinson on the next morning, July the 8th, had a talk with him, in order if possible to find out where Black Hawk was with his forces. The old blind or one eyed chief, told him that the Indians that we were in pursuit of, were still down on the island opposite the Burnt Village, where they shot the regular, and stated that if we did not find them there he would give General Atkinson leave to take his life. Upon this General Atkinson made a retrograde movement, and measured the ground and fathomed the muddy branches of the *celebrated* White Water, that we crossed the day before. We took up our abode that night on the same ground that we left before at the Burnt Village.

Next morning, July the 9th, Colonel Fry undertook to make a bridge across the almost impassable gulf. He was furnished with a number of the regulars, who were always ready for such undertakings. A strong guard was placed on the bank of the stream on the opposite side, for fear of those suffering who passed over on a raft. Captain Early, in the course of the day, took a part of his men and penetrated some distance into the island. They brought back word that they had seen a good deal of fresh sign, and were of opinion that the Indians were there. Colonel William S. Hamilton, who had a small band of Menominie Indians under his command, took them and went clear through the Island and hunted it out thoroughly. They returned in the evening, bringing the news that the Indians had left this Island. General Atkinson was again deceived by those treacherous Winnebagoes, but in place of putting the old one eyed chief to death, he still consulted him. He next told him that Black Hawk was still higher up the stream, on what was called the Tumbling Land. (Sometimes called "trembling lands." So called from the fact that when trod by man or beast, a trembling movement or sensation was observed, attributed to the surface being supported by muck or water instead of a subsoil.) Colonel Fry's bridge, that he had spent the best part of this day at with more than one hundred hands, was now kicked over and abandoned.

We now found that there was no dependence to be placed in those treacherous Winnebagoes. The men now had been marching through swamps for a considerable length of time without success; and no execution done, only what General Posey's men had done by killing the old blind Indian. We now plainly saw that Black Hawk knew we were in his neighbourhood. He knew all the passes between those swamps, and could evade our pursuit for some time; which discouraged our men very much.

Here his Excellency Governor Reynolds and his aids left us; likewise Colonel T. W. Smith, who had been promoted to the office of Adjutant General,—which office was not then of much service to us. Colonel A. P. Field, General Henry's aid, and Major Breese, also left us,—(some on furlough and some discharged,) and returned home: These men at this time did not believe, that there would be any fighting, or I think they would not have left the army.

We here were in another bad box. We were in a manner out of provision; and the nearest point to us, where we could get a supply was Fort Winnebago, which was about eighty miles distant from us; and to get it, we were compelled to go through the most swampy country that an army ever was marched through.

July 10th. General Atkinson this morning sent Colonel Ewing with his regiment down Rock River to Dixon's with Colonel Dunn, who was supposed to be mortally wounded.

General Posey with the rest of his brigade, was sent to Fort Hamilton, as a guard to that frontier part of the country, which was in a very exposed situation, on account of General Dodge having the troops from there with him.

General Henry and his brigade, General Alexander's brigade and General Dodge's squadron, were all this day sent to Fort Winnebago after provision. General Atkinson dropped down a short distance from our present encampment, near to the Koshkonong Lake, and there built a fort, which he called Fort Koshkonong, after the lake. (Present site of Fort Atkinson, Wisconsin.)

General Atkinson gave Generals Alexander, Henry, and Dodge, orders to return as soon as they drew provision. Here, when we got to Fort Winnebago, we were still surrounded by the Winnebagoes. A half breed Indian by the name of Poquet, told us he thought we might find Black Hawk by going around the head of Fox River, a stream of considerable size which empties into Green Bay; and offered to go with some of the Winnebagoes as a pilot.

At this place we met with a misfortune which we had been very much troubled with during our march, which I omitted mentioning before. Our horses were given to fright and running in a most fearful manner; the army was constantly in danger of suffering great damage by their taking those frights. There is no one can tell what a horrid sight it is, to see two thousand horses coming at full speed toward an encampment in the dead hour of night. This night they got more scared than common. There were about three hundred head on this night, that run about thirty miles before they stopped; and that, too, through the worst kind of swamps. This circumstance caused us to stay here two days, trying to recover our horses, but all could not be found. Our road back the way we had come, was hunted for upwards of fifty miles; and still a great number of them were missing.

Chapter 5

Narrative of the Imprisonment of the Two Miss Halls

The reader will recollect that, in a former chapter it was stated that two young and beautiful females were taken prisoners by the Indians, on Indian Creek, where they so inhumanly murdered and mutilated the families of Messrs. Hall, Daviess, and Pedigrew (Pettigrew) .

Reader, didst thou not shudder when you read of this horrid act, that was done in open day in our country? But, alas! if we shudder at the thought of this inhuman act, what must have been the feelings of those two young and unoffending women? Can I find language to describe them? No! The reader can better imagine, than pen can write it.

But reader, you shall have the narrative of their captivity as given to me by one of them in person, which was Silbey, (Sylvia), the eldest. I will give it in her own language, which I think will be more satisfactory to the reader; which is as follows:

> On the 20th of May, 1832, a party of Indians came to my father's house early in the morning. Mr. Pedigrew, one of the neighbours was there. They first shot him; they then commenced killing my father and mother, and the rest of the family that were at home, in the midst of which two Indians seized me, and two more my sister Rachel, by the arms, and bore us off as fast as possible. As we passed out of the door, we saw our mother sinking under the instruments of death. They compelled us to run on foot as fast as we were able, about one mile and a half, and about thirty Indians following to where their horses were left. There they awaited the arrival of those who staid back at the house to murder the family, during which delay they caught

and carried away several of my father's horses.

After the party that staid behind came up, we were mounted on horseback. The rest all at the same time mounted their horses. We rode in great haste until about midnight. They then halted and dismounted, and spread a blanket down, bidding us to sit on it. They then formed a circle around us. We rested here about two hours. They then mounted their horses, and rode at as fast a gait as we were able to go, until about ten o'clock in the morning, when they again dismounted and spread down their blankets, and bid us to sit upon them. We by this time were almost fatigued to death, and faint with hunger; they here scalded some beans, and eat them heartily. They gave some to us, telling us to eat; but to eat raw beans was what we could not do.

After they had satisfied themselves on the raw beans, they again mounted their horses, compelling us again to mount ours. The saddles were the common Indian saddles, just the tree, and a grained deer skin stretched over it, and the roughest going kind of horses. We thought every day it would be the last with us. We rode on this day, until about sun down, when they again halted. They here roasted a piece of prairie chicken and gave us to eat. I suppose we stayed here about an hour and a half. They then mounted again and rode until about three hours in the night, when they met the main army under Black Hawk.

We now fared a little better. When they found we were prisoners, they appeared to be much pleased, and presented us with their best diet, consisting of the kernels of hazelnuts and sugar mixed together, as a token of friendship; at the same time they gave us some tobacco and parched meal, making signs to us to burn it, which we did out of obedience to them. They also this night suffered us to sleep together, which they had before refused. They staid next morning until a late hour. They prepared red and black paints, and painted one side of our head and face red, and the other black. After this was done eight or ten of their leading warriors took us by the hand and marched round their encampment several times.

They then took us into the midst of the whole band of warriors, spread down some blankets, and set us down upon them. They then commenced dancing around us, singing and yelling in a most horrid manner. We here thought they intended to kill us. After they had danced until they were tired, and quit jumping around us, two squaws came to us and took us by the hand, and led us into one of their *wigwams*, where we staid undisturbed until they all could pack up and start, which they did in a very short time.—We now all took up the line of march together, and rode until about midnight, when we stopped. We were again separated, and had not the satisfaction of sleeping together.

Next morning, which was the fourth day of our captivity, they cleaned off a place fifteen or twenty feet round, and stuck a pole down in the middle of it. We were, as I stated before, again placed in the midst, and they danced around us, still singing their war song. They here staid all day, and the next morning took up the line of march again, and marched on until late in the evening, when they again cleared off another place as before, and placing us in it, commenced dancing around us, making us kneel down, and bow our faces to the earth.

Here once more, from their actions, we thought we were going to be killed; which we would almost as soon they would have done as not, for we were nearly exhausted with fatigue, on account of the long and forced marches that we had made. Next morning, which was the sixth day after our captivity, we were again mounted on our horses, and marched till in the afternoon, when they again stopped and went through the same wretched and disagreeable ceremony of clearing off a place, and dancing and singing around, while the squaws and young ones were generally engaged when we stopped, in gathering roots, which was our principal diet.

When they killed my father and mother, and the rest of the families, they took what coffee there was in the houses, parched it, and made it in the same manner that the white people do; we frequently got some of it to drink while it lasted.

On the next day four Winnebago Indians came to the place where we were encamped. Here a long council was held with the principal war chiefs or head men of the nation. After the talk was over, one of the Sacs came and took me by the hand, and led me up to where the Winnebagoes were seated, and where they had been for some time in council. The four Winnebagoes then all arose and shook me by the hand. Then one of them made signs for me to sit down by him, which I did. He then told me by signs that I belonged to him, and gave me to understand, in the same way, that I must go along with him. I then asked him if they were not going to let my sister go with me? which he understood. I now discovered that I had been purchased, but Rachel had not. The Indians who had purchased me, again renewed their talk with the Sacs and Foxes. Here another long council was held, and much warmth appeared to be excited on both sides. I thought several times they would not succeed in getting my sister. But at the close of the talk they came to where I was, leading Rachel by the hand, and sat her down by me. This was about an hour by sun in the evening. A number of the Sac and Fox Indians now came and shook us by the hands, and bid us goodbye.

We then started and rode until about an hour in the night, as fast as our horses were able to run, when we came to where their squaws were encamped: we here staid all night. Next morning we went up the Wisconsin River in canoes, and rowed on until about an hour by sun in the evening. Then they stopped and lay by that night and all next day, and till eleven or ten o'clock the third day; when twenty-four of the Winnebagoes started with us towards the settlements in Illinois; for they had I suppose, taken us a great way into the Michigan territory. We on this night came to another Indian encampment. We here were permitted once more to taste of food that we could eat a little of. They had pickle pork and Irish potatoes cooked up together. Our appetites by this time could take this food, although we were greatly distressed in mind.

Next day they travelled until nearly night, when they chanced to kill a deer. They cooked it, and devoured it in a very few minutes; but they gave us what we could eat of it. They had a little salt which they gave us to salt our part of the deer.

We on this evening got to the Blue Mounds, in the mining country. There was a small fort at this place, and a few families. It was an outside place of the inhabited part, and on the north side of the mining country, something like fifty miles north of the south line of Michigan territory.

Next morning we started on to Gratiot's Grove, as it was called, in company with two hundred and seventy-three soldiers, and the same twenty-four Winnebago Indians. In five or six miles we met Henry Gratiot, Indian agent, coming to meet us. We then understood that he and General Dodge had employed the

Indians that came after us, to do so.

I then inquired of her, if she knew how much the Winnebagoes had to pay for them. She replied:

I understood that General Dodge and Mr. Gratiot had given them, the Winnebagoes, two thousand dollars, paid in forty horses, *wampum* and other trinkets, to purchase us of the Sacs and Foxes.

We on this night reached the White Oak Grove in the settlement of the mines. Next day we reached Mr. Henry Grariot's. We here remained in the neighbourhood, at a small fort, at what was called the White Oak Springs, about two weeks. We then went to Galena and remained about one week.

I then inquired of her, if she did not think that some of the Indians that were engaged in taking them, were Pottawattomies? to which she replied, that "the four who took them by the hand at first, were Pottawattomies; for one of them she had frequently seen before."

Oh, reader, let us here stop and pause for one moment, and place ourselves in the situation of these two weak and feeble young women, who had just been prisoners in the hands of those barbarians for eleven days. Alas! go back to the scene of the massacre of their father, mother, brothers and sisters! What were their feelings? But, oh! how shall I begin to describe them? Alas! if I were only a Hervey, a Milton, or a Newton, I might then give a faint glimmer of one half of the anguish of their bursting hearts. Torn with violence, by frightful savages, from the abodes of peace and innocence; and, oh! still worse, to behold a bleeding mother, sinking under the sharp spear, pierced to her heart by the inhuman butchers; and to see a dear and beloved father struggling with death's last grasp to save his beloved family, who were shrieking around him, and beseeching the inhuman murderers to spare their lives!

The imagination can only think the pain they suffered; but it is impossible to write it. Forced on with all possible speed to where the butchers were prepared to lead them captive into a wilderness, where no friendly voice could salute their ears, no soothing comforter to pour the oil and balm of consolation into their swelling and almost bursting hearts. The yell of the war-song was all they heard, as they were forced away with all possible speed into the wilderness.

Solitude and sorrow appeared now to be their doom.—All their tears and entreaties were unheard. Their persecutors were deaf to any feeling for the anguish of soul that appeared to wring their bosoms. Yea, the sea of trouble and sorrow that they were engulfed in, never moved their savage hearts.

What was now the prospect of future happiness on earth?—their beloved friends inhumanly murdered, and they shut out from all the civilized world, far, far away in the wilderness, where the foot of a white man had scarcely ever trod—their meat and drink only bitter tears—nights passed in sorrow, mornings awaked to cares and fatigue—the few hours that they had to rest, the war dance around them harrowed up the most awful sensations in their breasts, expecting at every dance to become a prey to their vengeance. Oh, horrid thought! It is enough to start a tear in the eye of the most stout hearted to think of the swelling bosoms of those forlorn and disconsolate young women.

But let us with the poet say,

> *Why should we weep, why should we weep,*
> *When heaven throws such beams of love around,*
> *That, mingled with the darkest woes,*
> *The rays of hope are found?*
>
> *Why should we weep, when every storm*
> *That sweeps o'er ocean's breast,*
> *Awakes a gem whose sparkling form*
> *Had else remained at rest?*
>
> *Why should we weep, when every flower*
> *That closes with the night,*
> *Shall blush anew in beauty's power,*
> *When morn renews its light?*
>
> *Why should we weep, when placed on high,*
> *The bow, divinely sent,*
> *Still shows, when clouds obscure the sky,*
> *How quickly they are spent?*
>
> *Why should we weep, when dawning days*
> *And years so swiftly run?*
> *We only lose their setting light,*
> *To hail their brighter dawn.*

It appears that the Winnebagoes had much trouble to purchase Rachel, and from the best information that can be obtained on the subject, they had to use threats, and had to pay an additional sum of ten horses. A young warrior, it appears, claimed her as his prize, and at first positively refused to give her up. When he did so, he cut a lock of her hair out of her head. This I suppose he intended to keep as a trophy of his warlike exploits.

This now must have been the worst cut of all, to attempt a separation of them, as they now supposed, the only survivors of the family, and to take one away from the other, would be worse than death to them; but an all-wise Providence did not see fit to inflict this wound upon them. He had watched over them in the trying scene that they had already undergone, and he saw fit to release them from savage bondage. He heard their cries, and saw the distress they were in. They were now alone, and orphans in the world.

What now was most interesting to them, was peace of mind. To forget their murdered father and mother was impossible. Were all joys on earth now gone? Were they forsaken by all the world? Were none left to pour the oil of balm and comfort into their wounded bosoms? Yes, there were. The guardian angels of heaven had prepared a second father to take them by the hand, and point to them the path to happiness; and that path was an interest in the blood of a crucified Redeemer, which is a source of happiness to the mind when all earthly happiness fails, if there is such a thing as earthly happiness.

That person they found in the Reverend Mr. Horn. He had known them when they were children—he had been a companion and friend of their deceased father and mother; he felt now for the fatherless and unoffending orphans; with the affections of a father he flew to them to administer comfort to their heaving bosoms, which were wrung with the keenest pangs, when they thought of the loss of their friends. He now saw that there was only one way that they could see any degree of happiness, and that was, to point to them the comfort of religion, which he did by exhortation, entreating them to prepare to meet father, mother, brothers, and sisters, on the banks of deliverance beyond the grave, where the wicked cease from troubling, and the weary are at rest. They took the preacher's advice, and sought and obtained comfort in the blood of a crucified Redeemer, and, as I have every reason to believe, are now happy in the cause of religion, and preparing to meet their kindred friends in heaven.

One of them, Silbey, (Sylvia) the eldest, is married, and living with a second father indeed; his son William became a partner of her cares and sorrows. The younger, Rachel, is also married, to Mr. William Munson, and living in Putnam County, (as at time of first publication).

There is one thing more I cannot dismiss this subject and leave unnoticed. Although they were with the savage barbarians, and the worst of inhuman butchers that probably the earth affords, they never attempted to violate their chastity.

This is one of the noblest traits in the character of a savage, and one that appears to be held sacred and inviolate with them. But nevertheless, they are fond of making wives of prisoners. But it must be done agreeably to the custom of their nation. This they hold sacred, for they think if they were to violate this rule and practice, the Great Spirit would be offended with them.

Thus, reader, terminates the account of the two unfortunate Miss Halls, who suffered everything but death with those Indian barbarians.

It may not here be amiss and unprofitable to give the reader the following anecdote, which will go to show how easy the mind of a man can be alarmed, and the imagination wrought up to the highest pitch, and the great danger of excitement of this kind upon the female sex.

In travelling through the county of Fulton not long since, I chanced to stay all night with an elderly looking and familiar old gentleman; and with other subjects which we had talked not a little upon, we chanced to dwell upon the Black Hawk war. I asked Mr. F. if the people had forted in that neighbourhood during the great horror and alarm that were excited at the news of Major Stillman's defeat? to which he replied, that *he* had not; but had been much derided for being so foolhardy, as they called it, by several of his friends and neighbours; to which the good old man told me he replied to them, that if he could see a man running towards him with a bullet hole in him, and the blood running out of it, and hear unknown voices in pursuit, he then would think there was danger.

This declaration of the old gentleman made me almost think with his neighbours, until he stated to me the cause of it; which I here Would give in the good old man's own language, but as he understood the German language better than the English, I might not quote it precisely right. But what the old gentleman told me, and from his general character that I afterwards learnt from a number of his neighbours, his statement was true. (The so-called "Westerfield scare.")

As near as I could collect, both from him and his family, who joined in confirming what the old landlord stated, and which could be proven by a number of his neighbours, it was as follows: Soon after Stillman's defeat, a party of the troops from Fulton County, on their return home, when within a few miles of Canton, in said county, came across a gang of wolves, and having got into the settled part where they were not afraid, being from the seat of war, fired upon them, at the same time raising the war-whoop, which they had got by heart from the Indians in the memorable Indian school on the night of the fourteenth of May, on Sycamore Creek.

This frightful yelling, at a time when danger was expected, and accompanied with the firing of guns, was heard by another good old citizen of this county, away from the "far east," who happened to be out a little ways from home, who took the alarm, and supposed that it was the Indians killing his neighbours, made shift to get to the first of his horses that he came to, and putting on a bridle to guide it, never took time to consult the great benefit of a saddle in riding a long race, mounted bareback; and raising the cry of " murder" "murder!!" put his charger to the lash. He passed by home, and told his family to fly with all possible speed, who it appears was in the act of moving. But one of the family, who was not so badly alarmed by the shrieks of the dying neighbours, observed to him that he had left his son in the mill; to which he replied, "never mind my son, he is a cripple and cannot run,—they are certain to kill him—each one of you save yourselves if you can!"

So saying, he put his charger to it might and main, and at the same time crying out " murder!" "murder!!" to all he passed or met, he left all the world behind him, never dreaming that he was suffering for the want of a saddle until he had got many miles from the scene of action. He then beheld the blood trickling down his legs, from, I suppose the hard jolts of his charger, carrying a large body upon a sharp and bony back. But the ingenious old son of the pilgrim fathers soon found means to supply the want of a saddle. He had, a few days before the action took place, helped himself to a new hat; and not regarding the price of a hat when he expected every moment to hear the horrid war-whoop of an Indian behind him, he made a saddle of his new beaver, on which he rode, as Mr. F. informed me, until he came to Ross's Ferry, on the Illinois River, where as Mr. F. stated the citizens of that place stopped him, or he would, giving it in the good old Dutchman's own language, have been running yet; that is, if his horse and beaver saddle would have lasted so long.

This was about twenty-six miles from the scene of action, where he remained many days, apparently in a state of insanity. He was constantly trying to devise a plan to fix stirrups to his hat, and declared that if he only had a pair of stirrups hung to his beaver, he would not be in the least dread of an Indian ever overtaking him; but he was frequently heard to cry out "murder!" in his sleep, as at first, when he started on his race, and lamented the loss of the poor crippled mill boy.

But Mr. F. stated the poor crippled mill boy stood his ground, and his father having plenty of powder and lead in store, issued it out to those who were willing to fight in defence of the crippled boy and the women and children.

Now, reader, the laughable part of this story is over, but the sorrowful one has yet to come, which almost sickens my heart to relate, and I would fain hope it was false; but as I observed in the beginning of this story, it has come from too respectable a source for me to disbelieve it.

When the old frightened Mr. C. first started upon his race, he cried out "murder!" as before stated, and told the people as he went that the Indians were butchering and killing the people behind him; which, Mr. F. stated, frightened the neighbours in such a horrid manner that they took to flight. The women attempted to run, each carrying one of their children, or two of them, perhaps, if my memory serves me, on their hips; running in this way something like six miles. They all three expired in a few days, with fright and fatigue.

The other anecdote is something similar to the first; but it is no pain for me to relate it, as it was not of so serious a nature; for death was not produced by it.

Mr. F. stated, that some place on the eastern side of the state, perhaps near the Iroquois, a small stream in the north east corner of the state of Illinois, the people being much alarmed soon after the murder of the families on Indian Creek, the citizens sent out a spying party to the frontiers to see if they could see any signs of the enemy approaching toward the settlements where they lived. The men who had been spying for the enemy, on their return late in the evening, thought they saw some signs of Indians, and concluded to hasten and report danger to the neighbourhood. In a few minutes after they came to this conclusion, they heard a volley of guns fired in quick succession behind them, at the same time hallooing by a number of voices, and dogs barking behind them.

This was enough to confirm their fears. They put spurs to their horses; each one making for his family. As they proceeded, they cried out to the citizens to fly, and said the Indians were coming, murdering all before them, for they had heard them killing a family behind them; and that they had heard the shrieks of the dying. In this horrid rout that took place at this time, there was a family that lived near the river before mentioned; they had no horses, but a large family of small children; the father and mother each took a child; the rest were directed to follow on foot as fast as possible. The eldest daughter also carried one of the children that was not able to keep up. They fled to the river where they had to cross.

The father had to carry over all the children, at different times, as the stream was high, and so rapid the mother and daughter could not stem the current with such a burden. When they all, as they thought, had got over, they started, when the cry of poor little Susan was heard on the opposite bank, asking if they were not going to take her with them. The frightened father again prepared to plunge into the strong current for his child, when the mother, seeing it, cried out, "never mind Susan; we have succeeded in getting ten over, which is more than we expected at first and we can better spare Susan than you, my dear." So poor Susan, who was only about four years old was left to the mercy of the frightful savage.

But poor little Susan came off unhurt; one of the neighbours who was out a hunting, came along and took charge of little Susan, the eleventh, who had been so miserably treated by her mother.

When I commenced telling of these two anecdotes, I observed that the mind of man, when there was cause of fear or suspicion of danger, was frequently apt to suffer his imaginations to lead them him astray, which was the case at this time, as it was before with the good old cheese-maker. Now this last fright was occasioned by a parcel of boys who had assembled together to go squirrel hunting; for the squirrels at that season of the year were very bad at pulling up corn: it appears that they were very plenty, and several of them shot at or near the same time, and one of the boys wounding one, brought it to the ground, and the boys gave it chase. It was this, also which caused poor little Susan to weep and be forsaken by father and mother.

******

Note:—Adam Wilson Snyder was born in Connellsville, Fayette County, Pennsylvania, on the sixth day of October, 1799. In early life he learned the trade of wool carding, which he followed in Pennsylvania up to the day of his departure for the west.

He left Pennsylvania for the purpose of joining relatives in Indiana, but tiring of his long journey, which was made afoot, he tarried at a crossroads store in Knox County, Ohio, to engage with its solitary owner as clerk. There he remained until persuaded to remove to Illinois by Jesse Burgess Thomas, later United States Senator, for the purpose of undertaking the management of a woollen mill which had been erected by the latter a short while before. Once more turning his face westward, he arrived at Cahokia in June of the year 1817, footsore and weary. Under Judge Thomas, Snyder, who had steadfastly aspired to a professional career so soon as the moment became auspicious, began the study of law, and was admitted to practice in the year 1820, though he had not attained his majority.

In 1823 he was elected by the legislature to fill the office of District Attorney.

In 1830 and in 1832 he was elected state senator, and in 1836 he was elected Representative in Congress, defeating John Reynolds. This was regarded at the time as the greatest achievement in Illinois politics. Again, in 1840, he was elected state senator and a presidential elector.

On December 11, 1841, he was nominated for the office of governor by the Democratic convention, to which office he would have been elected beyond doubt, but his death occurred on May 14, 1842, from pulmonary consumption. Thomas Ford, who was appointed to assume his candidacy on the ticket, was elected.

Major John Dement. Few men, indeed, have been allowed the privilege of participating actively and influentially in the councils of their party and in the affairs of their state for a period of more than fifty years; yet such is the record of the commander of the Spy Battalion who met Black Hawk in person at Kellogg's Grove, and for the first time convinced the wily Sac that the whites could fight well. It is the fact, that from the time Major Dement stopped Black Hawk at Kellogg's Grove, that Indian was kept upon a constant retreat until his band was driven into the Mississippi River at the mouth of the Bad Axe. And for the commander's bravery, Black Hawk paid him the handsomest compliment to be found in the biography which the latter subsequently published.

John Dement was born at Gallatin, Sumner County, Tennessee, in April, 1804, where he lived until the family moved to Town Mound in Franklin County, Illinois, in 1817. In 1826 he was elected sheriff of Franklin County. In 1827 he served in the expedition sent from Illinois to assist in the Winnebago War. The same year he represented Franklin County in the General Assembly, as he did in the succeeding session of 1830.

In the first campaign against Black Hawk, in 1831, he was made aid to Governor Reynolds. During the same year, in the face of keen opposition, he was elected state treasurer, which office he continued to hold until 1836, when he resigned it at the solicitation of the friends of Vandalia, to enter the General Assembly and lead the fight against moving the capital to Springfield.

It is worthy of note that when his son, Hon. Henry D. Dement, became Secretary of State many years after, he found some of the reports of his father as state treasurer. They were written upon foolscap paper, and showed that $40,000 was collected for each of two years; but as the money then in circulation was worth but 25 cents on the dollar, the income of the State in reality was but $10,000 *per annum*.

Appointed Receiver of the Galena Land Office in 1837, he removed to Galena and remained there until the land office was moved to Dixon, in 1840, to which place he moved and remained till his death. In 1841, for political reasons, he was removed by President Harrison, but upon coming into office, President Polk reappointed him in 1845. He held the office again for four years, or until 1849, when a change of administration retired him for another four years. Again, in 1853, President Pierce reappointed him, and he held the office until it was abolished.

In 1834, while state treasurer, he was married to Miss Louise Dodge, daughter of the then General Henry Dodge, afterward Governor, Representative, and United States Senator in Congress from Wisconsin.

In 1844 he was made Presidential Elector for James K. Polk.

Major Dement was made a member of every Constitutional Convention held in Illinois up to the date of his death, with the exception of the first one, held in 1818, which of course met before he had reached his majority, and this too in the face of the fact that in 1862 and in 1870 his party at home was in a hopeless minority. Of those two conventions he was made the temporary presiding officer. In the last in stance the honour was unusual, for the reason that his party was in the minority.

On January 16, 1883, he died at his home in Dixon.

While at Vandalia, as state treasurer, Stephen A. Douglas made his appearance as a candidate for the office of district attorney, his first political aspiration. Almost destitute of friends and entirely destitute of money, Major Dement divided his room with young Douglas, and assisted him to what might now be denominated a meal-ticket. Better than either, he introduced the aspiring candidate to powerful friends, and before Douglas was ready to return home Dement had secured for him the desired appointment.

The late General Usher F. Linder has told a story wherein he credits Major Dement with saving both the life and honour of the former:

> General Linder had offended a desperate member of the state senate, for which a challenge very promptly followed through General James Turney, the senator's second. As Linder's second, Major Dement accepted, and replied that 'the fight must be with pistols at close quarters, each man holding a corner of the same handkerchief in his teeth.' General Turney was thunderstruck, and expostulated but to no purpose, that such a condition meant the deliberate murder of both. 'It don't matter,' answered Dement, 'your principal is cool, desperate, and deliberate, while my friend is nervous and excitable, and if he has to lose his life, your friend must bear him company.' The duel was called off without a moment's delay.

While receiver, Major Dement engaged in the business of smelting quite extensively, and during the latter years of his life, he was an extensive manufacturer of ploughs and flax bagging. At the time of his death, he was one of the largest landowners in the State.

Chapter 6

We Defeat the Enemy

Generals Henry and Dodge had by this time, come to the conclusion to go back around the head of Fox River, to see if they could not fall in with Black Hawk, and stop his passage to the north; as they supposed he was intending to make his way to the Chippeway nation.

General Alexander concluded that it was best to obey General Atkinson's order. He accordingly returned the same way we came, to join General Atkinson; taking with him twelve days' provision. We drew the same number of days' rations.

★★★★★★

Had Henry concluded to obey Atkinson's orders literally, by returning direct to Koshkonong as soon as the provisions had been drawn, the campaign would have ended in disgrace just as the others had ended. On receipt of news purporting to locate Black Hawk's forces, he called a council of war, at which Alexander declined to disobey orders. While Dodge was in favour of immediate pursuit, he maintained that his forces were so crippled and decimated that the plan was impossible so far as his command was concerned. Thereupon Henry declared he would pursue the enemy if he had to move alone.

At this juncture, the usual pusillanimity of the volunteers was displayed in the form of a remonstrance headed by Lieutenant Colonel Jeremiah Smith and other petty officers, in which they refused to obey their general. Henry ordered them under arrest and appointed Colonel Collins's regiment an escort to march the offenders back to Atkinson's headquarters, where, as he then told them, he had no doubt that every man would be shot. Such firmness was so unexpected, that the recalcitrants recoiled and in a body called upon Henry with an apology, protesting that ignorance alone was the cause. Henry as promptly forgave them. To their credit, be it said, they were among the very best fighters thereafter. The company of Captain James Craig arrived opportunely with its fresh horses and men, from Jo Daviess County, to join Dodge's squadron, which so strengthened the latter that he at once reported to Henry for duty.

Had Henry been given supreme command in the first instance, untrammelled by suggestions or orders from Reynolds, the Black Hawk War had ended at Old Man's Creek. In fact, it may be said that had it been possible to send Henry for Black Hawk when the latter was at the Prophet's village, defying Atkinson with messages that his heart was bad and that he would not return, the poor deluded old fellow would have returned with an impression left upon his mind that he had no further business east of the Mississippi River.

★★★★★★

July 15th. We took up the line of march on this day, with General Henry at our head, with the intention to try and see if we could not hunt out Black Hawk. But on account of our horses taking the fright on the night of the 12th, our brigade was very much weakened. The next morning after we started, the morning report was made out: General Henry had six hundred effective men; and Colonel Dodge's corps was reduced to one hundred and fifty, or nearly so; but their weakness did not discourage these true men, nor any of their officers.

We had now the brave General Henry at our head, and our intention was to find the enemy, if they were to be found in this region of the country. We now went with more speed than we had done before; the men appeared to have imbibed new spirit. They had a prospect of falling in with the enemy, and they well knew, that, if we went back to General Atkinson by the way we came to fort Winnebago, there would be but a very slight chance of ever seeing an Indian; for they now had been watching him some time; and being intimately acquainted with the situation of the country, they could dodge from swamp to swamp, and bid him defiance. We now thought that while they were watching General Atkinson, we could steal upon old Black Hawk, and take him by surprise.

We had Poquet, the half-breed, whom I have mentioned before, and twelve Winnebago Indians with us as pilots, and progressed with considerable speed. Nothing of importance occurred on our march from the 15th to the 18th. We this day came to a small Winnebago village, on Rock River; having reached that river once more, though some distance above General Atkinson.

Generals Henry and Dodge, (Wakefield inadvertently writes of Dodge as "General" in many places, which is an error, he was in 1832, a Colonel of volunteers for the Territory of Michigan, of which Wisconsin was then a part, and not a General until later years), here called a halt, and had a talk with this nation of the forest—for forest it really was. It might have been supposed, from the appearance of the place they were in, that they had tried to hide from all the world, as their bark *wigwams* were in the midst of a very large growth of timber, in a bend of the river, and the earth was covered with an almost impenetrable undergrowth.

General Dodge who was well acquainted with the Winnebagoes, attended strictly to the examination. They were asked where Black Hawk and his band were— They replied that they were above, on Rock River, at a place called the Cranberry Lake, about half a day's travel from where we then were. Generals Henry and Dodge consulted with the officers generally, in relation to the course most proper to pursue. They came to the conclusion to send an express to General Atkinson, informing him that they had learned where Black Hawk was, and that they would march against him on the next day. We were then, from the best information we could obtain from the Indians, about thirty-five miles above General Atkinson where he was still engaged in building a fort, at Lake Koshkonong.

It may not be considered a digression to state, here, the reasons we had for believing that the Winnebagoes were telling us the truth; for we had been a long time very suspicious that they were secret allies of Black Hawk, as we caught them in many lies. There was one fellow, who, on examination, stated that he had come from Black Hawk only two days before. He was then asked what he had been up there after. He replied that he had two sisters married to Sac men, and that each of his sisters had six daughters, who were also married to Sac men, and that he had been up to see them. This was a very reasonable story, and we thought that it might be true. But, at the same time, it went to show that they were to some extent, allies of the Sacs, as they were intermarried so much with each other.

Generals Henry and Dodge now made application for a pilot to go with two of our men to General Atkinson, to inform him where the Indians were, and that we were going in pursuit of them the next day. After some Indian chat among themselves, they reluctantly consented that Little Thunder should go. The next thing was, to get two of our men, possessed of sufficient courage and perseverance to go. Doctor E. H. Merryman, adjutant of Colonel Collins's regiment, and Mr. W. W. Woodbridge, adjutant of General Dodge's squadron, were the men who volunteered to perform this important and hazardous service. They started about 2 o'clock p. m., in company with Little Thunder as their pilot, intending to reach General Atkinson's camp that night; but they had not proceeded more than eight miles before they came upon a large fresh trail, which they soon learnt, by its appearance, and the signs and gestures of Little Thunder, their pilot, was that of Black Hawk and his whole army making their escape.—They pursued their course a little further, intending to go on with the message; but this Indian petitioned them to go back, intimating by signs that they would soon be killed if they went on.

The expresses could not speak his language, nor could he speak theirs; but they made signs for him to proceed with them, but they did not succeed in getting him more than two miles further, when he suddenly wheeled his horse to the right-about, and giving him timber, left them. It was now nearly night, and the country they were in impassable to a stranger; the ground being covered with prickly ash and white thorn; and in the midst of these thickets were the worst kind of swamps. They were therefore compelled to return to their camp. It was some time before they overtook their pilot, and after dark when they got back. On entering the encampment the sentinels fired at one of them, and came very near killing him. They now told the joyful news, that they had discovered the trail of Black Hawk and his band making out of the swamps, which seemed to give new life to every heart; as now there appeared to be a prospect of bringing our toils and troubles to a speedy issue.

Orders were accordingly given for all hands to be ready for an early march next morning in pursuit of the enemy. At the dawn of day the bugle sounded. All now were up, making ready with great eagerness for a march. Here we had to leave every thing that was calculated to retard our march. Five baggage waggons, sutlers' stores and a number of other valuable articles were left, in order that we should have nothing to impede us on our march.

July 19th. This day we had, for about twelve miles, the worst kind of road. To look at it, it appeared impossible to march an army through it. Thickets and swamps of the worst kind we had to go through; but the men had something now to stimulate them. They saw the Sac trail fresh before them, and a prospect of bringing our campaign to an end. There was no murmuring, no excuses made; none getting on the sick report. If we came to a swamp that our horses were not able to carry us through, we dismounted, turned our horses before us, and stepped in ourselves, sometimes up to our armpits in mud and water. In this way we marched with great celerity. In the evening of this day, it commenced thundering, lightening, and raining tremendously. We stopped not, but pushed on.

The trail appeared to be still getting fresher, and the ground better; which still encouraged us to overcome every difficulty found in the way. It continued raining until dark, and indeed until after dark. We now saw the want of our tents in the morning; a great number of us having left this necessary article behind, in order to favour our horses. The rain ceased before day, and it turned cold and chilly. In the morning we arose early, at the well known sound of the bugle, and prepared in a very short time our rude breakfast, dried our clothes a little, and by seven o'clock were on the march at a quick pace.

On this day some of our scouts took an Indian as a prisoner. On examination he was found to be a Winnebago. He stated that Black Hawk was but a little distance ahead of us, and that he had seen some of his party not more than two miles ahead. But it was a bad piece of conduct on our part, that this Indian was not kept as a prisoner of war, but was set at liberty, and let go: no doubt, he that night informed the Sacs of our pursuit.

We halted, and the order of battle was formed, as we expected we would overtake them this evening. The order was as follows: General Dodge and Major Ewing were to bring on the battle. Major Ewing was placed in the centre, with his spy battalion; Captain Gentry and Captain Clark's companies on our right; and Captain Camp and Captain Parkinson on our left. (The companies of Gentry, Clark, Camp, and Parkinson were Michigan companies belonging to Dodge's squadron.) Our own battalion (Major Ewing's) was reduced to two companies, (as Captain Webb and his company had been left at Fort Dixon;) Captain Lindsey, of our battalion, was placed on the right, and Captain Huston's company on the left; Colonel Fry and his regiment on the right; and Colonel Jones with his regiment on the left; and Colonel Collins in the centre. In this order we marched in quick time, with all possible speed, in hope that we would overtake the enemy on that evening. We were close to the Four Lakes, and we wished to come up with them before they could reach that place, as it was known to be a strong hold for the Indians; but the day was not long enough to accomplish this desirable object.

We reached the first of the Four Lakes about sundown. General Henry here called a halt, and consulted with Poquet, our pilot, as to the country we were approaching. Poquet, who was well acquainted with this country, told him he could not get through it after night; that we had to march close to the margin of the lake for some distance, as the underwood stood so thick, one man could not see another ten steps. General Henry concluded to encamp here until the break of day. General Dodge sent Captain Dixon (Joseph Dickson) on ahead with a few men, to see if they could make any discovery of the enemy, who returned in a very short time, and stated they had seen the enemy's rear guard about one mile and a half distant.

General Henry gave strict orders for every man to tie up his horse, so as to be ready to start as soon as it was daylight. The order was strictly obeyed, and after we took our frugal supper, all retired to rest, except those who had to mount guard; for we had marched a great way that day, and many were still wet by the rain that fell the preceding night; but being very much fatigued we were all soon lost in sleep, except those on guard.

July 21st. At the break of day the bugle sounded, and all were soon up, and in a few minutes had breakfast ready; and after taking a little food, we mounted our horses, and again commenced the pursuit.

We soon found that the pilot had told us no lie; for we found the country that the enemy was leading us into, to be worse if possible, than what he told us. We could turn neither to the right nor left, but were compelled to follow the trail the Indians had made; and that too, for a great distance at the edge of the water of the lake.

Here it may not be uninteresting to the reader, to give a small outline of those lakes. From a description of the country, a person would very naturally suppose that those lakes were as little pleasing to the eye of the traveller, as the country is. But not so. I think they are the most beautiful bodies of water I ever saw. The first one that we came to, was about ten miles in circumference, and the water as clear as crystal. The earth sloped back in a gradual rise; the bottom of the lake appeared to be entirely covered with white pebbles, and no appearance of its being the least swampy. The second one that we came to, appeared to be much larger. It must have been twenty miles in circumference. The ground rose very high all around;—and the heaviest kind of timber grew close to the water's edge.

If those lakes were anywhere else, except in the country they are, they would be considered among the wonders of the world. But the country they are situated in is not fit for any civilized nation of people to inhabit. It appears that the Almighty intended it for the children of the forest. The other two lakes we did not get close enough to for me to give a complete description of them; but those who saw them, stated that they were very much like the other. I am digressing and leaving my subject too long; so I will go back and pursue our march.

We had not marched more than five miles, before Doctor Philleo came back, meeting us, with the scalp of an Indian. (Philleo did not kill the Indian at all, though he scalped him. Many other complaints could be lodged against the man's pretensions.) He had been on ahead with the front scouts, and came on this Indian, who had been left as a rear guard to watch our movements. There were several shots fired at him about the same time, and I suppose all hit him, from the number of bullet holes that were in him; but Doctor Philleo scalped him; so he was called Philleo's Indian; which reminds me of the hunters: He who draws the first blood is entitled to the skin, and the remainder to the carcase, if there are several in the chase; which was the case at this time.

But I am not done with Doctor Philleo yet. I will show you that he is a good soldier, and something of an Indian fighter. The signs now began to get very fresh, and we mended our pace very much. We had not proceeded more than ten or fifteen miles further, before our fighting Doctor run afoul of two more Indians; he showed his bravery in assisting to kill them. I suppose he killed one, and Mr. Sample Journey the other; so there was a scalp for each. But one of those miserable wretches sold his life as dear as possible. He, in the act of falling after he was shot, fired, and shot three balls into a gentleman who was himself in the act of shooting at him. The balls were all small; one went through his thigh, one through his leg, and the other through his foot. I am sorry that I have for gotten the gentleman's name; he belonged to General Dodge's squadron.

We now doubled our speed, all were anxious to press forward, and as our horses were nearly worn out, we carried nothing, only what was actually necessary for us to eat; camp kettles, and many such articles, were thrown away.

The trail was now literally, in many places, strewed with Indian trinkets, such as mats, kettles, &c.; which plainly told us that they knew we were in pursuit. We too, saw from the face of the country that we were drawing close to the Wisconsin River, (Prairie du Sac, opposite which the battle was fought), and our object was to overtake them before they reached it; so we now went as fast as our horses were able to carry us;—but this was too severe for our poor horses; they began to give out; but even this did not stop a man. When ever a horse gave out, the rider would dismount, throw off his saddle and bridle, and pursue on foot, in a run, without a murmur. I think the number of horses left this day, was about forty.

The rear guard of the enemy began by this time (about three o'clock p. m.) to make feint stands; and as the timber stood thick, we did not know but that the whole army of Black Hawk was forming for action; in consequence of which, we got down and formed as often as twice, before we found out that their object was to keep us back until they could gain some strong position to fight from. Our front scouts now were determined not to be deceived any more; but the next they came to, they stopped not for their feigned manoeuvre, but pursued them to the main body of the enemy. They returned to us in great haste, and informed General Henry that the Indians were forming for action.

We all dismounted in an instant. The line of battle was then formed in the same order that it had been laid off the preceding day: General Dodge's corps and Major Ewing's spy battalion still in front. The horses were left, and every fourth man detailed to hold them; which gave seven horses to each man to hold.

We had scarcely time to form on foot, before the Indians raised the war-whoop, screaming and yelling hideously, and rushed forward, meeting us with a heavy charge. General Dodge and Major Ewing met them also with a charge, which produced a halt on the part of the enemy. Our men then opened a tremendous volley of musquetry upon them, and accompanied it with the most terrific yells that ever came from the head of mortals, except from the savages themselves. They could not stand this. They now tried their well-known practice of flanking: but here they were headed again by the brave Colonel Jones and his regiment who were on our left, where he met them in the most fear less manner, and opened a heavy fire upon them. Colonel Fry was placed on the extreme right. They tried his line, but were soon repulsed. Their strong position was on the left, or near the centre, where Colonels Jones, Dodge, and Ewing, kept up a constant fire upon them for something like half an hour.

The enemy here had a strong position. They had taken shelter in some very high grass, where they could lie down and load, and be entirely out of sight. After fighting them in this position for at least thirty minutes, during which time Colonel Jones had his horse shot from under him, and one of his men killed and several wounded. (Private Thomas J. Short of Captain Briggs's company killed, 8 men wounded in the engagement.) Colonels Dodge, Ewing and Jones, all requested General Henry to let them charge upon them at the point of the bayonet, which General Henry readily assented to, and gave the order, "charge!" which was obeyed by both men and officers in a most fearless manner. All were intent upon the charge. We had to charge up a rising piece of ground. When we got on the top, we then fired perfectly abreast. They could not stand this. They had to quit their hiding place, and made good their retreat. When they commenced retreating, we killed a great number.

Their commander, who, it was said, was Na-pope, was on a white pony on the top of a mountain in the rear of his Indians; who certainly had one of the best voices for command I ever heard. He kept up a constant yell, until his men began to retreat; when he was heard no more. Colonel Collins was kept during this engagement, in the rear, as a reserve, and to keep the enemy from flanking, and coming in upon us in the rear, which was a very good arrangement of General Henry.

It was now nearly sun down, and still raining as it had been all the evening; but so slow that we made shift to keep our guns dry. The enemy retreated toward the river with considerable speed. The ground they were retreating to, appeared to be low and swampy; and on the bank of the river there appeared to be a heavy body of timber, which the enemy could reach before we could bring them to another stand. So General Henry concluded not to pursue them any further that night, but remain on the battle ground until next morning; and then he would not be in danger of losing so many of his men; knowing that, in the dark, he would have to lose a number; for the Indians would have the timber to fight from, while we would have to stand in the open prairie.

Next morning, (July 22nd,) the troops were paraded, and put in battle order on foot, except Colonel Fry's regiment, and took up the line of march to the river; leaving Colonel Collins's regiment to guard the horses and baggage, and take care of the wounded.

We marched down to the river, which was about one mile and a half off; but before we reached the bank, we had a very bad swamp to go through, fifty or sixty yards on this side of the timber, which stood very high on the bank of the river. We now saw that General Henry had acted very prudently. If he had attempted to follow them the evening before, he would have lost a great many of his men.

When we got to the bank, we found they had made their retreat across the river during the night, leaving a great many articles of their trumpery behind. We also saw a good deal of blood, where their wounded had bled. We now returned to the camp; seeing there was no chance to follow them this day across the river.

We in this battle were very fortunate indeed. We had only one man killed and eight wounded; and we have learned since the battle, that we killed sixty-eight of the enemy, and wounded a considerable number; twenty-five of whom, they report, died soon after the battle.

We now were nearly out of provision, and to take up the line of march against them, in the condition our horses were in, told us plainly that we would suffer for something to eat before we could get it.

We buried the brave young man who was killed, with the honours of war. It was stated that he had just shot down an Indian, when he received the mortal wound himself. His name was John Short, and belonged to Captain Briggs's company from Randolph County. He had a brother and a brother-in-law in the same company, who witnessed his consignment to his mother earth. The wounded were all well examined, and none pronounced mortal.

We continued this day on the battle ground, and prepared litters for the wounded to be carried on. We spent this day in a more cheerful manner than we had done any other day since we had been on the campaign. We felt a little satisfaction for our toils, and thought that we had no doubt destroyed a number of the very same monsters that had so lately been imbruing their hands with the blood of our fair sex—the helpless mother and unoffending infant.

We dried our clothes which then had been wet for several days. This day was spent in social chat between men and officers. There were no complaints made; all had fought bravely; each man praised his officers, and all praised our general.

Late in the evening, some of our men, who had been out to see if there were any signs of the enemy still remaining near us, returned, and stated that they saw smoke across the river.

General Henry had been of the opinion through the day, that if the Indians did ever intend fighting any more, they would attack us that night, and this report went to confirm him in his belief more fully.

That night he had a larger guard than usual. He made use of another excellent precaution. He had fires made in advance of our lines, at least forty yards, and had them kept burning all night. Orders were given for every man to sleep upon his arms: so that he could be ready for action at the shortest notice, should an alarm be given. We had scarcely got to sleep, when we were alarmed by the running of our horses; we had to parade, as usual, to keep them from killing us. Men and officers now fully expected that it was the enemy who frightened them. Orders were now given, for no man to sleep that night, but for every man to stand to his arms, and be ready to receive the enemy. We all now expected to have hard fighting, and were prepared for the worst. There was not a man who shrunk from his duty. All punctually obeyed the orders of his officers, and made every preparation to receive the enemy, should he come.

About one hour and a half before day, on the same mountain from which the Indian chief had given his orders on the evening of the battle, we heard an Indian voice, in loud shrill tones, as though he was talking to his men, and giving them orders.

General Henry had his men all paraded in order of battle, in front of the tents, and the fires roused up. After all were paraded, General Henry addressed his men in the most beautiful manner I ever heard man speak on such an occasion. I am sorry I cannot give the precise words, but I will attempt an outline of them. The Indian was still yelling in the most loud and terrific manner. General Henry commenced:

> My brave soldiers, now is the critical and trying moment; hear your enemy on the same mountain from which you drove them only on the evening before last, giving orders for a charge upon you: there is no doubt but that they have mustered all their strength at this time: now let every mother's son be at his post:—Yes, my brave soldiers, you have stemmed the torrent of every opposition—you have stopped not for rivers, swamps, and, one might say almost impenetrable forests; suffered through the beating storm of night, amidst the sharpest peals of thunder, and when the heavens appeared a plane of lightning. My brave boys, hear their yells; let them not daunt you; remember the glory you won on the evening before last; be not now the tarnishers of this reputation, that you are so justly entitled to: remember that you are fighting a set of demons, who have lately been taking the lives of your helpless and unoffending neighbours.

Stand firm my brave Suckers, (a familiar name the Illinoisans are known by), until you can see the whites of their eyes, before you discharge your muskets, and then meet them with a charge as you have before done, and that too with great success.

The Indian all this time was talking as though he was addressing his men, and appeared to approach nearer. Every officer then on the ground, was at his post, and had his particular station assigned to him, and the ground he was to occupy during the action. In this order we stood until daylight. Just before day the Indian quit talking. When it was just light enough to discover a man a short distance, the brave and fearless Ewing took his battalion of spies, and mounted on horseback, we were soon at the top of the mountain to see who it was that had serenaded us so long, at that late hour of the night. We found only the sign of a few horse tracks, that appeared as though they had been made that night. We marched in quick time around every part of the mountain, and found no one. We took a circuitous route back to camp, but found no one on the way. What it was that made this Indian act so, was now a mystery that no one could solve. But before the reader gets through the history of this war, he will find out the cause. I cannot inform him now, as it does not come in its proper place.

It will be recollected that Doctor Merryman and Adjutant Woodbridge, were both started as express bearers by Generals Henry and Dodge, as soon as the Winnebagoes informed them that the Indians were at the Cranberry Lake; and had to return on account of Little Thunder (who was their pilot,) getting frightened. The day after that, late in the evening, they started again still in company with the same pilot. They now left the Sac trail, and this child of the forest was less afraid; so, knowing the country well, he took them on that night, amidst the storm, to General Atkinson's camp, or Fort Koshkonong, where General Atkinson was, with his infantry, and those of our volunteers, who had lost their horses at Fort Winnebago.

The next day Adjutants Woodbridge and Merryman, still with the same pilot, started back to General Henry, with an express from General Atkinson. They got to General Henry during the action, (July 21st,) but there was no time then for reading expresses; nor did those two men think of delivering expresses at that time; but immediately went to fighting. So those gentlemen performed a double duty, and deserve well of their country for the important services they rendered.

Now for the expresses. General Atkinson directed General Henry to pursue on the trail of Black Hawk until he could overtake him and to defeat or capture him, also stating, that he would start himself, with the infantry and General Alexander's Brigade; and that the rest of the volunteers who were with him under Lieutenant Colonel (P. H.) Sharp, would be left to guard the fort; and that they would go by way of the Blue Mounds; and directed us, if we got out of provision, to go to that place for a supply.

Chapter 7

General Engagement

We were now out of provisions, and were obliged to abandon further pursuit, and go to the Blue Mounds to procure a supply. Accordingly on the we got in motion again; not in pursuit of the enemy, but for bread and meat, to satisfy our appetites—as we were now out of every thing to eat.

Our wounded this day suffered very much on account of having rough ground to pass over, and some very muddy creeks. When they got to the Blue Mounds, they were very hospitably treated. There was a small fort and citizens plenty, who did not think it the least hardship to wait on those who had been shedding their blood to revenge the wrongs those people had suffered. For the Indians had killed three valuable men within one mile of this place; and one within view of the citizens who were in it,—a gentleman by the name of Green, of high standing in society, and who had recently emigrated from the east. I have forgotten the names of the other gentlemen, but can say that the citizens spoke in high terms of their worth, and seemed to lament their loss. (Emerson Green and George Force.)

We here found a part of General Posey's brigade, who had been sent from Fort Hamilton, to assist in guarding this frontier place. An express had been sent by General Atkinson to General Posey, to march as soon as possible to a small town on the Wisconsin River, to intercept the Indians, should any of them go down the river. So, in the afternoon, General Posey, from Fort Hamilton, passed on his way to Helena; and late in the evening General Atkinson and General Alexander arrived with their brigades; leaving Colonel Sharp, with those who had lost their horses, still at Fort Koshkonong; also Captain Low (Gideon Lowe), with one company of regulars.

We here drew three days' provision, and on the twenty-fifth we took up the line of march for Helena, on the Wisconsin River, where we intended to cross, again to take up the pursuit against the enemy. Accordingly we got to this place on the 26th, where we found General Posey with his brigade, busily employed in making rafts to cross on. This once bid fair to be a prosperous place; there were some tolerable good pine buildings that had been put up; the logs had been hewed, and of course were very light. So this deserted village was pulled down, and converted into rafts for the army to cross the river on. The river at this place is nearly as wide as the Mississippi; but not near so deep. There is a great number of islands and sand bars in it, which will always prevent it from being good for steam boat navigation.

We now once more had all the generals together, but not all the men; there had been a great falling off in all the brigades.

General Posey who commanded the first brigade, had but about two hundred men; a great number having lost their horses, and some being on the sick report. Colonel Ewing's regiment had been sent down to Dixon's, which weakened it very much.

The second brigade was nearly in the same condition; a great many being on foot, and some on the sick report. There were but about three hundred and fifty in this brigade.

General Henry's brigade was very much reduced, also. So the whole three brigades were not stronger than one of them was at first setting out in the campaign. There was now more dissatisfaction prevailing than I observed during the whole campaign. The general cry with all, appeared to be, that we would never again see an Indian—that they had been gone so long ahead of us, we would never be able to overtake them; and the men generally had become tired of hunting trails; and now we had to hunt this trail up again. So, there was nothing to stimulate the men, because all were of the opinion that the Indians were then near the Mississippi; as the distance was said not to be more than eighty miles; and as no one of us had ever been across, we had no idea of what kind of country we would have to pass through.

The army commenced crossing this stream on the 27th, and by twelve o'clock on the 28th, we were over, and ready to take up the line of march.

Two of our men at this place, whilst fishing, found a dead Indian, which no doubt had been killed at our battle on the Wisconsin; as I have no doubt the Indians threw many of their dead into the river during the night after the battle; and many that were wounded and died on that night; in order to keep us from scalping them; as those superstitious beings think it the greatest disgrace for one of their nation to lose his scalp.

Colonel William B. Archer had, on our arrival at this place, taken about twenty men, and gone up the river to our battle ground, to ascertain if they could discover any fresh signs of the Indians returning, or what direction they had gone from that place. They found no new sign of their crossing back. The remains of Mr. Short, who was killed in the battle, had not been interrupted, (*sic*.) which plainly showed, that they had not been back since we had left there; for if they had they would have dug up the corpse for the purpose of taking his scalp off; as they prize a scalp above any thing else in their warfare; and one that is so fortunate as to get a scalp, feels as proud as if he had killed a white man and lost the scalp.

Colonel Archer spent one day in searching for the main trail, but was not able to get upon it. The friendly Indians, who were sent with him as pilots, as usual, seemed to act cowardly. So he returned to the main army, and was ready to take up the line of march with us.

July 28th. We this day, at 12 o'clock, again got in motion, with General Atkinson at our head.

The brigades of Posey, Alexander and Henry, were all now together; and about four hundred and fifty regulars under the command of General Brady. The regular field officers were Colonel Taylor, Major W. Riley, (should be Bennet Riley, Morgan was Colonel Willoughby Morgan, Brady was General Hugh Brady), Major Morgan, and the others not recollected, Captain Johnson, and Thomas C. Brown, (volunteer aids,) *aides-de-camp* of General Atkinson; and Lieutenant Anderson, (General Robert Anderson of Fort Sumter fame), Brigade Major. The author is sorry that he cannot give the names of the other regular officers, as they were all deserving well of their country.

We had not this day marched more than five miles, before we came upon the main Indian trail. We had started up the river in order to get on it, opposite to where we had the battle, or near that place; as we were of opinion they would make up the river, rather than down. But here we were greatly disappointed. We got upon the trail much sooner than we expected, and found that we could follow it without any difficulty.

It appeared to be making down the river, too, which pleased us still better. We had understood that, north of us, the country was very mountainous, and almost impassable.

We followed the trail until a late hour this evening. Nothing of importance occurred this night. All now were once more satisfied, that we had again got on the trail, without having to hunt for it, as we heretofore had done. There was now a hope once more, of falling in with the enemy, all murmuring again ceased. The great object then was, with all, to push ahead, for fear the enemy—might cross the Mississippi before we could overtake them.

July 29th. We started this morning very early, and had proceeded but a short distance, before we came upon one of their encampments. We found that they were still killing their horses to eat. They here had killed the willing animal, that had carried them, no doubt for miles, and through many dangers. We now discovered that the enemy was about four days ahead of us, and were still flying from us with all speed.

July 30th. We this morning quickened our pace, and marched as fast as the nature of the case would admit of; but we soon found that the game that we were in chase of, had taken a track to the north; and our troubles, seemed to be returning on us. We discovered they were making up a bad swampy stream, apparently in order to find a crossing place. Before we succeeded in crossing this stream, we found ourselves going back, in the same direction we had come; but after we had crossed, we, not unlike a parcel of hounds after a fox, had to take another track to the south. We now found that we were leaving the Wisconsin River, and were getting into a miserable country. We had proceeded but a few miles, before we came to another stream, that appeared to be worse than any we had yet met with. We here had to make a retrograde movement, and go up a short distance, and make a bridge; which we soon did.

As soon as we crossed, we measured our course back to the trail, the general direction of which we now found, to be west by north west; but found that we were likely to get into a dreadful country. That, however mattered naught; we were on the trail of the enemy, and had, as we then thought, gone through the worst country in the known world. We had not the most distant thought that we would see another half as bad as that we had passed through. The idea that we would soon get into a more level, and better travelling country, encouraged us to push on, and surmount, for awhile, every difficulty that might come in our way.

We went on, that day, with considerable celerity, until about one o'clock, at which time some of our front scouts caught an Indian, who, upon examination, turned out to be a Winnebago. We here stopped and let our horses graze, while the Indian was undergoing an examination.

Captain Craig, (this is a mistake, Captain Craig joined Dodge at Fort Winnebago, as stated in chapter 1), from Galena, with a very respectable company from the county of Jo Daviess, came up and joined General Dodge's squadron, which added very much to the strength of it. The Indian that was taken here as a prisoner, said on examination, that the Indians had encamped close by there, and had been gone four days. He stated that they had a number of wounded that were laying on their horses, and that two of them died the night they staid here. We did not get much information from this son of the forest; nevertheless, we concluded to take him with us. He at first wanted to stay; but, after finding out that we would not injure him, and that there was a tolerable good chance to get plenty to eat, he went cheerfully.

There was another old fellow, taken as a prisoner, who was suffered to go away. He went to where the Winnebagoes had a small village. Three more of the children of these wild and dreary looking mountains came to us, after we had stopped to encamp. They came with a sort of white flag, which they carried on a stick. Mr. Chiler Armstrong, a gentleman belonging to General Dodge's corps, was the only one that could talk with them in their language. The Indians were examined respecting the country, but could not tell us any thing about it. They stated that they never knew of any person to cross these mountains but once; that was in the year 1827, when the Winnebagoes attacked Captain Lindsey's keel boats; the same Captain Lindsey who then commanded a company of spies belonging to Major Ewing's battalion; who, after their attack upon the keel boats, made their retreat across these mountains. We found the Sacs were keeping the same trail the Winnebagoes then made.

We had just entered those mountains; and as an all-wise Providence had so directed it, no one knew how bad they were; for if they had known the difficulty of crossing, and the distance across, them— and besides, that there was nothing for our horses to eat, but weeds— neither officers or men, would have undertaken to go through them.

But an all-wise Creator has ordained it, that man is not to know one day, that which he has to undergo on the next; for if he did, he would be a miserable, unhappy being; but as it is with man, he is kept in blindness as to his pilgrimage through life. But hope steps in, and tells him his path will be smoother by-and-by; so hope keeps the creature in good spirits, which causes him to pursue more diligently still thinking things will change for the better, and the rough path through life will become smooth, and then his toils will be over.

This was our situation at the time: no one knew, what a country we were now about to approach.

July 30th. We started early this morning, thinking that we would soon come to some good range for our horses, as we had encamped on the side of a mountain that was so barren, that it had no vegetation on it fit for a horse to eat. But to our extreme disappointment, we continued going from mountain to mountain; and in the place of getting better grazing, we found it getting worse. About twelve o'clock we were obliged to stop and refresh our horses, by letting them graze on weeds, and browse on such few things as they could get. The horses were not choice now, as to what they took hold of; they were extremely hungry, and soon filled their stomachs with whatever they could catch on the sides of the mountains; which were principally weeds, and a kind of a vine which grew close to the ground.

General Atkinson had succeeded in getting a waggon on thus far; but here it was found impossible to take it any further. The waggon contained his own private stores; but here all had to be left that could not be packed on horseback. A number of articles were packed on horses, that I never saw before: All medical stores, such as boxes and kegs were lashed on the packhorses, and carried over those almost impenetrable mountains.

We now saw ourselves enveloped in a mass of the tallest and steepest mountains we had ever seen, and no one to tell us how long it would be before we would get through them.

But the whole army was in good health, and in fine spirits. We were not like Bonaparte, when he crossed the Alps—we lost none of our men in heaps of snow, nor did any die with hunger.

General Atkinson had been famous from the commencement of the campaign, for providing plenty of provisions. We had our horses well packed with this necessary article. We also had a number of good beeves along; so we had no fear of starving.

On this day we began to find the trail strewed with the dead bodies of Indians, who had died with the wounds they had received in the battle near the Wisconsin River.

On the next day, which was July 31st, we were about the centre of those majestic mountains. It most certainly was a grand and majestic sight. They were very lofty, and generally covered with the largest kind of timber, with a thick undergrowth. This was truly a lonely and disheartening place. The *matin* song of the red bird, nightingale and sparrow were all that could be heard, and the only inhabitants of those grand and majestic looking mountains.

There are places, where we at once are at home with nature—where she seems to take us to her bosom, with all the fondness of a mother, although in a strange land. But not so here: There was nothing to entice the traveller to make a stop, except a view of the height and grandeur of those piles of earth, which do not seem to look as though they ever can be inhabited by any civilized people in the world.

There is not the smallest kind of bottom between those mountains. We generally found good water at the foot of them; but scarcely ever enough to have afforded ground for a small garden. So it appears that this country was formed by the great I-Am, for some purpose that the children of men have not yet found out.

It cannot be for those unhappy children of the forest, for they are disposed to reside where they can make their living by the chase. But here was no game for them to chase; no lakes or streams for them to paddle their canoes in, or fish to angle for. We were the first civilized people that ever had entered this tremendous pile of mountains. They are now found out, and I must leave them, for some person more able to describe further than I have done.

August 1st. We this day passed a number of dead Indians, who had died in consequence of wounds they had received at the battle near the Wisconsin River. There were five found, it is said, in going the distance of five miles.

About twelve o'clock this day, we came to a small river, which was called Kickapoo. We here found that the country was about to change. A short distance before we got to this stream, we came to a beautiful body of pine timber, which was tall and large. As soon as we crossed this stream, we found the mountains were covered with prairie grass. We here found the Indian trail was getting fresher. They had encamped at this creek.

We had now been three days in those mountains, and our horses had lived on weeds, except those that became debilitated and were left behind; for a great number had become so, and left to starve in this dreary waste.

We here for the first time in three days, had an opportunity of

BAD AXE BATTLE-GROUND

turning our horses out to graze. Accordingly we let them graze for about an hour, which they made good use of, and during which we took a cold check.—About one o'clock we started, at a faster gait than usual. We found from the face of the country, that we were not a great way from the Mississippi. The country was still hilly, but the hills of a small size, and almost barren; so we could get along with more speed. It gave the men new spirits. We now saw that our horses would not have to starve, as we had begun to think it probable that they would.

On this evening we came across the grave of an Indian chief, who was buried in the grandest style of Indian burials; painted, and otherwise decorated, as well as those wretched beings were able to do. He was placed on the ground, with his head resting against the root of a tree, logs were placed around him, and covered over with bark; and on top of which green bushes were laid; so intended, that we might pass by without discovering the grave. He was examined, and found to have been shot.

It was now late in the evening, and we had proceeded but a short distance from here, before some of our front spies, came across an Indian that had been left behind from some cause or other. The spies interrogated him about Black Hawk and his band. He stated that they would get to the river on that day, and would cross over on the next morning. The old sinner then plead for quarters; but that being no time to be plagued with the charge of prisoners, they had to leave the unhappy wretch behind, which appeared to be a hard case. But, no doubt, he had been at the massacre of a number of our own citizens, and deserved to die for the crimes which he had perpetrated, in taking the lives of harmless and unoffending women and children.

We this day made a tolerable push, having marched until eight o'clock at night before we stopped. We then halted, and formed our encampment: But it was for a short time only.

General Atkinson gave orders for all to confine their horses, and be ready to march by two o'clock in pursuit of the enemy.

We were now all tired and hungry: and something to eat was indispensably necessary. We had a long way to go after water, and the worst kind of a precipice to go down and up to procure it. All was now a bustle for a while to prepare something to sustain nature, and to do it in time to get a little rest, before we would have to march. About nine o'clock, the noise began to die away, so that, by ten o'clock, all was lost in sleep, but the sentinel who was at his post.

At the appointed hour the bugle sounded: all were soon up, and made preparations for a march at quick step; moving on to complete the work of death upon those unfortunate children of the forest.

General Atkinson, this morning, had the army laid off and arranged in the following manner: General Dodge, with his squadron was placed in front—the infantry next—the second brigade next, under the command of General Alexander—the first brigade next, under the command of General Posey—the third brigade next, under the command of General Henry.

In this order the march commenced. We had not proceeded more than four or five miles, before there was a herald sent back, informing us that the front spies had come in sight of the enemy's rear guard. The intelligence was soon conveyed to General Atkinson, and then to all the commanders of the different brigades. The celerity of the march was then doubled, and it was but a short time before the firing of the front spies commenced, about half a mile in front of the main army. The Indians retreated toward the Mississippi, but kept up a retreating fire upon our front spies for some time, until General Dodge, who commanded, began to kill them very fast. The Indians then retreated more rapidly, and sought refuge in their main army, which was lying on the bank of the Mississippi, where they had joined in a body to defend themselves, and sell their lives as dear as possible; for they now found that they could not get away from us, and the only chance for them, was, to fight until they died.

General Henry had this morning been put in the rear, but he did not remain there long. Major Ewing who commanded the spy battalion, sent his adjutant back to General Henry, informing him that he was on the main trail. Major Ewing, at the same time, formed his men in order of battle, and awaited the arrival of the brigade, which marched up in quick time. When they came up, General Henry had his men formed as soon as possible for action; he placed Colonel Jones and Major Ewing in front. General Atkinson called for one regiment from General Henry's brigade, to cover his rear. General H. dispatched Colonel Fry with his regiment. Colonel Collins formed on the right of Colonel Jones and Major Ewing; when all were dismounted and marched on foot in the main trail, down the bluff into the bottom.

Here it is worthy of remark, that Colonel E. C. March, who was the volunteer *aide* to General Atkinson, displayed the part of a good and fearless soldier; likewise Major McConnel. They went ahead and searched out the main trail of the enemy. We here had to charge for some considerable distance, over the worst kind of ground; the logs, and weeds being in some places as high as a man's head. All this did not stop us; General Henry, with his Aids, Majors Johnson, (Albert Sidney Johnston), and McConnel, in front, and the brave Colonel March leading the van.

We pursued on, until Colonel Jones and Major Ewing commenced a fire on the main body of the enemy; at which time General Henry sent back an officer to bring up Colonel Fry with his regiment. Colonel Collins was by this time in the heat of the action with his regiment. Captain Gentry from General Dodge's corps, was by this time also up, and opened a heavy fire. He fell into the lines of Colonel Jones and Major Ewing. Captains Gruer, (should be Abner Greer), and (John F.) Richardson, from General Alexander's brigade, with their companies, and a few scattering gentle men from General Dodge's corps, were also up; who all joined General Henry, and fought bravely.

Colonel Fry obeyed the call of his general, and was soon there with his regiment, who shrank not from their duty. They all joined in the work of death—for death it was. We were by this time fast getting rid of those demons in human shape.

About half an hour after the battle commenced, Colonel Taylor with the infantry, and General Dodge with his squadron, got on the ground, and joined in the battle with us. They had been thrown on the extreme right, by following the rear guard of the enemy.

******

When our army appeared in sight Black Hawk deployed a band of about twenty Indians to meet Atkinson, engage his attention, and gradually draw that general away from camp. They did their work so well that Atkinson was deceived and placed his forces to attack an enemy which in reality was far below him. Major Ewing discovered the main trail, and reporting it to Henry, that officer (who had been assigned to guard the baggage in the rear) followed it with such vigour that the fight was won before Atkinson could participate.

******

Those men are both brave officers, and would have gloried in being in front of the battle; but it appears that this was intended by the God of battles for our much beloved Henry, who here displayed the part of a General indeed. He was placed in the rear in the morning, and was first in battle. This may appear strange to the reader, but it was nevertheless the truth.

General Atkinson stationed Generals Posey and Alexander, up the river, on the extreme right, in order to prevent the Indians from making their escape in that direction; which appeared to be one of those hard cases, for the men had marched a great way, through swamps, over mountains, and through the worst kind of forests;—had suffered much with fatigue—and many other hardships which a person necessarily has to undergo in a campaign: and that, too, they had done without a murmur, in order that they might have it in their power to assist in expelling from their country, those wretched children of the forest.

The battle lasted about three hours: when we came upon the enemy, they were fixing their bark canoes to cross the river. Some of them had crossed; others had just launched their canoes; and some had not got them made; but I suppose all were busy in making the necessary arrangements to cross and get out of our way.

But the Ruler of the Universe, He who takes vengeance on the guilty, did not design those guilty wretches to escape His vengeance for the horrid deeds they had done, which were of the most appalling nature. He here took just retribution for the many innocent lives those cruel savages had taken on our northern frontiers.

It can never be ascertained how many were killed in this battle; but from the best calculation that could be made, I suppose we killed about one hundred and fifty; and I think it altogether probable, that as many more were drowned in attempting to cross the river. The river where they attempted to cross, was full of islands. A number of them succeeded in reaching one of those islands, and had taken shelter behind old logs and willows, where they kept up a constant fire upon us during the engagement. Colonel Taylor, (Zachary Taylor, who was then a lieutenant colonel in the regular establishment), ordered an officer and a part of his infantry to cross over to the island, and rout the enemy from this position; but it being the nature of an Indian to sell his life as dear as possible, they did so here. They killed five of the regulars, before they could drive them from their strong hold that they had got into; and then, it had to be done by a charge, which those men were not afraid to do. (This attack upon the Willow Island caused almost the entire number of casualties sustained by the whites, and the names of the United States officers which Wakefield did not remember were, Taylor himself in command, Major John Bliss, Captain W. S. Harney, and Captain Henry Smith.)

I am sorry, that, I cannot recollect the name of the officer who commanded and took this band of regulars into this island.

There were a number of gentlemen belonging to the militia, who crossed also into this island, and assisted in driving the enemy from this hiding place. Mr. William Bradford, adjutant of Major Ewing's spy battalion, and many other brave and fearless men from the militia, crossed.

The part of the river they had to wade, took a man up to his armpits; but even this appeared to be no obstacle in their way. The enemy were there, doing mischief by annoying us, and they had to be routed or killed. The latter was most desirable, and was nearly done, there being but few who made their escape from the place.

During the engagement we killed some of the squaws through mistake. It was a great misfortune to those miserable squaws and children, that they did not carry into execution the plan they had formed on the morning of the battle—that was, to come and meet us, and surrender themselves prisoners of war. It was a horrid sight to witness little children, wounded and suffering the most excruciating pain, although they were of the savage enemy, and the common enemy of the country.

It was enough to make the heart of the most hardened being on earth to ache.

We took about fifty prisoners, principally women and children. They during the engagement, had concealed themselves in the high weeds and grass, and amongst old logs and brush, which lay very thick in the bottom, and some had buried themselves in the mud and sand in the bank of the river, just leaving enough of their heads out to breathe the breath of life. The soldiers drew them out, and brought them to what was then called head quarters, the place where the officers were principally assembled, and where the surgeons and surgeon's mates were busily engaged in dressing and examining the wounded. We lost here in killed and wounded twenty-seven men.

Three of the wounded died next day, among whom was Lieutenant (Samuel) Bowman. He had command of the company, the captain being absent. The loss of this officer was very much lamented by his men and brother officers. He fought bravely until he received the mortal wound. He belonged to Colonel Fry's regiment. I have been told that he had a wife and one child to lament his death; but the child can have it to say, when he arrives to the years of maturity, that his father died fighting the battles of his country, and he was proud that he had a father that died in such a cause.

As soon as the battle was over, all the wounded were collected to one place, and, with those of our enemy, were examined, and their wounds dressed; there was no difference here between our men and our enemy. The different surgeons did their best for both. They were no longer able to do us any harm, but were in our power, and begging for mercy, and we acted like a civilized people, although it was with the worst kind of enemies, and one that had done so much mischief, and had taken away so many of the lives of our fellow citizens.

After the Indians were all collected together that we had taken prisoners, they were examined respecting many things; and among others what it was that the Indian chief was saying when he talked so long on the mountain at the Wisconsin. They stated, that he was telling us in the Winnebago language, that they had their squaws and children with them, and that they were starving for something to eat, and were not able to fight us; and that if we would let them pass over the Mississippi, they would do no more mischief. They stated that he spoke this in the Winnebago language, believing that the same Winnebagoes that were with us in the battle, were still there. But here he was mistaken: as soon as the battle was over, the Indians, with our pilot Poquet, all left us; so there was no one among us, that understood the Winnebago language.

CHAPTER 8

March Down to Prairie du Chien

Soon after the battle was over, the steamboat *Warrior* arrived. When she came near to where we were, she commenced raking the island with a six pounder. We in return fired a salute, thinking she was apprised of our battle, and that she was firing us a salute; but the truth was, she had the first fight with the enemy herself and was then raking the island with her six pounder, not knowing but the enemy were still there. (The *Warrior's* fight was on the day before. Captain John Throckmorton commanded her.) When she came up, we then learnt that on the evening before, she had been there for the express purpose of preventing the Indians from crossing, until the main army might get up with them.

Lieutenant Kingsbury, who commanded, stated that they hoisted a white flag, but would not send aboard the steamboat. He told them if they did not do it, he would fire upon them; but they still refused, and appeared to be making preparation for action; so, accordingly, he fired his six pounder, and likewise opened a fire of musquetry upon them, when they commenced a heavy fire upon the boat.

The battle now became general, and lasted for some time, as the boat was anchored. All were at their posts, and would have, it is stated, continued at this place until the main army got up, if they had not been out of wood. So she had to drop down, in order to lay in wood; but it is stated, she killed five in this action and, I suppose, wounded a number; but the number I do not think has been ascertained; but Lieutenant Kingsbury and all the other officers deserve great credit for the bravery and industry they made use of, in trying to prevent the Indians from crossing until the army could come up with them; they dropped down that night as low as Prairie du Chien, and took in wood, and returned to the scene of action the next day, by twelve o'clock, a distance of forty miles or upwards.

But when they got back to their old play place, the boys that they had been sporting with the day before, were no more. We had killed and wounded a great many of these wretched wanderers, that have no home in the world, but are like the wild beasts more than man wandering from forest to forest, and not making any improvement in the natural mind. All their study is, how to proceed in the chase, or take scalps in time of war. But although they are a miserable race of people, and live a wretched life, they are much frightened when they see death stare them in the face; which was the case at this time. When we came upon the squaws and children, they raised a scream and cry loud enough to affect the stoutest man upon earth. If they had shown themselves, they would have come off much better, but fear prevented them; and in their retreat, trying to hide from us, many of them were killed; but contrary to the wish of every man, as neither officer nor private intended to have spilt the blood of those squaws and children.

But such was their fate; some of them were killed, but not intentionally by any man; as all were men of too much sense of honour and feeling to have killed any but those who were able to harm us. We all well knew the squaws and children could do us no harm; and could not help what the old Black Hawk and the other chiefs did. The prisoners we took seemed to lament their ever having raised arms against the United States, and appeared to blame the Black Hawk and the Prophet, for the miserable condition that their tribe was then in; but at the same time, appeared to rejoice that they were prisoners of war, which plainly showed that they had some faith in our humanity, and that they would exchange the life they then were living, for any other.

They appeared to manifest every token of honesty in their examination. They stated that Black Hawk had stolen off up the river, at the commencement of the battle, with some few of his warriors, and a few squaws and children. I think the number of warriors was ten, and thirty-five women and children, or, in other words, four lodges, which is the Indian phrase as they do not know how to count by numbers.

They were examined respecting the first battle we had with them on the Wisconsin, and they stated that we killed sixty-eight on the field of action; and that twenty-five had died since with their wounds; making in all ninety-three that we are certain we killed in that battle, besides a number more, that there is no doubt still lingered and died with their wounds. Putting together what were killed in the two battles, and all the little skirmishes, we must have destroyed upwards of four hundred of these unhappy and miserable beings, which was occasioned, no doubt, by the superstitious ideas which were instilled into their minds by the Prophet.

******

The Prophet was a cross-bred Winnebago-Sac, whose village in what is now Whiteside County, Illinois, it will be remembered, was burned by Whiteside's men in passing that point.
There is no doubt about the fact that his evil genius had much to do with influencing Black Hawk's conduct.

******

Although I have already stated that those unhappy wanderers make no improvement in the natural mind, they still, by instinct, believe in an over-ruling Providence, and are the most credulous people upon earth. They pay much attention to their dreams, and if one of their nation dreams much, he soon takes the name of prophet, as they believe it to be a visitation of the Great Spirit.

One morning I chanced to rise very early; and taking a walk through the encampment, accidently wandered to where the Indians were encamped. It was just at the dawn of day, and they were just beginning their morning worship of the Great Spirit. I had often heard that these uninformed children of the forest, believed that there was a God, and tried to worship him, which made me call a halt to see if what I had heard respecting this unhappy people was true. They commenced by three of them standing up with their faces to the east; one of them commenced a kind of talk, as though he was talking to some person at a distance, at the same time shaking a gourd, which, from the rattling, I should have taken to be full of pebbles or beans.

The other two stood very still, looking towards the east; the others were all sitting round in the most perfect silence, when the old priest, prophet, or whatever they called him, commenced a kind of song, which, I believe, is the common one sung by the Indians on all occasions. It was, as near as I could make out, in the following words. *He-aw-aw-he-aw-how-he-aw-hum*—with a great many elevations and falls in their tone, and beating time with the gourd of pebbles. When this song was sung they commenced a kind of prayer, which I thought the most solemn thing I had witnessed. It was a long, monotonous note, occasionally dropping by a number of tones at once, to a low and unearthly murmur.

When he had done he handed the gourd of pebbles to one of the two that stood by him, who went, as near as I could ascertain, through the same ceremony, still shaking the gourd. When he had done, he handed it to the third, who went through the same motions, and making use of the same words that the first two had done, which I suppose was a supplication or prayer to the Great Spirit to give them plenty to eat, and strength to conquer their enemies. It is stated, by those who are acquainted with this race of people, that they are very much afraid of offending the Great Spirit. If they have bad luck in hunting, they think it is caused by their having offended the Great Spirit, and they make an atonement, by offering up or making a sacrifice of something that they set much store by, such as burning their tobacco, (this ceremony is very similar to those performed around the Hall girls during their captivity), or something else that they dote upon very much, but there is nothing in this world that they think more of than tobacco, as smoking they think is almost as indispensably necessary as eating. I must now return to the battle ground with my subject.

After the battle was all over, and the wounded all attended to, the prisoners and the wounded of both parties, were put on board of the steamboat *Warrior*, and taken down to Prairie du Chien, where the wounded were taken to the hospital, and the prisoners put in confinement. The boat returned to us the next morning. We were still at the battle ground, or near it; whilst we lay there, our men were still picking up scattering Indians. They brought in an old chief who was wounded. He was very poor, was between six and seven feet high; what hair was on his head was gray, but that was not much, as the most of it was shaved off, just leaving enough for hand hold to scalp him by; as these superstitious beings think it would be a mark of cowardice to cut off this tuft of hair, which they call their scalp.

These superstitious beings believe that if they are maimed or disfigured in this world, they will appear in the next in the same form, which is the reason they scarcely ever bury their dead. If he should chance to lose his scalp, they think that it would show in the next world that he had been conquered and scalped by an enemy, which would go to show that he was not a great warrior.

******

This disposition of the scalp-lock was very common among Indians of the Mississippi River and Valley. Travellers up and down the valley during the early part of the nineteenth century have unanimously testified to the fact. The boast of inviting an enemy to come and take it, so frequently made by Black Hawk, was pure fiction. With the same show of reason he might have claimed that plucking out the beard was peculiar to his individuality alone.

★★★★★★

General Atkinson now thought that he had taken just retribution for the blood these Indians had spilt on our frontiers, and saw that it would be useless to cross the river in pursuit of those wretched beings, for they were now scattered and hid in the swamps, so that it was an impossible thing to take many of them. He finally came to the conclusion, to drop down to Prairie du Chien, and have a talk with the Winnebagoes; for it was now manifest that they had been allies to the Sacs and Foxes; for the prisoners that we took in this action, put all doubts to rest on this score.

We had a long time believed that they were acting treacherously, and General Atkinson now thought that it was time to bring them to an account for their conduct. He, accordingly, on the second day after the battle, which was the fourth of August, took up the line of march for Prairie du Chien; but before General Atkinson left the battle ground, he provisioned a number of Sioux and some Winnebagoes, and sent them in search of Black Hawk to see if they could not capture him, and bring him in as a prisoner, which the Sioux appeared to be anxious to do, as the Sacs and they had been at variance a long time; and they saw that there was no chance of taking revenge for the many injuries the Sacs had done them.

★★★★★★

The Sioux inhabited the western bank of the Mississippi River. Finding their ancient enemies, the Sacs, crushed, they asked the privilege of pursuing those fugitives who had made their escape to the west side of the river. Without thought of the possible consequences, General Atkinson unfortunately granted them such permission. The scene of slaughter which followed was reported to be sickening.

★★★★★★

General Atkinson and the infantry went down on the steam boat Warrior, and reached Prairie du Chien on the same day we started. The mounted men, baggage and all went down by land, and reached Prairie du Chien the next day, which was the fifth of August. On entering the settlement of Prairie du Chien, we witnessed a very novel scene. The Menominie Indians were rejoicing at the defeat of the Sacs and Foxes, and were expressing it by music and dancing. They had obtained several scalps, amongst which were some of the squaws, which they always give to their squaws. They had given their squaws several of them, and were making music for them to dance around them. It was, as near as I could observe, in the following way:

The men all stood in a row with gourds in their hands, shaking them in very regular order, while one old fellow was beating on the head of a kind of drum, which is generally a deer skin stretched over a hollow gum, sawed to the length of our drums. They never use but one stick, and that very slow.

The squaws were all paraded in front of the men, facing them, and the squaws who were related to those whom the Sacs and Foxes killed in 1831, held the scalps of the Sacs and Fox squaws on long poles, and stood in the centre between the two lines, shaking them, while the other squaws and the men danced around them, apparently trying to keep time with the rattling of the gourds, and sound of the drum, and all at the same time singing the song usually sung by all nations of Indians, consisting only of a few simple words that I have already repeated; but they rise and fall very singular, and always beat time to the song with their feet; when the song gets to the highest pitch, they jump up very high, and sometimes stamp with their feet. They generally bend forward toward each other, sometimes with their noses so close as to touch.

The squaws appeared to exert all the power they were master of, in shaking the scalps, and using their feet at the same time, with the drummer and the gourd-shakers; and, from their countenances, they appeared to be perfectly happy.—General Atkinson, on the second day after we arrived at Prairie du Chien, had the principal chiefs of the Winnebagoes, and a few of the Menominies, at General Street's, the Indian Agent at Prairie du Chien, and had a talk with them. He told them that they had given him reason to think they were not true to him, as he had caught them in many lies, which they tried to deny.

He then accused Wisshick of aiding the Sacs, and inquired of him where his two sons were. The answer of Wisshick was, that he did not know where they were. General Atkinson then asked him if they were not with Black Hawk. His answer was, that one had been with him, but he did not know where he was then. General Atkinson then ordered him to be put in prison until his sons could be produced. He then had a talk with the Menominies, who had never been at war with the United States. They professed all the friendship in the world for our government; and stated that they had never done us any harm, and did not tell lies, and that if they wanted to do any harm now, they would not know how.

This was a little Menominie chief whose name I do not recollect. General Atkinson talked very friendly to him, and advised him to pursue the same friendly course towards the United States, and they would be well treated. When this chief was done, he made a request of General Atkinson, whom he termed father, to give each of his young men a pair of shoes, and stated that their feet were worn out with walking. He then went on to explain, that when he said shoes, he meant horses, and stated that his young men had been promised a horse apiece, and had not got them.

General Atkinson promised that they should have them, or that he would see to it, I do not recollect which. On the next day about eleven o'clock, Wisshick's sons were brought in, both badly wounded, which went to confirm that he and his sons were allies to the Sacs and Foxes. They had been wounded in the battle on the Mississippi. They were put in confinement July 7th.

General Scott and suite arrived this morning in the steamboat *Warrior*, and assumed the command of the whole army, to which station he had been appointed some time previous, but was unable to come on sooner in consequence of the cholera breaking out in his army. He came past several posts, and discharged the men wherever he found them.

******

The progress of General Scott with his army around the lakes; the spread of the cholera among his men, and his heroic efforts to stamp it out, should be read in full by every person who loves to read of noble deeds. Another notable name should be added at this point, that of Lieut. Joseph E. Johnston, Gen. Scott's aid, who accompanied the latter.

******

General Scott concluded to discharge the army (or the Mounted Volunteers) that were then in the field, and demanded Black Hawk of Keokuck, (the impression prevailed at the time among the United States army officers that Keokuk had been aiding and abetting Black Hawk in secret, and he was even then suspected of harbouring him from capture, an unjust and cruel suspicion); as both men and horses were nearly worn out with fatigue. Accordingly, on the 8th day of August, we left the tented fields, and took up our line of march to Dixon's on Rock River, the place appointed for us to be discharged at (or mustered out of the service of the United States.) All now were eager to press forward.

We had turned our faces toward our respective homes; and notwithstanding that we as well as our horses, were nearly worn out with the fatiguing marches through the swamps, and over the mountains, yet all were cheerful, and every heart seemed to leap for joy at the thought of being free from the toils and hardships of a soldier, to return again to the embraces of a wife and children, or a father and mother, brothers and sisters, and to mingle once more, in the walks and society of the fair sex—which appears to be a sovereign balm to man in all his afflictions.

On this day just at night, we met about three hundred Menominie Indians, in company of an American Officer from Green Bay, (Colonel S. C. Stambaugh), coming to join in pursuit of the Sac and Fox Indians. We happened to meet them in a prairie. The officer advanced and met us, or we certainly would have fired upon them. When we came up to them, they appeared almost to lament, that they had not got in before we had the last battle, in order that they could have had an opportunity of assisting us in the work of death to our common enemy. For they are, as I have already stated, great enemies to the Menominie Indians.

When they left us, they seemed to press forward with more vigour, as it was their object to pursue the balance of the Sacs and Foxes, who had made their escape.

On the next day, we began to reach the settlements in the mining country. This was again a solemn scene. The farms had mostly been sown in grain of some kind or other. Those that were in small grain, were full ripe for the sickle; but behold! the husbandman was not there, to enjoy the benefits of his former labour—by thrusting in the scythe and sickle, and gathering in his grain, which was fast going to destruction. All appeared to be solitary, and truly presented a state of mourning.

But as we advanced a little further into the more thickly settled parts, we would occasionally see the smoke just beginning to make its appearance from the tops of the chimneys; as some of the inhabitants thought that it would be as well to risk dying by the tomahawk and scalping knife, as to lose their grain, and die by famine; and others had received information that we had slain in battle their trouble some enemy, who had driven them from their homes, and had slain many of their neighbours. Whenever we approached a house, there is no telling the joy it would give to the desolate man who had lately emerged from some fort, and had left his wife and children still in it, while he ventured to his home, to save something for them to subsist upon.

I must confess, that it filled my heart with gratitude and joy, to think that I had been instrumental, with many others, in delivering my country of those merciless savages, and restoring those people again to their peaceful homes and firesides, there to enjoy in safety the sweets of a retired life; for a fort is to a husband man, what a jail is to a prisoner. The inhabitants of this district of the country had been shut up in forts for the last three months, through fear of becoming a prey to Indian barbarity.

Nothing very interesting occurred on our march to Dixon's. Lieutenant Anderson, (later General Robert Anderson), of the United States Army, met us at this point, and by the 17th of August, mustered us all out of the service of the United States. We sheathed our swords, and buried our tomahawks, and each man again became his own commander, and shaped his own course towards his home, to enjoy the social society of his relatives and friends, in the pursuit of their different avocations in life.

CHAPTER 9

Description of Black Hawk and the Prophet

When General Atkinson dropped down to Prairie du Chien, after the battle on the Mississippi, he made the following report to Major General Macomb, Commander in Chief at Washington City.

Headquarters, 1st A. Corps, N. Western Army
Prairie du Chien, Aug. 5, 1832.

Sir—I have the honour to report to you, that I crossed the Wisconsin on the 27th and 28th *ult.*, with a select body of troops, consisting of the regulars under Colonel Taylor, four hundred in number, part of Henry's, Posey's and Alexander's brigades, and Dodge's battalion of mounted volunteers; amounting in all to thirteen hundred men; and immediately fell upon the trail of the enemy, and pursued it by forced marches through a mountainous and difficult country, till the morning of the second instant, when we came up with his main body, on the left bank of the Mississippi, nearly opposite the mouth of the Iowa; which we attacked, defeated, and dispersed, with a loss on his part of about one hundred and fifty men killed, and thirty-nine women and children prisoners.

The precise number could not be ascertained, as the greater portion was slain after being forced into the river. Our loss in killed and wounded, which is stated below, is very small in comparison with the loss of the enemy; which may be attributed to the enemy's being forced from his positions by a rapid charge at the commencement, and through the engagement. The remnant of the enemy, cut up and disheartened, crossed to the opposite side of the river, and has fled into the interior, with a view it is supposed of joining Keokuck and Wapilo's, (should be Wa-pel-lo., emphasis on the first syllable), bands of Sacs and Foxes.

The horses of the volunteer troops being exhausted by long marches, and the regular troops without shoes, it was not thought advisable to continue the pursuit. Indeed a stop to the further effusion of blood seemed to be called for, until it might be ascertained if the enemy would not surrender.

It is ascertained from our prisoners, that the enemy lost in the Battle of Ouisconsin, sixty-eight killed, and a very large number wounded. His whole loss does not fall short of three hundred. After the Battle of the Ouisconsin, the enemy's women and children, and some who were dismounted, attempted to make their escape by descending that river, but judicious measures being taken here by Captain Loomis and General Street, and Indian Agent, thirty-two women and children, and four men, have been captured, and some fifteen killed by the detachment under Lieutenant Ritner.

The day after the battle on this river, I fell down with the regular troops to this place by water, and the mounted men will join us to day. It is now my purpose to direct Keokuck to demand a surrender of the remaining principal men of the hostile party; which, from the large number of women and children we hold as prisoners, I have every reason to believe will be complied with. Should it not, they should be pursued and subdued; a step Major General Scott will no doubt take on his arrival.

I cannot speak too highly of the conduct of the regular and volunteer forces engaged in the last battle, and the fatiguing march that preceded it.

As soon as the reports of the officers of brigades and corps are handed in, they shall be submitted with further remarks.

  I have the honour to be, with great respect,
    Your obedient servant,
      H. Atkinson, Bt. Bgdr. General U. S. A.
Major General Macomb, Commander in Chief,
Washington City.

The reader will recollect that I have, in a preceding chapter, given the substance of a talk between General Atkinson and General Street, agent for the Winnebagoes, and several Winnebago chiefs, on our arrival at Prairie du Chien, after the battle on the Mississippi near the Bad-Axe. In this talk, General Street told the principal chiefs that if they would bring in the Black Hawk and the Prophet, it would be well for them, and that the government of the United States would hold them in future as friends, and treat them kindly, and not any more consider them friends to the Sacs and Foxes.

On this declaration the old one-eyed chief, called the Decorri, and Cheater, (Cha-e-tar, pronounced in three syllables), took some of their men with them and went in pursuit of these Sac chiefs, in order if possible to take them prisoners, and bring them and deliver them up to the Indian agent at Prairie du Chien.

Accordingly, on the 27th of August, these two Winnebago chiefs returned, bringing with them the Black Hawk and the Prophet, the principal movers and instigators of the war. The interview with them on their arrival at Prairie du Chien, I have been told, was a very interesting scene. I will give the reader the substance of their talk with General Street and Colonel Taylor, which will go to show how vigilant, and with what perseverance, these Winnebago chiefs acted to take these prisoners. They were upwards of twenty days gone after they left Prairie du Chien before they returned with them.

When they arrived, Black Hawk desired to speak to General Street. The amount of what he said was, that he was not the originator of the war; that he was going where he would meet Keokuck, and then he would tell the truth; that he would then tell all about this war, which had caused so much trouble; that there were chiefs and braves of his nation, who were the cause of the continuance of the war; that he did not want to hold any council with him; that when he got where Keokuck was, he would tell the whole of the origin of the difficulties, and of those who continued it; that he wanted to surrender long ago, but others refused: that he wanted to surrender to the steamboat *Warrior*, and tried to do so until the second fire; that he then ran and went up the river, and never returned to the battleground; that his determination then was to escape if he could; that he did not intend to surrender after that, but that, when the Winnebagoes came upon him, he gave up—and that he would tell all about the disturbance when he got to Rock Island.

******

It is regrettable that when confronted by Keokuk, Black Hawk had forgotten all about the promised disclosures. His neglect in that particular gives plausibility to the theory that there was no truth to his assertions. Keokuk was found trying at all times to persuade Black Hawk to abandon his shadow chasing when at liberty, and when confined in Jefferson Barracks he sought to make Black Hawk's confinement bearable by taking him presents and ultimately bringing to him his wife and family.

Some measure of gratitude should have been manifested for such favours; but prior to 1832 the record is not illuminated with many examples of gratitude from Black Hawk.

******

The one eyed Decorri and the Cheater both in like manner addressed General Street, whom they term their father; which almost all the Indians do their agents.

The one eyed Decorri rose first, and addressed him in the following manner:

My father, I now stand before you. When we parted, I told you we would return soon; but I could not come any sooner. We had to go a great distance, (to the Dale on the Wisconsin River, above the Portage;) you see we have done what you sent us to do. These are the two you told us to get, (pointing to Black Hawk and the Prophet.) We always do what you tell us to do, because we know it is for our good. My father, you told us to get these men, and it would be the cause of much good to the Winnebagoes. We have brought them, but it has been very hard for us to do it; that one, Macatamish Kakacky, was a great way off. You told us to bring them alive; we have done so. If you had told us to bring their heads alone, we would have done so; and it would have been less difficult for us to do, than what we have done.

My father, we deliver these men into your hands; we would not deliver them even to our brother, the chief of the warriors, but to you, because we know you, and believe you are our friend. We want you to keep them safe. If they are to be hurt, we do not wish to see it, wait until we are gone before it is done. My father, many little birds have been flying about our ears of late, and we thought they whispered to us, that there was evil intended for us; but now we hope the evil birds will let our ears alone.

My father, we know you are our friends, because you take our part; this is the reason we do what you tell us to do.

My father, you say you love your red children; we think we love you as much or more than you love us.

My father, we have been promised a great deal if we would take these men, that it would do much good for our people, we now hope to see what will be done for us.

My father, we have come in haste, and are tired and hungry, we now put these men in your hands; we have done all you told us to do.

General Street then said:

My children, you have done well; I told you to bring these men to me, and you have done so. I am pleased at what you have done. It will tend to your good, and for this reason I am well pleased. I assured the great chief of the warriors that if these men were in your country, you would find them, and bring them to me; that I believed you would do what I directed you to do. Now I can say much for your good. I will go down to Rock Island with the prisoners, and I wish you who have brought these men especially to go with me, and such other chiefs and warriors as you may select. My children, the great chief of the warriors, when he left this place, directed me to deliver these and all other prisoners to the chief of the warriors, Colonel Taylor, who is by my side.

Some of the Winnebagoes on the south side of the Wisconsin River have befriended the Sacs, and some of the Indians of my agency have given them aid; this was wrong, and displeased the great chief of the warriors and your great father the president, and was calculated to do you much harm. My children, your great father the president, at Washington, has sent a great war chief from the far east, General Scott, with a fresh army of soldiers, who is now at Rock Island.

Your Great Father has sent him and the Governor of Illinois, to hold a council with the Indians at Rock Island; he has sent a speech to you; and wishes the chiefs and warriors of the Winnebagoes, to meet him in council, on the 10th of September next; I wish you to be ready to go along with me to Rock Island.

My children, I am well pleased that you have taken Black Hawk and the Prophet, and so many others; because it will enable me to say much for you to the great chief of the warriors, and your great father the president. I shall now deliver these two men, Black Hawk and the Prophet, to the chief of the warriors here, Colonel Taylor, who will take good care of them until we start to Rock Island.

Colonel Taylor then said:

The great chief of the warriors told me to take the prisoners, when you should bring them, and send them to Rock Island to him; I will take them, and keep them safe, but use them well, and will send them by you and General Street when you go down to the council, which will be in a few days. Your friend General Street advised you to get ready and go down soon, and so do I. I tell you again, I will take the prisoners and keep them safe, but will do them no harm. I will deliver them to the great chief of the warriors, and he will do with them and use them in such manner as he may be ordered by your Great Father the president.

Cheater, a Winnebago, said to General Street,

My father, I am young, and don't know how to make speeches. This is the second time I ever spoke to you before the people. My father, I am no chief. I am no orator, but I have been allowed to speak to you. My father, if I should not speak as well as others, still you must listen to me.

My father, when you made the speech to the chiefs, Waughkon-decorri, Carimanee, the one-eyed Decorri, and others, the other day, I was there. I heard you. I thought what you said to them, you also said to me. You said, if these two (pointing to Black Hawk and the Prophet), were taken by us, and brought to you, there would never any more a black cloud hang over your Winnebagoes. My father, your words entered into my ears, into my brains, and into my heart. I left here that very night, and you know you have not seen me since, until now.

My father, I have been a great way. I had much trouble; but when I remembered what you said, I know you was right. This made me keep on, and do what you told me to do. Near the Dale on the Wisconsin River, I took Black Hawk. No one did it but me. I say this in the ears of all present, and they know it; and I now appeal to the Great Spirit, our Grand Mother, for the truth of what I say. My father, I am no chief, but what I have done is for the benefit of my own nation, and, I hope, for the good that has been promised us. My father, that one, Wabokishick, is my relation. If he is to be hurt, I do not wish to see it. My father, soldiers sometimes stick the ends of their guns (bayonets) into the backs of Indian prisoners, when they are going about in the hands of the guard. I hope this will not be done to these men.

So ended this long talk of the uninformed savage, which goes to show that they have a warm feeling for their red brethren.

It appears that they at this time were true friends to our government; but they were, I have no doubt, frightened into this friendship by the first talk at Prairie du Chien, which Generals Street and Atkinson held with them, on our arrival at that place, after the battle of BadAxe.

It may not here be uninteresting to the reader, to give a description of those two distinguished prisoners, respecting whom so much has been said. No doubt they were the sole movers and cause of the late war. Black Hawk is a Pottawattomie, by birth, but raised by the Sacs. (This is a mistake, he was a full-blood Sac.) He appears to be about sixty years old; has a small bunch of grey hair on the crown of his head, the rest of which is bare; has a high forehead; a Roman nose; and full mouth, which generally in clines to be a little open; has a sharp chin; no eye brows, but a very fine eye. His head is frequently thrown back on his shoulders. He is about five feet four or five inches high; at present he is thin, and appears much dejected; but now and then he assumes the aspect of command. He held in his left hand a white flag; in the other, the tail with the back, skin, head, and beak of the Caumet Eagle. With this he frequently fans himself. His Indian name is Mucatamish-ka-kack. (The name given in his autobiography is Ma-ka-tai-me-she-kia-kiak.)

The Prophet, a half Sac and half Winnebago, is about forty years old; nearly six feet high; is stout and athletic; has a large broad face; short blunt nose; large full eyes; broad mouth; thick lips; with a full suit of hair. He wore a white cloth head-dress which rose several inches above the top of his head; the whole man exhibiting a deliberate savageness; not that he would seem to delight in honourable war, or fight; but making him as the priest of assassination, or clerical murder. He had in one hand a white flag, while the other hung carelessly by his side. They were both clothed in very white dressed deer skin, fringed at the seams with short cuttings of the same. His Indian name is Wabokie-shick, (the White Cloud.)

According to the directions of General Street and Colonel Taylor, those two chiefs (or braves,) accompanied by the Winnebago chiefs, and braves, went down to Rock Island at the stipulated time, under the command of Colonel Taylor. (Wakefield is in error. Lieutenant Jefferson Davis took the prisoners down to Jefferson Barracks, near St. Louis. Lieutenant Colonel Taylor was not present on the trip.) But when they got to this point, which had been the place designated to hold the treaties with those nations of Indians, the cholera prevailed to such an extent, that they found it was impossible to treat at that point; so General Scott, Governor Reynolds, and those concerned in the treaty, dropped down the Mississippi to Jefferson Barracks, where a number of other chiefs and braves were brought to them, amongst which was Napope, a celebrated Sac chief, also Wisshick, who it appears celebrated himself at the battle on the Mississippi, for it appears he had the command at that place, and from his own statement did much execution himself.

Here the commissioners made and concluded treaties both with the Sacs and Foxes, and the Winnebagoes, which the reader will find in the appendix of this book. (Appendix A 6 and 7.) It was a fair equitable treaty; the government purchased all the claims they had to lands in the state of Illinois, and paid them a liberal sum for the same. They kept Black Hawk, Napope, Wisshick, and the Prophet, as hostages for the good behaviour of the rest of the nation of Sacs and Foxes.

Thus terminated a short but laborious war, between the United States and those nations of Indians; but it was not without the loss of some of our valuable citizens, that peace was again restored to our country. In the accomplishment of this desired object, it is just to remark, that both officer and soldier did all that lay in their power to bring this unhappy war to a close as soon as possible.

Our citizen soldiers hesitated not when the sound of alarm was given, to forsake all other interests, dear as it must have been to some, to defend the rights of their common country. They at once saw that these Indians had violated the solemn obligations of a solemn treaty, entered into but a few months before. This bold and daring defiance of us, and unprovoked outrage upon the provisions of the treaty, aroused the indignation of the whole country; it was more than the free sons of Illinois could think of bearing. They immediately at the call of their

GENERAL HENRY ATKINSON

chief, flew to arms. Their governor was with them, and one of the first in the field, who, together with his efficient adjutant general, organised the troops in as quick time as ever it was done in any country, notwithstanding they laboured under many difficulties on account of the great scarcity of provisions in our state at that time; for a visitation of Providence had almost entirely cut off our crops the last two years.

To provision this army was very perplexing at this time. What was Governor Reynolds to do? At this critical moment our state was invaded by a savage foe, and he knew not how soon the help less citizens on the frontiers might become an easy prey to their barbarity. But justice says to my pen, write it down, and say to your reader, that he flew to one of the ablest and most efficient men, Colonel March. (The efficiency of Colonel Enoch C. March in the campaigns has been universally pronounced marvellous.) Provisions, forage, arms, munitions of war, and every thing that was necessary was soon furnished and conveyed up the Illinois and Mississippi Rivers, to such points as Governor Reynolds directed him. There were provisions in St. Louis, and this energetic and unsurpassable man got them, let the prices be what they might please to ask. There was no lack of provision.

But the first campaign proved unsuccessful; but such is the fate of war, and none ought to lay the blame on the commander-in-chief, which some have had the boldness to do, but I think unjustly. I was an eye witness a greater part of the campaign, and I thought he did not spare time or pains to hunt out the enemy, and chastise them for their temerity. I think he must be a man of a reckless disposition, who would charge the ill success to him in this first campaign. Those who were out on the second can testify to the many difficulties we had to encounter before we fell in with the enemy. But did the governor, when the first campaign proved unsuccessful, fold his arms in this trying and critical moment, and abandon the bleeding frontier to the merciless savages? Did he abandon the camp for a life of ease, in the repose of his own domestic habitation?

The answer, I think, reader, will be No! by all who know anything of the first and last campaigns. Did he not see that a fair portion of the State, which he had the honour to govern, was exposed to the midnight and noon day assassination by the ruthless savage? Were the cries of his people listened to unheeded? No! he left a devoted band under the command of those heroic soldiers, Henry and Fry, and issued a proclamation to his countrymen to come forth to the frontier and protect the rights of their country.

Was this appeal, too, unheeded by the gallant sons of Illinois? Did they turn a deaf ear to the cries of the people of the mining country, when the savage had killed some of its choice citizens in open day?

Look at the massacre on Indian Creek, of the Halls, Daviess, and Penigrew families; the highway murder of St. Vrain, Durley, Howard, Green, Hall, and many others. Who could see or hear of all those massacres, and not turn out in defence of his country? Or what governor would tamely lose one moment, before he would fly with all its force to its relief? Was not this the case at this time? Did not Governor Reynolds a second time invoke the patriotism of his people for a fresh supply of troops? The people heard, and abandoned their ploughs, when in the act of planting their corn; the courts of justice were suspended; the lawyer quit the bar; the minister of divine truth forsook the pulpit for the tented fields of a soldier's life. They plainly saw, that if the arm of succour was not held out to those frontiers, the country bordering on the Mississippi and Illinois, and the Mining District, would soon be left a barren wilderness, and present a blaze of conflagration, and the voice of our friends and neighbours heard no more.

Our chief gave the word, "to arms" and that was sufficient; all were soon at the place of rendezvous; none slumbered by the way; they were going forth to avenge the murders of their butchered brethren.

In obedience to the call of their governor, in two weeks there was a force of nearly four thousand assembled at Fort Wilbourn, a distance of at least three hundred and fifty miles from the homes of some of the volunteer companies. Here we again found our governor in arms in defence of his country. The army was soon organised, by the aid of Adjutant General Berry, into three brigades. We wanted a Bruce or a Wallace to lead us to victory. Such a man was the brave James D. Henry, (see note at end of chapter), to become. He was elected Brigadier General of the third brigade, as I have before mentioned. Generals Posey and Alexander are like wise deserving men, and stand high in the estimation of their country. But an all-wise Providence saw fit to crown the Bruce-like Henry with the glory of avenging our country's wrongs, and restoring peace to its citizens.

I must next speak of General Atkinson, who has a thousand times received the thanks of Illinois and the general government. He had the command of all the north-western army, until succeeded by General Scott; which was not until after the last battle was fought, and the enemy completely conquered. This officer is also deserving well of his country, for the long and vigilant perseverance in pursuing the enemy through every difficulty that presented itself. He can truly have it to say, that he marched an army over a country that cannot be surpassed in the inhabited world, and one that no white man ever approached before.

Not even the savage himself attempts to penetrate this country, only when he is forced, then he resorts to this mountainous forest to evade pursuit, thinking that no white man can penetrate it. This was done as I have before remarked, in the year eighteen hundred and twenty-seven, by the Winnebagoes, after they attacked Captain Lindsey's boats on the Mississippi.

But General Atkinson stopped not at this time for the tall and lofty mountains, or the low and marshy swamp. His word of command to his generals, was "onward, march"—and at the sound of the morning bugle, he was one of the first to rise and prepare for the pursuit. Although stricken in years, he would leap off his charger, when he would come to an impassable mud hole or precipice, like a boy of sixteen. This officer, throughout the whole of this long campaign, which lasted for three months, used every precaution to save the lives of his men, when danger was expected, his men never failed to have breast works thrown up when they encamped, for fear of a surprise at the dead hour of the night.

Thus, by his perseverance, and the gallant officers under him, and a brave and chivalrous set of soldiers, the war was brought to an end, with honour to both men and officers.

But whilst we rejoice at the honourable result of the close of this war, we cannot at the same time help lamenting the loss of so many valuable citizens, who were either massacred at their own private dwellings, or assassinated on the highway, or fell in fighting the battles of their country.

The author has been led to the foregoing reflections, from seeing in many of the eastern prints, that many erroneous statements have gone abroad, respecting the origin and management of this war; and some of them casting reflections on the Governor of our State, and crying out, "poor Indians." But as I have before observed, none but the reckless and abandoned hearted man, would have the hardihood to cast imputations upon our Executive, and cry out, "poor Indians," after a thorough perusal of the many outrages these hell-hounds committed on our frontier settlements.

✶✶✶✶✶✶

Note:—James Dougherty Henry has been styled by so respectable an authority as Judge Joseph Gillespie as the most remarkable man in Illinois down to the day of his death at New Orleans, March 4, 1834.

Born in Pennsylvania, he removed to Delaware, Ohio, in 1816, and there remained until the year 1822, when in a rage he whipped three or four fellow-workmen. That unwarrantable act compelled him to leave the place in haste. By keel boat he reached the mouth of Wood River, from which point he went to Edwardsville, and at once began work at his trade of shoemaker. To overcome his educational deficiencies, and gratify a passion for knowledge, he attended night school taught by William Barrett, beside which he induced the boy, Joseph Gillespie, to read to him during the day, while at work, biographies of such military heroes as Alexander the Great, Hannibal, Caesar and Napoleon. Meagre as were those sources, his advancement in learning was phenomenal.

In 1826, Mr. Jonathan Atwater established him in business at Springfield, where he was enabled to take his first ambitious step. He was made sheriff of the county.

His nature was composed of numerous and painfully abnormal contrarieties. He was melancholy, retiring, and withal insanely ambitious for military renown. The same Judge Gillespie has said, "He was as mild as a May morning and as terrible as a tornado." Once, at Edwardsville, he suspected a negro named Jarrett, the slave of Joseph Conway, of doing him an injury, a wholly unjust suspicion. Henry dragged the unfortunate wretch to the barn of Rowland P. Allen, stripped him to the waist, tied him to a hayrack, and proceeded to lash him with hickory withes.

The crowd of men which gathered stood helplessly and stupidly watching the act, afraid to antagonise the giant form of Henry and his fiendish rage; but when the cries of the negro reached the ears of Mrs. Allen, she seized a carving-knife from her table and rushed between the slave's bleeding body and Henry, who recoiled in astonishment, while Mrs. Allen cut the cords and led the negro to safety.

While that brutishness mellowed and at last disappeared almost entirely, its reappearance at Fort Winnebago, together with his powerful physique, awed an army and permitted him to advance and win the battles of the Wisconsin and the Bad Axe, the latter in the face of the fact that Atkinson purposely relegated him to the rear of the army in charge of the baggage, in a spirit of jealousy for having, contrary to orders, pursued Black Hawk, and whipped him at the Wisconsin.

The man was a fatalist, said to have been accentuated by reason of the misfortune of his birth, and when the Winnebago war, the 1831 campaign, and the first half of the 1832 campaign ended without presenting to him the opportunity to win fame, he was inconsolable.

Rugged as he had been, the severities of the last campaign undermined his health. Early in 1834 he sought relief in the milder climate of New Orleans, but without avail, and he passed away so quietly that until it became noised about that General Henry was dead, his presence in the city was almost unknown. Before departing he had been nominated by a "People's Party" for governor, and so reliable an authority as Governor Ford has stated that nothing but his death could have prevented his election by 20,000 majority. The coincidence might be called remarkable that two of the Black Hawk heroes were nominees for the office of governor when death snatched away the honour.

Appendix A

1

The author must now begin with the Sac and Fox nations of Indians; and it is his intention to confine himself principally to the war between them and the general government.

In order to show the cause of hostilities between those Indians and the United States, he has to trouble the reader with petitions sent by the settlers near Rock Island, to his Excellency Gov. Reynolds, praying for protection; and then the course pursued to dissuade those Indians from their evil designs, by General Clark, Gov. Reynolds, General Gaines, and the Indian Agent, without a resort to arms. But it would not do; a resort to arms was indispensably necessary to restore peace and safety to our citizens. The letters and petitions are as follows:

April 30, 1831.

His Excellency the Governor of the State of Illinois:

We the undersigned, being citizens of Rock River and its vicinity, beg leave to state to your honour, the grievances which we labour under, and pray your protection against the Sac and Fox tribe of Indians, who have again taken possession of our lands near the mouth of Rock River and its vicinity. They have, and now are, burning our fences, destroying our crops of wheat now growing, by turning in all their horses. They also threaten our lives if we attempt to plant corn, and say they will cut it up; that we have stolen their lands from them; and they are determined to exterminate us, provided we don't leave the country. Your honour no doubt is aware of the outrages that were committed by said Indians, heretofore. Particularly last fall, they almost destroyed all our crops, and made several attempts on the owners' lives when they attempted to prevent their depredations, and actually wounded one man by stabbing him in several places. This spring they act in a much more outrageous and menacing manner, so that we consider ourselves compelled to beg protection of you; which the agent and garrison on Rock Island refuse to give, inasmuch as they say they have no orders from government; therefore, should we not receive adequate aid from your honour, we shall be compelled to abandon our settlement, and the lands which we have purchased of government.

Therefore, we have no doubt but that your honour will better anticipate our condition, than it is represented, and grant us immediate relief in the manner that to you may seem most likely to produce the desired effect. The number of Indians now among us, is about six or seven hundred. They say there are more coming, and that the Pottawattomies and some of the Winnebagoes will help them in case of an irruption with the whites. The warriors now here, are the Black Hawk's party, with other chiefs, the names of whom we are not acquainted with. Therefore, looking up to you for protection, we beg leave to remain, yours, &c.

John Wells,	B. F. Pike,	H. McNeil,
Albert Wells,	Griffith Ausbury,	Thomas Gardiner,
J. Vandruff,	S. Vandruff,	John L. Bain,
Horace Cook,	David B. Hail,	John Barrel,
William Henry,	Arastus Kent,	Levi Wells,
Joel Wells,	Michael Bartlet,	Huntington Wells,
Thomas Davis,	Thomas Lovitt,	William Heans,
Charles French,	M. S. Hulls,	Eri Wells,
Asaph Wells,	G. V. Miller,	Edward Burner,
Joel Thompson,	Joel Wells, Jun.,	J. W. Spencer,
Joseph Danforth,	William Brasher,	Jonah H. Case,
Samuel Wells,	Charles French,	Benjamin Goble,
Gentry McCall.		

2

It will be seen that this petition was sent to the governor on the 30th of April. The citizens waited until the 19th of May, when they found they would have to send a second embassy to his Excellency by express, in as much haste as possible, as they were hourly in danger of being all massacred by those Indians. They accordingly drew up the following petition and sent it by one of the most respectable of their citizens, who was able in person to lay before the governor their grievances.

Farnhamburg, May 19th, 1831.

To His Excellency the Governor of the State of Illinois:

We the undersigned, citizens of Rock River and its vicinity, having previously sent a petition to your honour, praying your protection against these Sac Indians, who were at that time doing every kind of mischief, as was set forth and represented to your honour: but feeling ourselves more aggrieved, and our situation more precarious, we have been compelled to make our distress known to you by sending one of our neighbours, who is well acquainted with our situation. If we do not get relief speedily, we must leave our habitations to these savages, and seek safety for our families, by taking them down into the lower counties, and suffer our houses and fences to be destroyed; as one of the principal war chiefs has threatened, if we do not abandon our settlement, his warriors should burn our houses over our heads.

They were, at the time we sent our other petition, destroying our crops of wheat, and are still pasturing their horses in our fields; burning our fences, and have thrown the roof off one house. They shot arrows at our cattle, killed our hogs; and every mischief. We have tried every argument to the agent for relief, but he tells us they are a lawless band, and he has nothing to do with them until further orders; leaving us still in suspense, as the Indians say, if we plant we shall not reap, a proof of which we had last fall; they almost entirely destroyed all our crops of corn, potatoes, &c. Believing we shall receive protection from Your Excellency, we shall go on with our farms until the return of the bearer; and ever remain your humble supplicants, &c.

I omit giving the names of the signers of this petition as it was signed by nearly the same citizens who signed the first.

I will next give the reader the deposition of Benjamin F. Pike, the bearer of the above petition to Gov. Reynolds, and also the depositions of Hirah Sanders and Ammyson Chapman, taken before John H. Dennis, a Justice of the Peace for St. Clair, and Stephen Dewey a Justice of the Peace for Fulton County.

STATE OF ILLINOIS, ST. CLAIR COUNTY.

Present, Benjamin F. Pike, before me, a Justice of the Peace in and for the said county, and made oath and deposed, that he has resided in the vicinity of Rock River, in the State of Illinois, for almost three years last past; that he is well acquainted with the band of Sac Indians, whose chief is the Black Hawk, and who have resided and do now reside near the mouth of Rock River in this State; that he understands so much of the said Indian language, as to converse with the said Indians intelligibly; that he is well satisfied that said Indians, to the amount of about three hundred warriors, are extremely unfriendly to the white people; that said Indians are determined; if not prevented by force, to drive off the white people, who have some of them purchased land of the United States, near said Indians; and said Indians to remain the sole occupiers of the said country.

That said Indians do not only make threats to this effect, but have, in various instances, done much damage to said white inhabitants, by throwing down their fences, destroying the fall grain, pulling off the roofs of houses, and positively asserting that if the whites did not go away, they would kill them; that there are about forty inhabitants and heads of families in the vicinity of said Indians, who are immediately affected by said band of Indians; that said Pike is certain that said forty heads of families, if not protected, will be compelled to leave their habitations and homes from the actual injury that said Indians will commit on said inhabitants.

That said band of Indians, consist, as above stated, of about three hundred warriors, and that the whole band is actuated by the same hostile feelings towards the white inhabitants; and that, if not prevented by an armed force of men, will commit murders on said white inhabitants. That said Indians have said, that they would fight for their country where they reside, and would not permit the white people to occupy it at all. That said white inhabitants are desirous to be protected, and that immediately, so that they may raise crops this spring and summer.

Benjamin F. Pike.

Sworn and subscribed before me, this 26th May, 1831.

John H. Dennis, J. P.

The deposition of Hirah Sanders and Ammyson Chapman, taken

before Stephen Dewey, Esq., a Justice of the Peace for Fulton County.

STATE OF ILLINOIS, FULTON COUNTY.

Personally appeared before me, Stephen Dewey, an acting Justice of the Peace in and for the said county of Fulton, and State of Illinois, Hirah Sanders, and Ammyson Chapman, of the aforesaid county and State, and made oath that some time in the month of April last, they went to the old Indian Sac town, about thirty miles up Rock River, for the purpose of farming and establishing a ferry across said river, and the Indians ordered us to move away, and not to come there again, and we remained there a few hours. They then sent for their chief, and he informed us that we might depart peaceably, and if we did not that he would make us go. He therefore ordered the Indians to throw our furniture out of the house; they accordingly did so, and threatened to kill us if we did not depart. We therefore discovered that our lives were in danger, and consequently moved back again to the above county. We supposed them to be principally Winnebagoes.

H. Sanders,
A. Chapman.

Sworn and Subscribed this 11th day of May, 1831.

Stephen Dewey, J. P.

There were several other petitions sent the governor from Henderson River and elsewhere, which I will not trouble the reader with at this time; likewise a number of depositions were taken, the substance of which will be found in General Gaines's report to the President of the United States.

I will trouble the reader with those documents, in order to show that Governor Reynolds and General Gaines did not act premature, but acted with too much forbearance towards those Indians. Likewise I hope it will put the seal of disapprobation upon many false reports that have gone abroad, to the prejudice of those men, making out that justice has not been done them, as I have before stated. I think if they are to blame at all, it is for not calling out an armed force sooner than what they did, for the citizens certainly suffered very much by the annoyance of those Indians. It has been plainly proven that those lands were sold by those Indians to the United States, and the United States had sold many of them to those individuals, which they had paid their money for, and as individuals are bound to protect their government, and support its laws. It also is the duty of the government to protect them.

I will next give the reader the correspondence that took place between Governor Reynolds, General Clark, and General Gaines, which goes fully to show that those Indians were not to be persuaded to surrender the idea of taking those lands by force, only by an army superior to themselves in numbers.

Copy of a letter to General Clark, Superintendent of Indian Affairs.
Belleville, May 26, 1831.

General Clark, Superintendent, &c.

Sir: In order to protect the citizens of this State, who reside near Rock Island, from Indian invasion and depredation, I have considered it necessary to call out a force of militia of this State, of about 700 strong, to remove a band of the Sac Indians, who reside now about Rock Island. The object of the government of the State is to protect those citizens by removing those Indians, peaceably if they can, but forcibly if they must. Those Indians are now, and so I have considered them, in a state of actual invasion of the State.

As you act as the general agent of the United States in relation to said Indians, I consider it my duty to inform you of the above call on the militia, and that in or about fifteen days a sufficient force will appear before said Indians to re move them, dead or alive, over to the west side of the Mississippi. But to save all this disagreeable business, perhaps a request from you to them, for them to remove to the west side of the river, would affect the object of procuring peace to the citizens of the State. There is no disposition on the part of the people of this State to injure those unfortunate savages, if they will let us alone; but a government that does not protect its citizens, deserves not the name of a government.

Please correspond with me on this subject.
Your obedient servant,
John Reynolds.

Superintendency of Indian Affairs,
St. Louis, May 28, 1831.

Sir: I have the honour to acknowledge the receipt of your letter of the 26th inst. informing me of your having considered it necessary to collect a force of militia of about seven hundred, for the protection of the citizens of Illinois who reside near

Rock Island, from Indian invasion; and for the purpose of removing a band of Sac Indians, who are now about Rock Island. You intimate that to prevent the necessity of employing this force, perhaps a request from me to those Indians to remove to the west side of the Mississippi, would effect the object of procuring peace to the citizens of your State. In answer to which, I would beg leave to observe, that every effort on my part has been made to effect the removal from Illinois of all the tribes who had ceded their lands.

For the purpose of affording you a view of what has been done (in part) in relation thereto, I enclose herewith extracts from the reports of the agent of the Sac and Fox tribes, by which it will be seen that every means has been used short of actual force to effect their removal.

I have communicated the contents of your letter to General Gaines, who commands the Western Division of the army, and has full power to execute any military movement deemed necessary for the protection of the frontier. I shall also furnish him with such information, regarding the Sac and Foxes, as I am possessed of; and would beg (cave to refer you to him for any further proceedings in relation to this subject. I have the honour to be,

    With high respect,
        Your most obedient servant,

                      Wm. Clark.

His Excellency, John Reynolds,
Governor of the State of Ill.

Copy of a letter to Major General Gaines.
                Belleville, May 28, 1831.

General Gaines:

Sir: I have received undoubted information, that the section of this State near Rock Island, is actually invaded by a hostile band of the Sac Indians, headed by Black Hawk; and in order to repel said invasion, and to protect the citizens of the State, I have, under the provisions of the Constitution of the United States, and the laws of this State, called on the militia, to the number of seven hundred men, who will be mounted and ready for service in a very short time. I consider it my duty to lay before you the above information, so as you, commanding the military forces of the United States in this part of the Union, may adopt such measures in regard to said Indians as you deem right.

The above mentioned mounted volunteers (because such they will be) will be in readiness immediately to move against said Indians, and, as Executive of the State of Illinois, respect fully solicit your co-operation in this business. Please honour me with an answer to this letter.

With sincere respect for your character,
I am, your obedient servant,
John Reynolds.

Copy of a letter of Major General Gaines.

H. Q. Western Department, May 29, 1831.

His Excellency, Governor Reynolds:

Sir: I do myself the honour to acknowledge the receipt of your letter of yesterday's date, advising me of your having received undoubted information that the section of the frontier of your State near Rock Island, is invaded by a hostile band of Sac Indians, headed by a chief called Black Hawk. That in order to repel said invasion, and to protect the citizens of the State, you have called on the militia to the number of seven hundred militiamen, to be in readiness immediately to move against the Indians, and you solicit my co-operation.

In reply, it is my duty to state to you, that I have ordered six companies of the regular troops stationed at Jefferson Barracks, to embark tomorrow morning, and repair forthwith to the spot occupied by the hostile Sacs. To this detachment I shall, if necessary, add four companies from Prairie du Chien, making a total of ten companies. With this force I am satisfied that I shall be able to repel the invasion, and give security to the frontier inhabitants of the State.

But should the hostile band be sustained by the residue of the Sac, Fox, and other Indians, to an extent requiring an augmentation of my force, I will, in that event, communicate with your Excellency by express, and avail myself of the co-operation which you propose. But, under existing circumstances, and the present aspect of our Indian relations on the Rock Island section of the frontier, I do not deem it necessary or proper to require militia, or any other description of force, other than that of the regular army at this place and Prairie du Chien.

I have the honour to be, very respectfully,
Your obedient servant,
Edmund P. Gaines,
Major General by Brevet Commanding.

3

General Gaines to Governor Reynolds.

Headquarters, Rock Island, 5th June, 1831.

John Reynolds, Governor of Illinois:

Sir: I do myself the honour to report to Your Excellency the result of my conference with the chiefs and braves of the band of Sac Indians, settled within the limits of your State near this place.

I called their attention to the facts reported to me of their disorderly conduct towards the white inhabitants near them. They disavow any intention of hostility, but at the same time adhere with stubborn pertinacity, to their purpose of remaining on the Rock River land in question.

I notified them of my determination to move them peaceably if possible, but at all events to move them to their own side of the Mississippi River; pointing out to them the apparent impossibility of their living on lands purchased by the whites without constant disturbance. They contended that this part of their country had never been sold by them. I explained to them the different treaties of 1804, '16 and '25, and concluded with a positive assurance that they must move off, and that I must as soon as they are ready assist them with boats.

I have this morning learned that they have invited the Prophet's band of Winnebagoes on Rock River, with some Pottawattomies and Kickapoos, to join them. If I find this to be true I shall gladly avail myself of my present visit to see them well punished; and therefore, I deem it to be the only safe measure now to be taken to request of Your Excellency the battalion of mounted men, which you did me the honour to say would co-operate with me. They will find at this post a supply of rations for the men, with some corn for their horses; together with a supply of powder and lead.

I have deemed it expedient under all the circumstances of the case, to invite the frontier inhabitants to bring their families to this post until the difference is over.

I have the honour to be, with great respect,
Your obedient servant,

Edmund P. Gaines,
Major General by Brevet Commanding.

P. S. Since writing the foregoing remarks, I have learned that the Winnebagoes and Pottawattomie Indians have actually been invited by the Sacs to join them. But the former evince no disposition to comply; and it is supposed by Colonel Gratiot, the agent, that none will join the Sacs, except perhaps some few of the Kickapoos. E. P. G.

4

Articles of agreement and capitulation, made and concluded this thirtieth day of June, one thousand eight hundred and thirty one, between E. P. Gaines, Major General of the United States Army, on the part of the United States, John Reynolds, Governor of Illinois, on the part of the State of Illinois, and the chiefs and braves of the band of Sac Indians, usually called the British band of Rock River, with their old allies of the Pottawattomie, Winnebago, and Kickapoo nations.

Witnesseth, that whereas, the said British band of Sac Indians, have, in violation of the several treaties entered into between the United States and the Sac and Fox nations, in the years 1804, 1816, and 1825, continued to remain upon, and to cultivate the lands on Rock River, ceded to the United States by the said treaties, after the said lands had been sold by the United States, to individual citizens of Illinois and other States: And whereas, the said British band of Sac Indians, in order to sustain their pretensions to continue upon the said Rock River lands, have assumed the attitude of actual hostility towards the United States, and have had the audacity to drive citizens of the State of Illinois from their homes, destroy their corn, and invite many of their old friends of the Pottawattomie, Winnebago, and Kickapoos to unite with them (the said British band of Sacs) in war, to prevent their removal from said lands: And whereas, many of the most disorderly of their several tribes of Indians, did actually join the said British band of Sac Indians prepared for war against the United States, and more particularly against the State of Illinois; from which purpose they confess that nothing could have restrained them but the appearance of force far exceeding the combined strength of the said British band of Sac Indians, with such of their aforesaid allies as had actually joined them; but being now convinced that such a war would tend speedily to annihilate them, they have voluntarily abandoned their hostile attitude and sued for peace.

Peace is therefore granted them upon the following conditions, to which the said British band of Sac Indians, with their aforesaid allies agree; and for the faithful execution of which the undersigned chiefs and braves of the said band and their allies mutually bind themselves, their heirs and assigns for ever.

2. The British band of Sac Indians are required peaceably to submit to the authority of the friendly chiefs and braves of the United Sac and Fox nations, and at all times hereafter to reside and hunt with them upon their own lands west of the Mississippi River, and be obedient to their laws and treaties, and no one or more of the said band shall ever be permitted to recross said river to the place of their usual residence, nor to any part of their old hunting ground east of the Mississippi, without the express permission of the President of the United States, or the Governor of the State of Illinois.

3. The United States will guarantee to the united Sac and Fox nations, including the said British band of Sac Indians, the integrity of all the lands claimed by them west of the Mississippi river pursuant to the treaties of the years 1825 and 1830.

4. The United States require the united Sac and Fox nations, including the aforesaid British band, to abandon all communication and cease to hold any intercourse with any British post, garrison or town, and never again to admit among them any agent or trader who shall not have derived his authority to hold commercial or other intercourse with them from the President of the United States or his authorised agent.

5. The United States demand an acknowledgment of their right to establish military posts and roads within the limits of the said country guaranteed by the third article of this agreement and capitulation, for the protection of the frontier inhabitants.

6. It is further required by the United States, that the principal friendly chiefs and headmen of the Sacs and Foxes bind themselves to enforce as far as may be in their power, the strict observance of each and every article of this agreement and ca-

pitulation, and at any time they may find them selves unable to restrain their allies the Pottawattomies, Kickapoos or Winnebagoes, to give immediate information thereof to the nearest military post.

7. And it is finally agreed by the contracting parties, that henceforth permanent peace and friendship be established between the United States and the aforesaid band of Indians.

(Signed)   Edmund P. Gaines,
Major General by Brevet Commanding.

(Signed)   John Reynolds,
Governor of the State of Illinois.

(Sac) Chiefs.

Pashepaho, or Stabbing Chief, his **X** mark.
Weeshat, or Sturgeon Head, his **X** mark.
Chakinpoxepaho, or Little Stabbing Chief, his **X** mark.
Chicohalico, or Turtle Shell, his **X** mark.
Pemexee, or The one that flies, his **X** mark.

Warriors and Braves.

Mucata Muhicatak, or the Black Hawk, his **X** mark.
Menacon, or The Lead, his **X** mark.
Kakekamah, or All Fish, his **X** mark.
Crepesh, or Water, his **X** mark.
Casamesan, or The one that flies too fast, his **X** mark.
Paunenanee, or Paune Man, his **X** mark.
Wawapalosa, or White Walker, his **X** mark.
Wapaquat, or White Horse, his **X** mark.
Keokuck, or Walker, his **X** mark. (Not the principal chief of that name.)

Fox Chiefs.

Wapello, or The Prenee, his **X** mark.
Katemse, or The Eagle, his **X** mark.
Pawsheet, or The one who threw, his **X** mark.
Namer, or The one that has gone, his **X** mark.

Fox Braves and Warriors.

Allotoh, or Morgan, his **X** mark.
Kakakew, or The Crow, his **X** mark.
Shesveguanas, or Little Guard, his **X** mark.
Kokaskee, his **X** mark.
Takona, or The Prisoner, his **X** mark.
Crakiskowa, or The one that meets, his **X** mark.

Pametekeh, or The one that clouds about, his **X** mark.
Tapokea, or The Light, his **X** mark.
Moransot, or The one that has his hair pulled, his **X** mark.
Kakenekapeo, or Setting in the Grass, his **X** mark.
Witnesses.
Jos. M. Street, United States Indian Agent, Prairie du Chien; Aby. (W.) Morgan, Colonel U. S. Infantry; J. Bliss, Bvt. Maj. 3rd Infantry; Geo. A. McCall, Aidecamp; Saml. Whiteside; Felix St. Vrain, Indian Agent; John S. Greathouse; M. K. Alexander; A. S. West; Antoine Le Claire, Interpreter; Joseph Danforth; Daniel S. Witter; Benj. F. Pike.

5

H. Q. Western Department,
Nashville, Tenn. Aug. 10, 1831.
Sir: I have the honour to report for the information of the President of the United States, the several depositions and original letters, to which I have hitherto referred, since the date of my last, of the first *ultimo*. In relation to the late disorderly conduct of the British band of Sac Indians, in attempting to retake and hold possession of the Rock River lands; and for this purpose to enter into alliances, and form combinations with the most disorderly of their red neighbours, against the States of Missouri and Illinois and the Territory of Michigan, *viz*:
No. 1. The deposition of Rennah Wells, Samuel Wells, Benjamin Pike, Joseph Danforth, Moses Johnson, John Wells, John W. Spencer, Joseph H. Case, and Charles Case, sworn to and subscribed June 10th, 1831, before

William T. Brasher, J. P.

No. 2. The deposition of John Wells, sworn to the 10th of June, 1831, before

Joel Wells, J. P.

No. 3. The deposition of Rennah Wells, and Samuel Wells, sworn to and subscribed the 10th of June, 1831, before

Joel Wells, J. P.

No. 4. The deposition of Nancy Wells and Nancy Thompson, sworn to and subscribed the 10th of June, 1831, before

William T. Brasher, J. P.

No. 5. The deposition of Joseph Danforth, sworn to and subscribed the 10th of June, 1831, before

Joel Wells, J. P.

No. 6. The copy of a letter from P. L. Chouteau, Indian Agent for the Osage nation, to General William Clark, Superintendent of Indian affairs, dated the 27th of June, 1831.

No. 7. A letter from Felix St. Vrain, agent for the Sac and Fox Indians, dated the 15th of June, 1831.

No. 8. A letter from Colonel Henry Gratiot, sub-agent for the Winnebago Indians, dated the 11th of June, 1831.

No. 9. A letter from Colonel Henry Gratiot, sub-agent for the Winnebago Indians, dated the 22nd of June, 1831, with a copy of a communication from John Dixon to J. G. Soulard, dated the 17th of June, 1831.

No. 10. A letter from Colonel Henry Gratiot, dated 1st July, 1831, enclosing a talk, or communication, signed by some of the chiefs of the Winnebago nation of his subagency.

These depositions numbered one to five inclusively, and which are in substance similar to those on which Governor Reynolds's communication of the 29th of May last was based, and which he promised to forward to the War Department, sufficiently establish the facts of the return of the British band of Sac Indians to the place of their former residence on Rock River, after the lands had been sold, surveyed, and in part inhabited by several of these deponents; and the hostile conduct of this band with determined purpose forcibly to hold those lands, in violation of the several treaties of 1804, 1816, and 1825. The second article of the last mentioned treaty, clearly shows that the Sac and Fox Indians have no claim to any lands whatsoever east of the Mississippi River, and it puts an end to all doubt or cavil that might possibly arise under the seventh article of the treaty of 1804; inasmuch as, by the aforesaid second article of treaty of 1825, the Sac and Fox Indians expressly relinquished all their claims to land east of the Mississippi River.

The enclosed No. 6 copy of a letter from Colonel P. L. Chouteau, U. S. agent for the Osage Indians, to General Clark, with enclosure No. 7, a letter from Felix St. Vrain, taken in connection with the other letters herewith, Nos. 8, 9, and 10, together with the enclosed depositions, established, as clearly as could be desired, the long continued restlessness and enmity of this band of Sac Indians against the United States, as well as the great exertions and systematic efforts on the part of the offenders, to organise an opposition, as formidable as the Indians near us have ever wielded against us when aided by the forces of England, as in 1812 and 1813, for their object was, as extravagant as it may seem, to make a simultaneous attack upon, and break up the whole line of frontier settlements from Detroit along our western border to the Sabine or Texas.

Long as I have known our southern and western Indians, and often as I have witnessed their lamentable ignorance of our strength, and of the utter impossibility of their affecting, without the aid of a civilized power, any thing like a formidable array of force against us, I found among the Winnebago and Sac Indians, a still greater degree of ignorance and arrogance and stupidity.

The reports which first reached me, of the Sac Indians having sent a deputation to the Osage and nations to the south west as far as Texas, with a view to invoke their aid in a war against the United States, seemed too extravagant to merit the least notice. Nor did I place any reliance on the report, until it was confirmed by the evidence of their interpreters and traders, with the assurance of Colonel Gratiot and other persons long acquainted with those Indians; that they frequently indulge in the habit of boasting, that they have always beaten our troops in battle, often when their number were much inferior to ours; and that they believed that more red men can be brought out against us than we can oppose to them white men.

This impression is of course confined to the Indians who have never visited the interior of our middle and eastern states. Those who have visited the city of Washington, are generally better informed; but these have not that influence among their more savage brethren, which superior information would seem to entitle them to; and they are, moreover, much influenced in their views and policy by the prevailing impression, that, let the Indians do what they may towards us in violation of existing treaties, they have nothing to do but to sue for peace whenever they please, and by a new treaty, give us satisfaction, and obtain for themselves rations, presents, annuities, &c.

I take this occasion to remark, that, though satisfied of the necessity of my movement, and of the employment, under the circumstances of the case, of the volunteers called for, even whilst without definite information as to the extent of the arrangements by the Sac Indians; to obtain the assistance of their old brother warriors, who served with them under Tecumseh, in the years 1812 and 1813, the information obtained by me at Rock Island in the early part of the month of June, and more especially that which I enclose herewith, convinced me that without the increased force brought out by Governor Reynolds, the lives of many of our frontier families would in all probability have been lost in an Indian war, in that quarter, before the close of the present summer.

If my measures shall have contributed to arrest a calamity so much and so justly to be deprecated, I shall rejoice at the result, inasmuch as I have acted in accordance with a maxim which has borne me through the most difficult service. I have hitherto encountered the maxim which requires that in pre paring against Indian or other foes, we should rely for success mainly on our own strength and vigilance, rather than upon the supposed feebleness of our adversary.

I have delayed this report in expectation of receiving and forwarding with the enclosed, some additional statements of facts designating more particularly the different notions or tricks of Indians, applied to, or engaged by the Sac deputation, but the last mail from the west having brought me nothing upon this subject, I deem it proper to make no further delay.

   All which is respectfully submitted,
 (Signed)   E. P. Gaines,
        Major General by Bt. Commanding

The following is the substance of the depositions of sun dry citizens of the Rock River settlement, taken before William Brasher, J. P. and Joel Wells, J. P. on the 10th of June, 1831.

1. John Wells, John W. Spencer, Jonah H. Case, Rennah Wells, Samuel Wells, Benjamin T. Pike, Joseph Danforth, and Moses Johnson, before William Brasher, J. P., swore that the Sac Indians, did through the last year repeatedly threaten to kill them for being on their ground, and acted in the most outrageous manner, threw down their fences, burnt or destroyed their rails, turned horses into their cornfields, and almost destroyed their crops, stole their potatoes, killed and ate their hogs, shot arrows into their cattle, and put out their eyes, thereby rendering them

useless to the owners, saying the land was theirs, and that they had not sold it. In April they ordered the deponents to leave their houses, and turned from fifty to one hundred horses into one man's wheat field, threatening that the fields should not be reaped, although the owners should plough them, and although said owners had purchased the land of the United States Government. The Indians also levelled deadly weapons at the citizens, and on some occasions hurt some of the said citizens, for attempting to prevent the destruction of their property.

Also that the Indians stole their horses, some of which were returned by the agent six or eight months after, and in a miserable condition; others were never heard of again. Nearly fifty Indians headed by their notorious war chief, all armed and equipped for war, came to the house of Rennah Wells, and ordered him to be off, or they would kill him, which, for the safety of his family, he obeyed. They then went to another house, rolled out a barrel of whisky, and destroyed it, as well as committing many other outrages, to the knowledge of the deponents.

2. John Wells, before Joel Wells, J. P., swore, That on the 30th of September, 1830, he saw two Sac Indians throwing down his fence, who said they were doing it for the purpose of going through, in which they persisted although forbidden by the owner, and when the owner attempted to prevent them, one of them made a pass at him with his fist, and drew his knife on him.

3. Rennah and Samuel Wells, before Joel Wells, J. P., swore, That on the 29th of May, a party of Sac Indians, calling themselves chiefs, with Black Hawk at their head, came to the house of Rennah Wells, near the mouth of Rock River, and said that he must let the squaws cultivate his field, which Wells refusing, they became much displeased, and told him to go off; upon Wells's refusal they went away. That on the next day the same chiefs, with about fifty warriors, came, armed, and told Wells that he must move, or they would cut the throats of himself and family, and making motions to that effect, upon which said Wells told them that he would take counsel, and tell them at three o'clock the next day what would be his determination. They consented, and went away; at the appointed time they returned, and told Wells that he must go off; which he accord-

ingly did, leaving all his possessions to the Indians.

4. Nancy Thompson, and Nancy Wells, before W. J. Brasher, swore, That in October, 1830, two Indians, residing in the village forty or fifty miles above the mouth of Rock River, and called Sacs or Winnebagoes, came to the house of Rennah Wells, and commenced chasing some sheep, as if they would kill them; those Indians were ordered to desist, upon which they drew their knives and made at the women, who being alarmed, called for assistance, Samuel Wells being sick in the house at the time, ran out with a pitchfork, and the Indians pursued no farther. London L. Case heard the alarm given, and joined. The Indians then returned to the river bank eighty or one hundred yards distant; when Case, thinking they were still in pursuit of the sheep, went to ascertain the truth, and coming near the Indians they wounded him severely in three places with a knife and tomahawk.

5. Joseph Danforth, before Joel Wells, J. P., swore, that he saw Sacs at a fence belonging to John Wells, who forbid them going through, when they continued throwing down the fence. Wells attempted to prevent them, when one of the Indians struck him with his fist, and drew his knife; Danforth got a stick, and the Indians making several attempts towards Danforth, he (Danforth) knocked one of them down with his stick. The Indian rose several times and made at Danforth with his knife, and finally deserted the ground, leaving his knife.

The above is the substance of the depositions above mentioned.

6

Whereas, a treaty between the United States of America and the Winnebago nation of Indians, was made and concluded at Fort Armstrong, in the State of Illinois, on the fifteenth day of September, one thousand eight hundred and thirty-two, by Winfield Scott and John Reynolds, commissioners on the part of the United States, and certain chiefs, headmen, and warriors of the Winnebago nation, on the part of the said nation, which treaty is in the words following, to wit:

Articles of a treaty made and concluded at Fort Armstrong, Rock Island, Illinois, between the United States of America, by their Commissioners, Major General Winfield Scott, of the

United States' Army, and his Excellency John Reynolds, Governor of the State of Illinois, and the Winnebago nation of Indians, represented in general Council by the undersigned Chiefs, Headmen, and Warriors.

ART. I. The Winnebago nation hereby cede to the United States, forever, all the lands to which said nation have title or claim, lying to the south and east of the Wisconsin River, and the Fox River of Green Bay; bounded as follows, *viz*: beginning at the mouth of Pee-kee-tol-a-ka River; thence, up Rock River to its source; thence, with a line dividing the Winnebago nation from other Indians east of the Winnebago Lake, to the Grand Chute; thence, up Fox River to the Winnebago Lake, and with the north-western shore of said lake, to the inlet of Fox River; thence up said river to Lake Puckaway, and with the eastern shore of the same to its most south easterly bend; thence with the line of purchase made of the Winnebago nation, by the treaty at Prairie du Chien, the first day of August, one thousand eight hundred and twenty-nine, to the place of beginning.

ART. II. In part consideration of the above cession, it is hereby stipulated and agreed, that the United States grant to the Winnebago nation, to be held as other Indian lands are held, that part of the tract of country on the west side of the Mississippi, known, at present, as the neutral ground, embraced within the following limits, *viz*: beginning on the west bank of the Mississippi River, twenty miles above the mouth of the upper Ioway River, where the line of the lands purchased of the Sioux Indians, as described in the third article of the treaty of Prairie du Chien, of the fifteenth day of July, one thousand eight hundred and thirty, begins; thence with said line, as surveyed and marked, to the eastern branch of the Red Cedar Creek; thence down said creek, forty miles, in a straight line, but following its windings, to the line of purchase, made of the Sac and Fox tribe of Indians, as designated in the second article of the before recited treaty; and thence along the southern line of said last mentioned purchase, to the Mississippi, at the point marked by the surveyor, appointed by the President of the United States, on the margin of said river; and thence up said river to the place of beginning. The exchange of the two tracts of country to take place on or before the first day of June next; that is to say, on or before that day, all the Winnebagoes now residing within the country ceded by them as above, shall leave the said country, when and not before, they shall be allowed to enter upon the country granted by the United States, in exchange.

ART. III. But, as the country hereby ceded by the Winnebago nation is more extensive and valuable than that given by the United States in exchange; it is further stipulated and agreed, that the United States pay to the Winnebago nation, annually, for twenty-seven successive years, the first payment to be made in September of the next year, the sum of ten thousand dollars in specie; which sum shall be paid to the said nation at Prairie du Chien and Fort Winnebago, in sums proportional to the numbers residing most conveniently to those places respectively.

ART. IV. It is further stipulated and agreed, that the United States shall erect a suitable building, or buildings, with a garden or field attached, somewhere near Fort Crawford, or Prairie du Chien, and establish and maintain therein, for the term of twenty-seven years, a school for the education, including clothing, board and lodging, of such Winnnebago children as may be voluntarily sent to it; the school to be conducted by two or more teachers, male and female, and the said children to be taught reading, writing, arithmetic, gardening, agriculture, carding, spinning, weaving; and sewing, according to their ages and sexes, and such other branches of useful knowledge as the President of the United States may prescribe; Provided, That the annual cost of the school shall not exceed the sum of three thousand dollars.

And, in order that the said school may be productive of the greatest benefit to the Winnebago nation, it is hereby subjected to the visits and inspections of His Excellency the Governor of the State of Illinois for the time being; the United States' General Superintendents of Indian affairs; of the United States' agents who may be appointed to reside among the Winnebago Indians, and of an officer of the United States' Army, who may be of, or above the rank of Major: Provided that the commanding officer of Fort Crawford shall make such visits and inspections frequently, although of an inferior rank.

ART. V. And the United States further agree to make to the said nation of Winnebago Indians the following allowances, for the period of twenty-seven years, in addition to the considerations hereinbefore stipulated; that is to say; for the support of six agriculturists, and the purchase of twelve yokes of oxen, ploughs and other agricultural implements, a sum not exceeding two thousand five hundred dollars *per annum*; to the Rock River band of Winnebagoes, one thousand five hundred pounds of tobacco, *per annum*; for the services and attendance of a physician at Prairie du Chien, and of one at Fort Winnebago, each, two hundred dollars *per annum*.

ART. VI. It is further agreed that the United States remove and maintain, within the limits prescribed in this treaty, for the occupation of the Winnebagoes, the blacksmith's shop, with the necessary tools, iron, and steel heretofore allowed to the Wrnnebagoes, on the waters of the Rock River, by the third article of the treaty made with the Winnebago nation, at Prairie du Chien, on the first day of August, one thousand eight hundred and twenty-nine.

ART. VII. And it is further stipulated and agreed by the United States, that there shall be allowed and issued to the Winnebagoes, required by the terms of this treaty to remove within their new limits, soldiers' rations of bread and meat, for thirty days: Provided, that the whole number of such rations shall not exceed sixty thousand.

ART. VIII. The United States, at the request of the Winnebago nation of Indians, aforesaid, further agree to pay, to the following named persons, the sums set opposite their names respectively, *viz*:

To Joseph Ogee, two hundred and two dollars and fifty cents;

To William Wallace, four hundred dollars, and

To John Dougherty, four hundred and eighty dollars; amounting in all, to one thousand and eighty-two dollars and fifty cents, which sum is in full satisfaction of the claims brought by said persons against said Indians, and by them acknowledged to be justly due.

ART. IX. On demand of the United States' Commissioners, it is expressly stipulated and agreed, that the Winnebago nation shall promptly seize and deliver up to the commanding officer of some United States' military post, to be dealt with according to law, the following individual Winnebagoes, *viz*: Koo-zee-ray-Kaw, Moy-che-nun-Kaw, Tshik-o-ke-maw-kaw, Ah-hun-see-Kaw, and Waw-zee-reekay-hee-wee-kaw, who are accused of murdering, or of being concerned in the murdering of certain American citizens, at or near the Blue Mounds, in the territory of Michigan; Nausaw-nay-he-kaw, and Toag-ra-naw-koo-ray-see-ray-kaw; who are accused of murdering or of being concerned in murdering, one or more American citizens, at or near Kellogg's Grove, in the State of Illinois; and also Waw-kee-aun-shaw and his son who wounded, in attempting to kill, an American soldier, at or near Lake Koshkonong, in the said territory; all of which offences were committed in the course of the past spring and summer. And till these several stipulations are faithfully complied with by the Winnebago nation, it is further agreed that the payment of the annuity of ten thousand dollars, secured by this treaty, shall be suspended.

ART. X. At the special request of the Winnebago nation, the United States agree to grant, by patent, in fee simple, to the following named persons, all of whom are Winnebagoes by blood, lands as follows: To Pierre Paquette, three sections; to Pierre Paquette, junior; one section, to Therese Paquette, one section; The lands to be designated under the direction of the President of the United States, within the country ceded by the Winnebago nation.

ART. XI. In order to prevent misapprehensions that might disturb peace and friendship between the parties to this treaty, it is expressly understood that no band or party of Winnebagoes shall reside, plant, fish, or hunt after the first day of June next, on any portion of the country herein ceded to the United States.

ART. XII. This treaty shall be obligatory on the contracting parties, after it shall be ratified by the President and Senate of the United States.

Done at Fort Armstrong, Rock Island, Illinois, this fifteenth day of September, one thousand eight hundred and thirty-two.

Winfield Scott,
John Reynolds.

Prairie du Chien Deputation.
Tshee-o-nuzh-ee-kaw, War Chief, (Kar-ray-mau-nee) his **X**

mark.
Wau-kaun-hah-kaw, or Snake Skin, (Day-kan-ray) his **X** mark.
Khay-rah-tshoan-saip-kaw, or Black Hawk, his **X** mark.
Wau-kaun-kaw, or Snake, his **X** mark.
Sau-sau-mau-nee-kaw, or He who walks naked, his **X** mark.
Hoantsh-skaw-skaw, or White Bear, his **X** mark.
Hoo-tshoap-kaw, or Four Legs, his **X** mark.
Mau-hee-her-kar-rah, or Flying Cloud, son of Dog Head, his **X** mark.
Tshah-shee-rah-wau-kaw, or he who takes the leg of a deer in his mouth, his **X** mark.
Mau-kee-wuk-kaw, or Cloudy, his **X** mark.
Ho-rah-paw-kaw, or Eagle Head, his **X** mark.
Hash-kay-ray-kaw, or Fire Holder, his **X** mark.
Eezhook-hat-tay-kaw, or Big Gun, his **X** mark.
Mau-wau-ruck, or The Muddy, his **X** mark.
Mau-shoatsh-kaw, or Blue Earth, his **X** mark.
Wee-tshah-un-kuk, or Forked Tail, his **X** mark.
Ko-ro-ko-ro-he-kaw, or Bell, his **X** mark.
Haun-heigh-kee-paw-kaw, or The Night that meets, his **X** mark.

Fort Winnebago Deputation.

Hee-tshah-wau-saip-skaw-skaw, or White War Eagle, De-kaw-ray sr. his **X** mark.
Hoo-wau-nee-kaw, or Little Elk, (orator) one of the Kay-ra-men-nees, his **X** mark.
Wau-kaun-tshah-hay-ree-kaw, or Roaring Thunder, Four legs Nephew, his **X** mark.
Mau-nah-pey-kaw, or Soldier, (Black Wolf's son) his **X** mark.
Wau-kaun-tsha-ween-kaw, or Whirling Thunder, his **X** mark.
Wau-nee-ho-no-nik, or Little Walker, son of Fire Brand, his **X** mark.
To-shun-uk-ho-nik, or Little Otter, son of Sweet Corn, his **X** mark.
Tshah-tshun-hat-tay-kaw, or Big Wave, son of Clear Sky, his **X** mark.

Rock River Deputation.

Kau-ree-kaw-see-kaw, White Crow, (the blind) his **X** mark.
Mo-rah-tshay-kaw, or Little Priest, his **X** mark.

Mau-nah-pey-kaw, or Soldier, his **X** mark.
Ho-rah-hoank-kaw, or War Eagle, his **X** mark.
Nautsh-kay-peen-kaw, or Good Heart, his **X** mark.
Keesh-koo-kaw, his **X** mark.
Wee-tshun-kaw, or Goose, his **X** mark.
Wau-kaun-nig-ee-nik, or Little Snake, his **X** mark.
Hoo-way-skaw, or White Elk, his **X** mark.
Hay-noamp-kaw, or Two Horns, his **X** mark.
Ee-nee-wonk-shik-kaw, or Stone Man, his **X** mark.

              Signed in presence of,

R. Bache, Captain Ord. Secretary to the Commission.
Jos. M. Street, United States Indian Agent.
John H. Kinzie; Sub Agt. Indian Affairs.
Abrm. Eustis.
H. Dodge, Major U. S. Rangers.
Alexr. R. Thompson, Major United States Army.
William (S.) Harney, Capt. 1st Infantry.
E. Kirby, Paymaster United States Army.
Albion T. Crow.
John Marsh.
Pierre Paquette, Interpreter, his **X** mark.
P. H. Gait, Assistant Adjutant General.
S. W. Wilson.
Benj. F. Pike.
J. B. F. Russell, Captain 5th Infantry.
S. Johnson, Captain 2nd Infantry.
John Clitz, Adj. 2nd Infantry.
Jno. Pickell, Lieutenant 4th Artillery.
A. Drane, A. Qr. U. S. A.
J. R. Smith, 1st Lieutenant 2nd Infantry.
H. Day, Lieutenant 2nd Infantry.
William Maynadier, Lieutenant and A. D. C.
P. G. Hambaugh.
S. Burbank, Lieutenant 1st Infantry.
J. H. Prentiss, Lieutenant 1st Artillery.
E. Rose, Lieutenant 3rd Artillery.
L. J. Beall, Lieutenant 1st Infantry.
Antoine Le Claire.

Now, therefore, be it known that I, Andrew Jackson, President of the United States of America, having seen and considered said Treaty, do, by and with the advice and consent of the Senate, as expressed by their resolution of the ninth instant, accept, ratify and confirm the same, and every clause and article thereof.

In testimony whereof, I have caused the seal of the United States to be hereunto affixed, having signed the same with my hand.

Done at the City of Washington, this thirteenth day of February, in the year of our Lord one thousand eight hundred and thirty-three, and of the Independence of the United States, the fifty-seventh.

Andrew Jackson.

By the President:
Edw. Livingston, Secretary of State.

7

Whereas a treaty, between the United States of America and the confederated tribes of Sac and Fox Indians, was made and concluded at Fort Armstrong, in the State of Illinois, on the twenty-first day of September, one thousand eight hundred and thirty-two, by Winfield Scott, and John Reynolds, commissioners on the part of the United States, and certain chiefs, headmen and warriors of the confederated tribes of Sac and Fox Indians, on the part of said tribes, which Treaty is in the words following, to wit:

> Articles of a Treaty of peace, friendship and cession, concluded at Fort Armstrong, Rock Island, Illinois, between the United States of America, by their Commissioners, Major General Winfield Scott, of the United States Army, and his Excellency John Reynolds, Governor of the State of Illinois, and the confederated tribes of Sac and Fox Indians, represented in general Council, by the undersigned chiefs, headmen and warriors.
>
> Whereas, under certain lawless and desperate leaders, a formidable band, constituting a large portion of the Sac and Fox nation, left their country in April last, and, in violation of treaties, commenced an unprovoked war upon unsuspecting and defenceless citizens of the United States, sparing neither age nor sex; and whereas, the United States, at a great expense of treasure have subdued the said hostile band, killing or capturing all its principal chiefs and warriors—the said States, partly as indemnity for the expense incurred, and partly to secure the

future tranquillity of the invaded frontier, demand of the said tribes, to the use of the United States, a cession of a tract of the Sac and Fox country, bordering on said frontier, more than proportional to the numbers of the hostile band who have been so conquered and subdued.

ART. I. Accordingly the confederated tribes of Sacs and Foxes hereby cede to the United States forever, all the lands to which the said tribes have title, or claim, (with the exception of the reservation hereinafter made,) included within the following bounds, to wit: Beginning on the Mississippi River, at the point where the Sac and Fox northern boundary line as established by the second article of the treaty of Prairie du Chien, of the fifteenth of July, one thousand eight hundred and thirty, strikes said river; thence, up said boundary line to a point fifty miles from the Mississippi, measured on said line: thence, in a right line to the nearest point on the Red Cedar of the Ioway, forty miles from the Mississippi River; thence, in a right line to a point in the northern boundary line of the State of Missouri, fifty miles, measured on said boundary, from the Mississippi River; thence, by the last mentioned boundary to the Mississippi River, and by the western shore of said river to the place of beginning. And the said confederated tribes of Sacs and Foxes hereby stipulate and agree to remove from the lands herein ceded to the United States, on or before the first day of June next; and, in order to prevent any future misunderstanding, it is expressly under stood, that no band or party of the Sac or Fox tribes shall reside, plant, fish, or hunt on any portion of the ceded country after the period just mentioned.

ART. II. Out of the cession made in the preceding article, the United States agree to a reservation for the use of the said confederated tribes, of a tract of land containing four hundred square miles, to be laid off under the directions of the President of the United States, from the boundary line crossing the Ioway River, in such manner that nearly an equal portion of the reservation may be on both sides of said river, and extending downwards, so as to include Keokuck's principal village on its right bank, which village is about twelve miles from the Mississippi River.

ART. III. In consideration of the great extent of the foregoing cession the United States stipulate and agree to pay to the said confederated tribes, annually, for thirty successive years, the first payment to be made in September of the next year, the sum of twenty thousand dollars in specie.

ART. IV. It is further agreed that the United States shall establish and maintain within the limits, and for the use and benefit of the Sacs and Foxes, for the period of thirty years, one additional black and gunsmith shop, with the necessary tools, iron and steel, and finally make a yearly allowance for the same period, to the said tribes, of forty kegs of tobacco, and forty barrels of salt, to be delivered at the mouth of the Ioway River.

ART. V. The United States, at the earnest request of the said confederated tribes, further agree to pay to Farnham and Davenport, Indian traders at Rock Island, the sum of forty thousand dollars without interest, which sum will be in full satisfaction of the claims of the said traders against the said tribes, and by the latter was, on the tenth day of July, one thousand eight hundred and thirty-one, acknowledged to be justly due, for articles of necessity, furnished in the course of the seven preceding years, in an instrument of writing of said date, duly signed by the chiefs and headmen of said tribes, and certified by the late Felix St. Vrain, United States' Agent, and Antoine Le Claire, United States' Interpreter, both for the said tribes.

ART. VI. At the special request of the said confederated tribes, the United States agree to grant, by patent, in fee simple, to Antoine Le Claire, interpreter, a part Indian, one section of land opposite Rock Island, and one section at the head of the first rapids above said Island, within the country herein ceded by the Sacs and Foxes.

ART. VII. Trusting to the good faith of the neutral bands of Sacs and Foxes, the United States have already delivered up to those bands the great mass of prisoners made in the course of the war by the United States, and promise to use their influence to procure the delivery of other Sacs and Foxes, who may still be prisoners in the hands of a band of Sioux Indians, the friends of the United States; but the following named prisoners of war, now in confinement, who were chiefs and headmen, shall be held as hostages for the future good conduct of the late hostile bands, during the pleasure of the President of the United States, *viz*. Mukka-ta-mish-a-ka-kaik (or Black Hawk) and his two sons; Wau-ba-kee-shik (the Prophet) his brother and two sons; Napope; We-sheet Ioway; Pamaho; and Cha-kee-pa-shipa-ho (the little stabbing Chief.)

ART. VIII. And it is further stipulated and agreed between the parties to this treaty, that there shall never be allowed in the confederated Sac and Fox nation, any separate band, or village, under any chief or warrior of the late hostile bands; but that the remnant of the said hostile bands shall be divided among the neutral bands of the said tribes according to blood—the Sacs among the Sacs, and the Foxes among the Foxes.

ART. IX. In consideration of the premises, peace and friendship are declared, and shall be perpetually maintained between the United States and the whole confederated Sac and Fox nation, excepting from the latter the hostages before mentioned.

ART. X. The United States, besides the presents delivered at the signing of this treaty, wishing to give a striking evidence of their mercy and liberality, will immediately cause to be issued to the said confederated tribes, principally for the use of the Sac and Fox women and children, whose husbands, fathers and brothers, have been killed in the late war, and generally for the use of the whole confederated tribes, articles of subsistence as follows: thirty-five beef cattle; twelve bushels of salt; thirty barrels of pork; and fifty barrels of flour, and cause to be delivered for the same purposes, in the month of April next, at the mouth of the lower Ioway, six thousand bushels of maize or Indian corn.

ART. XI. At the request of the said confederated tribes, it is agreed that a suitable present shall be made to them on their pointing out to any United States agent, authorized for the purpose, the position or positions of one or more mines, supposed by the said tribes to be of a metal more valuable than lead or iron.

ART. XII. This treaty shall take effect and be obligatory on the contracting parties, as soon as the same shall be ratified by the President of the United States, by and with the consent of the Senate thereof.

Done at Fort Armstrong, Rock Island, Illinois, this twenty-first day of September, in the year of our Lord one thousand eight hundred and thirty-two, and of the Independence of the United States the fifty-seventh.

Winfield Scott,
John Reynolds.

Sacs.

Kee-o-kuck, or He who has been every where, his **X** mark.
Pa-she-pa-ho, or the Stabber, his **X** mark.
Pia-tshe-noay, or the Noise Maker, his **X** mark.
Wawk-kum-mee, or Clear Water, his **X** mark.
O-sow-wish-kan-no, or Yellow Bird, his **X** mark.
Pa-ca-to-kee, or Wounded Lip, his **X** mark.
Winne-wun-quai-saat, or the Terror of Men, his **X** mark.
Mau-noa-tuck, or He who controls many, his **X** mark.
Wau-we-au-tun, or the Curling Wave, his **X** mark.

Foxes.

Wau-pel-la, or He who is painted white, his **X** mark.
Tay-wee-mau, or Medicine Man, (Strawberry) his **X** mark.
Pow-sheek, or the Roused Bear, his **X** mark.
An-nau-mee, or the Running Fox, his **X** mark.
Ma-tow-e-qua, or the Jealous Woman, his **X** mark.
Mee-shee-wau-quaw, or the Dried Tree, his **X** mark.
May-kee-sa-mau-ker, or the Wampum Fish, his **X** mark.
Chaw-co-saut, or the Prowler, his **X** mark.
Kaw-kaw-kee, or the Crow, his **X** mark.
Mau-que-tee, or the Bald Eagle, his **X** mark.
Ma-she-na, or Cross Man, his **X** mark.
Kaw-kaw-ke-moute, or the Pouch, (running bear) his **X** mark.
Wee-she-kaw-ka-skuck, or He who steps firmly, his **X** mark.
Wee-ca-ma, or Good Fish, his **X** mark.
Paw-qua-nuey, or the Runner, his **X** mark.
Ma-hua-wai-be, or Wolf Skin, his **X** rnark.
Mis-see-quaw-kaw, or Hairy Neck, his **X** mark.
Waw-pee-shaw-kaw, or White Skin, his **X** mark.
Mash-shen-waw-pee-teh, or Broken Tooth, his **X** mark.
Nau-nah-que-kee-she-ko, or Between Two Days, his **X** mark.
Paw-puck-ka-kaw, or Stealing Fox, his **X** mark.
Tay-e-sheek, or the Falling Bear, his **X** mark.
Wau-pee-maw-ker, or the White Loon, his **X** mark.
Wau-co-see-nee-me, or Fox Man, his **X** mark.

In presence of R. Bache, Cap. Ord. Sec. to the Commission; Abrm. Eustis 5 Alex. Cummings, Lt. Col. 2nd Infantry; Alex. R.

Thompson, Major U. S. Army; B. Riley, Major U. S. Army; H. Dodge, Major; W. Campbell; Hy. Wilson, Major 4th U. S. Infantry; Donald Ward; Thos. Black Wolf; Sexton G. Frazer; P. H. Gait, Ast. Adj. Gen.; Benj. F. Pike; Wm. Henry; James Craig; John Aukeney; J. B. F. Russell; Isaac Chambers; John Clitz, Adj. Inf. John Pickell, Lieut. 4th Arty.; A. G. Miller, Lt. 1st Inf.; Geo. Davenport, Asst. Q. Mas. General Ill.. mil.; A. Drane, Æneas Mackay, Capt. U. S. Army; I. R. Smith, 1st Lt. id Inf.; Wm. Maynadier, Lt. and A. D. C.; I. L. Gallagher, 1st Lt. A. C. S.; N. B. Bennet, Lt. 3rd Arty.; Horatio A. Wilson, Lt. 4th Arty.; H. Day, Lt. 2nd Inf.; Jas. W. Penrose, Lt. 2nd Infy.; J. E. Johnston, Lt. 4th Arty.; S. Burbank, Lt. 1st Infy.; I. H. Prentiss, Lt. 1st Arty.; L. I. Beale, Lt. 1st Infy.; Addison Philleo; Thomas L. Alexander, Lt. 6th Infy.; Horace Beale, Actg. Surg. U. S. Army; Oliver W. Kellogg; Jona. Leighton, Actg. Surg. U. S. Army; Robt. C. Buchanan, Lt. 4th Infy.; Jas. S. Williams, Lt. 6th Infy.; John W. Spencer; Antoine Le Claire, Interpreter.

Now therefore, be it known, that I, Andrew Jackson, President of the United States of America, having seen and considered said Treaty, do, by and with the advice and con sent of the Senate, as expressed by their Resolution of the ninth instant, accept, ratify and confirm the same and every clause and article thereof.

In testimony whereof, I have caused the seal of the United States to be hereunto affixed, having signed the same with my hand.

Done at the City of Washington, this thirteenth day of February in the year of our Lord one thousand eight hundred and thirty-three, and of the Independence of the United States the fifty-seventh.

Andrew Jackson.

By the President:
    Edw. Livingston, Secretary of State.

Appendix B

1

Articles of a treaty made at St. Louis, in the district of Louisiana, between William Henry Harrison, Governor of the Indiana Territory and of the District of Louisiana, Superintendent of Indian affairs for the Territory and District, and Commissioner Plenipotentiary of the United States, for concluding any treaty or treaties which may be found necessary, with any of the north-western tribes of Indians, of the one part, and the chiefs and head men of the united Sac and Fox tribes of Indians of the other part.

ART. I. The United States receive the United Sac and Fox tribes into their friendship and protection, and the said tribes agree to consider themselves under the protection of the United States, and no other power whatsoever.

ART. II. The general boundary line between the lands of the United States and of the said Indian tribes, shall be as follows, to wit: Beginning on a point on the Missouri River, opposite to the mouth of the Gasconade River, thence in a direct course, so as to strike the River Jefferson at a distance of thirty miles from its mouth, and down the said Jefferson, to the Mississippi, thence up the Mississippi, to the mouth of the Ouisconsin River, and up the same, to a point which shall be thirty-six miles in a direct line from the mouth of said river; thence by a direct line to a point where the Fox River, a branch of the Illinois, leaves the small lake called Lakacgan; thence down the Fox River, to the Illinois River, and down the same to the Mississippi. And the said tribes, for and in consideration of the friendship and protection of the United States, which is now extended to them, and of goods to the value of two thousand two hundred and thirty-four dollars and fifty cents, which are now delivered, and of the annuity hereinafter stipulated to be paid, do hereby cede and relinquish forever to the United States, all the lands included within the above described boundary.

ART. III. In consideration of the cession and relinquishment of land made in the preceding article, the United States will deliver to the said tribes, at the town of St. Louis, or some other convenient place on the Mississippi, yearly and every year, goods suited to the circumstances of the Indians, of the value of one thousand dollars, six hundred of which are intended for the Sacs and four hundred for the Foxes, reckoning that value at the first cost of the goods in the city or place in the United States, where they shall be procured; and if the said tribes shall hereafter, at an annual delivery of the goods afore said, desire that a part of their annuity should be furnished in domestic animals, implements of husbandry, and other utensils convenient for them, or in compensation to useful artificers who may reside with or near them, and be employed for their benefit; the same shall, at the subsequent annual delivery, be furnished accordingly.

ART. IV. The United States will never interrupt the said tribes in the possession of the lands which they rightfully claim; but will, on the contrary, protect them in the quiet enjoyment of the same against their own citizens, and against all other white persons who may intrude upon them; and the said tribes do hereby engage that they will never sell their lands or any part thereof, to any sovereign power but the United States, nor to the citizens or subjects of any other sovereign power, nor to the citizens of the United States.

ART. V. Lest the friendship which is now established between the United States and the said Indian tribes should be interrupted by the misconduct of individuals, it is hereby agreed, that for injuries done by individuals, no private revenge or retaliation shall take place, but instead thereof, complaints shall be made by the party injured to the other, by the said tribes, or either of them, to the superintendent of Indian affairs, or one of his deputies, and by the superintendent or other person appointed by the president, to the chiefs of the said tribes; and it shall be the duty of the said chiefs, upon complaint being made as aforesaid, to deliver up the person or persons against whom the complaint is made, to the end that he or they may be punished agreeably to the laws of the State or Territory where the offence may have been committed; and in like manner, if any robbery, violence, or murder shall be committed on any Indian or Indians belonging to said tribes, or either of them, the person or persons so offending, shall be tried, and if found guilty, shall be punished in like manner, as if the injury had been done to a white man;.

And it is further agreed, that the chiefs of the said tribes, shall, to the utmost of their power, exert themselves to recover horses or other property which may be stolen from any citizen or citizens of the United States, by any individual or individuals of their tribes; and the property so recovered, shall be forthwith delivered to the superintendent, or other person authorized to receive it, that it may be restored to the owner, and in cases where the exertions of the chiefs shall be ineffectual in recovering the property stolen as aforesaid, if sufficient proof can be obtained that such property was actually stolen by any Indian or Indians belonging to the said tribes, or either of them, the United States may deduct from the annuity of the said tribes, a sum equal to the value of the property which has been stolen, and the United States hereby guaranty to any Indian or Indians of the said tribes, a full indemnification for any horses or other property which may be stolen from them, by any of their citizens; provided the property so stolen cannot be recovered, and that a sufficient proof is produced that it was actually stolen by a citizen of the United States.

ART. VI. If any citizen of the United States, or other white person, should form a settlement upon lands which are the property of the Sac and Fox tribes, upon complaint being made there of to the superintendent, or other person having charge of the affairs of the Indians, such intruder shall forthwith be removed.

ART. VII. As long as the lands which are now ceded to the United States remain their property, the Indians belonging to the said tribes shall enjoy the privilege of living and hunting upon them.

ART. VIII. As the laws of the United States regulating trade and intercourse with the Indian tribes are already extended to the country inhabited by the Sacs and Foxes, and as it is provided by those laws, that no person shall reside as a trader in the Indian country, without a license under the hand and seal of the superintendent of Indian affairs; or other person appointed for the purpose by the president, the said tribes do promise and agree that they will not suffer any trader to reside amongst them without such license, and that they will from time to time give notice to the superintendent, or to the agent for their tribes, of all the traders that may be in their country.

ART. IX. In order to put a stop to the abuses and impositions which are practiced upon the said tribes by the private traders, the United States will, at a convenient time, establish a trading house or factory, where the individuals of said tribes can be supplied with goods at a more reasonable rate than they have been accustomed to procure them.

ART. X. In order to evince the sincerity of their friendship and affection for the United States, and a respectful deference for their advice, by an act which will not only be acceptable to them, but to the common Father of all nations of the earth, the said tribes do hereby solemnly promise and agree, that they will put an end to the bloody war which has heretofore raged between their tribes and those of the Great and Little Osages; and for the purpose of burying the tomahawk, and renewing the friendly intercourse between themselves and the Osages, a meeting of their respective chiefs shall take place, at which, under the direction of the above named commissioner, or the agent of Indian affairs, residing at St. Louis, an adjustment of all their differences shall be made, and peace established upon a firm and lasting basis.

ART. XI. As it is probable that the government of the United States will establish a military post at or near the mouth of the Wisconsin River; and as the land on the lower side of the river may not be suitable for that purpose, the said tribes hereby agree that a fort may be built either on the upper side of the Wisconsin, or on the right bank of the Mississippi, as the one or the other may be found most convenient, and a tract of land not exceeding two miles square shall be given for that purpose; and the said tribes do further agree that they will, at all times, allow to traders and other persons travelling through their country, under the authority of the United States, a free and safe passage for themselves and their property of every description, and that for such passage they shall at no time, and on no account whatever, be subject to any toll or exaction.

ART. XII. This treaty shall take effect, and be obligatory on the contracting parties, as soon as the same shall have been ratified by the president, by and with the advice and consent of the Senate of the United States.

ADDITIONAL ARTICLE. It is agreed that nothing in this treaty contained shall affect the claim of any individual or individuals, who may have obtained grants of land from the Spanish government; and which are not included within the general boundary line laid down in this treaty, provided that such grants have at any time been made known to the said tribes and recognised by them.

Ratified the 25th of February, 1805.

Recognitions of the preceding Treaty which was held at St. Louis 13th May, 1816.

Treaty with the Sacs of Rock River and the United States, by William Clark, Ninian Edwards and Auguste Chouteau.

(*This appears to be a Treaty of amity, but the following article is considered proper to be inserted.*)

ART. I. The Sacs of Rock River, and the adjacent country, do hereby unconditionally assent to, recognise, re-establish, and confirm the treaty between the United States of America and the united tribes of Sacs and Foxes, which was concluded at St. Louis, on the 3rd of November, 1804, as well as all other contracts and agreements heretofore made between the Sac tribe or nation and the United States."

2

Treaty with the Sacs residing on Missouri River, by William Clark, Ninian Edwards and Auguste Chouteau, at Portage de Sioux, 13th Sept., 1815.

ART. I. The undersigned chiefs and warriors, for themselves, and that portion of the Sacs which they represent, do hereby assent to the treaty between the United States of America, and the United tribes of Sacs and Foxes, which was concluded at St. Louis, on the 3rd of November, 1804, and they moreover promise to do all in their power to re-establish and enforce the same.

Treaty with the Fox tribe, by William Clark, Ninian Edwards, and Auguste Chouteau.

ART. IV. The Fox tribe or nation do hereby assent to, recognise, re-establish and confirm, the treaty of St. Louis, concluded on the 3rd of November, 1804, to the full extent of their interest in the same, as well as all other contracts and agreements between the parties; and the United States promise to fulfil all the stipulations contained in the said treaty in favour of the Fox tribe or nation."

Treaty with the Sac and Fox tribes of Indians, concluded at the City of Washington, the 4th of August, 1824.

To perpetuate peace and friendship between the United States and the Sac and Fox tribes or nations of Indians, and to remove all future cause of dissensions which may arise from undefined territorial boundaries, the President of the United States of America, by Wm. Clark, Superintendent of Indian affairs, and sole commissioner, specially appointed for that purpose, of the one part, and the undersigned chiefs and head men of the Sac and Fox tribes or nations fully deputized to act for and in behalf of their said nations of the other part, have entered into the following articles and conditions, *viz.*

ART. I. The Sac and Fox tribes or nations of Indians, by their deputations in council assembled, do hereby agree, in consideration of certain sums of moneys, &c., to be paid to the said Sac and Fox tribes, by the government of the U. States, as hereinafter stipulated, to cede and forever quit claim, and do, in behalf of their said tribes or nations, hereby cede, relinquish, and forever quit claim unto the United States, all right, title, interest, and claim to the lands which the said Sac and Fox tribes have or claim within the limits of the State of Missouri, which are situated, lying and being, between the Mississippi and Missouri Rivers, and a line running from the Missouri at the entrance of the Kansas River, north one hundred miles to the north-west corner of the State of Missouri, and from thence east of the Mississippi.

It being understood, that the small tract of land lying between the Rivers Des Moine and the Mississippi, and the section of the above line between the Mississippi and the Des Moine is intended for the use of the half breeds belonging to the Sac and Fox Nations; they holding it, however, by the same title, and in the same manner that other Indian titles are held.

ART. II. The chiefs and headmen who signed this convention, for themselves and in behalf of their tribes, do acknowledge the lands east and south of the lines described in the first article, so far as the Indians claimed the same, to belong to the United States, and that none of their tribes shall be permitted to settle or hunt upon any part of it, after the first day of January, 1826, without special permission from the Superintendent of Indian affairs.

ART. III. It is hereby stipulated and agreed on the part of the United States, as a full consideration for the claims and lands ceded by the Sac and Fox tribes in the first article, there shall be paid to the Sac and Fox Nations within the present year, one thousand dollars in cash or merchandise; and, in addition to the annuities stipulated to be paid to the Sac and Fox tribes, by a former treaty, the United States do agree to pay to the said Sac tribe, five hundred dollars, and to the Fox tribe five hundred dollars, annually, for the term of ten succeeding years; and at the request of the chiefs of the said Sac and Fox Nations, the commissioner agrees to pay to Maurice Blondeau, a half breed Indian of the Fox tribe, the sum of five hundred dollars, it being a debt due by the said nation, to the aforesaid Blondeau for property taken from him during the late war.

ART. IV. The United States engage to provide and support a blacksmith for the Sac and Fox nations, so long as the President of the United States may think proper, and to furnish the said nations with such farming utensils, and cattle, and to employ such persons to aid them in their agriculture, as the president may deem expedient.

ART. V. The annuities stipulated by the third article are to be paid either in money, merchandise, provisions, or domestic animals, at the option of the aforesaid tribes, and when the annuities, or part thereof is paid in merchandise, it is to be delivered to them at the first cost of the goods at St. Louis, free from cost of transportation.

ART. VI. This treaty shall take effect and be obligatory upon the contracting parties so soon as the same shall be ratified by the President of the United States, by and with the advice and consent of the Senate thereof.

Ratified the 18th of January, 1825.

ALSO FROM LEONAUR
AVAILABLE IN SOFTCOVER OR HARDCOVER WITH DUST JACKET

AN APACHE CAMPAIGN IN THE SIERRA MADRE by John G. Bourke—An Account of the Expedition in Pursuit of the Chiricahua Apaches in Arizona, 1883.

BILLY DIXON & ADOBE WALLS by Billy Dixon and Edward Campbell Little—Scout, Plainsman & Buffalo Hunter, *Life and Adventures of "Billy" Dixon* by Billy Dixon and *The Battle of Adobe Walls* by Edward Campbell Little (*Pearson's Magazine*).

WITH THE CALIFORNIA COLUMN by George H. Petis—Against Confederates and Hostile Indians During the American Civil War on the South Western Frontier, *The California Column, Frontier Service During the Rebellion* and *Kit Carson's Fight With the Comanche and Kiowa Indians*.

THRILLING DAYS IN ARMY LIFE by George Alexander Forsyth—Experiences of the Beecher's Island Battle 1868, the Apache Campaign of 1882, and the American Civil War.

THE NEZ PERCÉ CAMPAIGN, 1877 by G. O. Shields & Edmond Stephen Meany—Two Accounts of Chief Joseph and the Defeat of the Nez Percé, *The Battle of Big Hole* by G. O. Shields and *Chief Joseph, the Nez Percé* by Edmond Stephen Meany.

CAPTAIN JEFF OF THE TEXAS RANGERS by W. J. Maltby—Fighting Comanche & Kiowa Indians on the South Western Frontier 1863-1874.

SHERIDAN'S TROOPERS ON THE BORDERS by De Benneville Randolph Keim—The Winter Campaign of the U. S. Army Against the Indian Tribes of the Southern Plains, 1868-9.

GERONIMO by Geronimo—The Life of the Famous Apache Warrior in His Own Words.

WILD LIFE IN THE FAR WEST by James Hobbs—The Adventures of a Hunter, Trapper, Guide, Prospector and Soldier.

THE OLD SANTA FE TRAIL by Henry Inman—The Story of a Great Highway.

LIFE IN THE FAR WEST by George F. Ruxton—The Experiences of a British Officer in America and Mexico During the 1840's.

ADVENTURES IN MEXICO AND THE ROCKY MOUNTAINS by George F. Ruxton—Experiences of Mexico and the South West During the 1840's.

AVAILABLE ONLINE AT **www.leonaur.com**
AND FROM ALL GOOD BOOK STORES

www.ingramcontent.com/pod-product-compliance
Lightning Source LLC
Chambersburg PA
CBHW030227170426
43201CB00006B/139